ECONOMIC COMMISSION FOR EUROPE
Committee on Environmental Policy

# ENVIRONMENTAL PERFORMANCE REVIEWS

# THE FORMER YUGOSLAV REPUBLIC OF MACEDONIA

UNITED NATIONS
New York and Geneva, 2002

# Environmental Performance Reviews Series No.17

**NOTE**

Symbols of United Nations documents are composed of capital letters combined with figures. Mention of such a symbol indicates a reference to a United Nations document.

The designations employed and the presentation of the material in this publication do not imply the expression of any opinion whatsoever on the part of the Secretariat of the United Nations concerning the legal status of any country, territory, city or area, or of its authorities, or concerning the delimitation of its frontiers or boundaries.

| ECE/CEP/88 |
| --- |

| UNITED NATIONS PUBLICATION |
| --- |
| *Sales No.* E.03.II.E.21 |
| ISBN 92-1-116836-8 |
| ISSN 1020-4563 |

# *Foreword*

The Environmental Performance Reviews are intended to assist countries in transition to improve their management of the environment by establishing baseline conditions and making concrete recommendations for better policy implementation and performance and to integrate environmental policies into sectoral policies at the national level. Through the Peer Review process, they also promote dialogue among UNECE member countries and harmonization of environmental conditions and policies throughout the region.

This work was initiated by ministers at the second Ministerial Conference "Environment for Europe," in Lucerne, in 1993. Acting on the request of the ministers, the UNECE Committee on Environmental Policy, meeting in special session in January 1994, decided to make the Environmental Performance Reviews a part of its regular programme. As a voluntary exercise, the Environmental Performance Review is undertaken only at the request of the country itself at the ministerial level.

The studies are carried out by international teams of experts from the region, working closely with national experts from the reviewed country. Through a process of broad consultations, the experts carry out a comprehensive assessment of a wide range of issues related to the environment, covering three broad themes: the framework for environmental policy and management, management of pollution and natural resources and economic and sectoral integration. The team's final report contains recommendations for further improvement, taking into consideration the country's progress in the current transition period.

The teams also benefit from close cooperation with other organizations in the United Nations system, including the United Nations Development Programme, the United Nations Environment Programme, the World Bank and the World Health Organization.

This Environmental Performance Review is the seventeenth in the series published by the United Nations Economic Commission. I hope that this Review will be useful to all countries in the region, to intergovernmental and non-governmental organization and, especially, to the former Yugoslav Republic of Macedonia, to its Government, all national stakeholders, to its people.

Brigita Schmögnerova
Executive Secretary

# *Preface*

The Environmental Performance Review (EPR) of the former Yugoslav Republic of Macedonia began with a preparatory mission in February 2001, during which the structure of the report was established. Thereafter, the review team of international experts was constituted. It included experts from Belgium, Bulgaria, Canada, Croatia and Switzerland, together with experts from the secretariat of the United Nations Economic Commission for Europe (UNECE), the United Nations Environment Programme (UNEP) Regional Office for Europe, UNEP/Grid-Arendal, and the European Centre for Environment and Health of the World Health Organization (WHO).

The review mission took place in February 2002. In October 2002 the draft was submitted for expert review to the ad hoc EPR Expert Group of the UNECE Committee on Environmental Policy. During this meeting, the Expert Group discussed the report in detail with representatives of the Government of the former Yugoslav Republic of Macedonia, focusing in particular on the conclusions and recommendations. The EPR report, as amended by the Expert Group, was then submitted for peer review to the UNECE Committee on Environmental Policy at its annual session in Geneva on 4-6 November 2002. A high-level delegation from the Government of the former Yugoslav Republic of Macedonia participated in the peer review. The Committee adopted the recommendations as set out in this report.

The review of the former Yugoslav Republic of Macedonia's environmental performance is evidence of the country's commitment to improving environmental management, restructuring the related institutions and, in the context of its pre-accession agreement, developing new national legislation adapted to European Union standards. However, the report also points out a number of constraints to implementation and enforcement that slow down the pace of progress. The EPR team, with the assistance of national experts, prepared an analysis and offered recommendations for future action in a number of areas, including the decision-making framework, economic instruments and financing, environmental information and public participation, waste management, air management, water management, agriculture and biodiversity, industry, energy, spatial planning, transport and human health. The report stresses that the environment should become a priority and should be integrated into the decision-making processes of all sectors.

The UNECE Committee on Environmental Policy and the UNECE review team would like to thank both the Government of the former Yugoslav Republic of Macedonia for its invitation to carry out this review and the many excellent national experts who worked with the international experts and contributed with their knowledge and assistance. UNECE wishes the former Yugoslav Republic of Macedonia success in carrying out the tasks before it to meet its environmental objectives, including implementation of the recommendations contained in the present report.

UNECE would also like to express its appreciation to the Governments of Denmark, Germany, the Netherlands and Switzerland for their support, and to the United Nations Development Programme (UNDP) office in Skopje, the UNEP Regional Office in Europe, the WHO European Centre for Environment and Health (ECEH), and UNEP/Grid-Arendal for participating in this Environmental Performance Review.

# LIST OF TEAM MEMBERS

| | | |
|---|---|---|
| Ms. Mary Pat SILVEIRA | (ECE secretariat) | Team Leader |
| Mr. Ivan NARKEVITCH | (ECE secretariat) | Project Coordinator |
| Mr. Antoine NUNES | (ECE secretariat) | Project Coordinator |
| Mr. Jyrki HIRVONEN | (ECE secretariat) | Introduction |
| Ms. Vanya GRIGOROVA | (BULGARIA) | Chapter 1 |
| Ms. Vanya GRIGOROVA | (BULGARIA) | Chapter 2 |
| Ms. Mijke HERTOGHS | (ECE secretariat) | Chapter 3 |
| Ms. Ieva RUCEVSKA | (UNEP/ GRID-Arendal) | Chapter 4 |
| Mr. Harald EGERER | (UNEP) | Chapter 5 |
| Ms. Catherine MASSON | (ECE secretariat) | Chapter 6 |
| Mr. Michel HOUSSIAU | (BELGIUM) | Chapter 7 |
| Mr. René NIJENHUIS | (ECE secretariat) | Chapter 8 |
| Ms. Elisabeth CLÉMENT-ARNOLD | (SWITZERLAND) | Chapter 9 |
| Ms. Stella SATALIC | (CROATIA) | Chapter 10 |
| Ms. Charlotte GRIFFITHS | (ECE secretariat) | Chapter 11 |
| Ms. Sasha TSENKOVA | (CANADA) | Chapter 12 |
| Ms. Louise GRENIER | (CANADA) | Chapter 13 |
| Ms. Bettina MENNE Ms. Francesca RACIOPPI | (WHO/ECEH) | Chapter 14 |

The preparatory mission for the project took place from 8 to 9 February 2001. The review mission was organized from 4 to 15 February 2002.

# LIST OF NATIONAL CONTRIBUTORS

## The former Yugoslav Republic of Macedonia

| | |
|---|---|
| Mr. Metodija DIMOVSKI | Ministry of Environment and Physical Planning |
| Ms. Jadranka IVANOVA | Ministry of Environment and Physical Planning |
| Mr. Ljupco AVRAMOVSKI | Fund for the Environment and Nature Protection and Promotion |
| Ms. Svetlana GJORGEVA | Ministry of Environment and Physical Planning |
| Ms. Menka SPIROVSKA | Ministry of Environment and Physical Planning |
| Ms. Marionka VILAROVA | Ministry of Environment and Physical Planning |
| Ms. Lence KURCIEVA | Ministry of Environment and Physical Planning |
| Mr. Dimitar ROLEVSKI | Ministry of Environment and Physical Planning |
| Ms. Teodora OBRADOVIC-GRNCAROVSKA | Ministry of Environment and Physical Planning |
| Mr. Saso APOSTOLOV | Ministry of Environment and Physical Planning |
| Ms. Nada TASKOVSKA-ARSOVA | Ministry of Environment and Physical Planning |
| Mr. Sokol KLINCAROV | Ministry of Environment and Physical Planning |
| Ms. Gordana KOZUHAROVA | Ministry of Environment and Physical Planning |

# TABLE OF CONTENTS

**PART III:**    **ECONOMIC AND SECTORAL INTEGRATION**

**ANNEXES**

---------

# LIST OF FIGURES

# LIST OF TABLES

# LIST OF BOXES

## ACRONYMS AND ABBREVIATIONS

| | |
|---|---|
| BOD | Biological oxygen demand |
| CARDS | Community Assistance for Reconstruction |
| CITES | Convention on International Trade in Endangered Species of Wild Fauna and Flora |
| COD | Chemical oxygen demand |
| CPI | Consumer price index |
| DEM | Environmental Movement (NGO) |
| DO | Dissolved oxygen |
| EBRD | European Bank for Reconstruction and Development |
| EC | European Commission |
| ECEH | European Centre for Environment and Health |
| EEA | European Environment Agency |
| EIA | Environmental impact assessment |
| EIB | European Investment Bank |
| EIONET | European Environment Information and Observation Network |
| EMEP | Cooperative Programme for Monitoring and Evaluation of the Long-range Transmission of Air Pollutants in Europe |
| EPR | Environmental Performance Review |
| ESP | Electrostatic precipitator |
| EU | European Union |
| GDP | Gross domestic product |
| GEF | Global Environment Facility |
| GHG | Greenhouse gas |
| GIS | Geographic information system |
| GTZ | Gesellschaft für Technische Zusammenarbeit GmbH |
| HCFCs | Hydrochlorofluorocarbons |
| HESME | Health, Environment and Safety Management in Enterprises |
| HPP | Hydropower plant |
| IAEA | International Atomic Energy Agency |
| IFI | International financing institution |
| IMF | International Monetary Fund |
| IPPC | Integrated pollution prevention and control |
| ISC | Institute for Sustainable Communities |
| ISDE | International Society of Doctors for the Environment |
| ISO | International Standardization Organization |
| IUCN | World Conservation Union |
| JICA | Japan International Cooperation Agency |
| LEAP | Local environmental action plan |
| LEHAP | Local Environmental Health Action Plans |
| MAC | Maximum allowable concentration |
| MEA | Multilateral environmental agreement |
| NEAP | National Environmental Action Plan |
| NEHAP | National Environment and Health Action Plan |
| NGO | Non–governmental organization |
| ODS | Ozone-depleting substances |
| OECD | Organisation for Economic Co-operation and Development |
| OSCE | Organization for Security and Co-operation in Europe |
| PAH | Polyaromatic hydrocarbon |
| PCB | Polychlorinated biphenyl |
| PEBLDS | Pan-European Biological and Landscape Diversity Strategy |
| POP | Persistent organic pollutant |
| PPI | Producer price index |
| PWME | Public water management enterprise |
| REC | Regional Environmental Center for Central and Eastern Europe |
| REReP | Regional Environmental Reconstruction Programme |

| | |
|---|---|
| RON | Research octane number |
| SAC | Special Area of Conservation |
| SCI | Site of Community Interest |
| SEA | Strategic environmental assessment |
| SECI | Southeast European Cooperation Initiative |
| SoE | State of the Environment |
| SPM | Suspended particulate matter |
| UCTE | Union for the Co-ordination of Transmission of Electricity |
| UNDP | United Nations Development Programme |
| UNECE | United Nations Economic Commission for Europe |
| UNEP | United Nations Environment Programme |
| UNFPA | United Nations Population Fund |
| UNICEF | United Nations Children's Fund |
| UNIDO | United Nations Industrial Development Organization |
| USAID | United States Agency for International Development |
| VAT | Value-added tax |
| VOC | Volatile organic compound |
| WHO | World Health Organization |
| WUA | Water users associations |

## SIGNS AND MEASURES

| | |
|---|---|
| .. | not available |
| - | nil or negligible |
| . | decimal point |
| ha | Hectare |
| kt | Kiloton |
| g | Gram |
| kg | Kilogram |
| mg | Milligram |
| mm | Millimetre |
| $cm^2$ | square centimetre |
| $m^3$ | cubic metre |
| km | Kilometre |
| $km^2$ | square kilometre |
| toe | ton oil equivalent |
| l | Litre |
| ml | Millilitre |
| min | Minute |
| s | Second |
| m | Metre |
| ºC | degree Celsius |
| GJ | Gigajoule |
| $kW_{el}$ | kilowatt (electric) |
| $kW_{th}$ | kilowatt (thermal) |
| $MW_{el}$ | Megawatt (electric) |
| $MW_{th}$ | Megawatt (thermal) |
| MWh | Megawatt-hour |
| GWh | gigawatt-hour |
| TWh | terawatt-hour |
| Bq | Becquerel |
| Ci | Curie |
| MSv | millisievert |
| Cap | Capita |
| Eq | Equivalent |
| H | Hour |
| kv | Kilovolt |
| MW | Megawatt |
| Gcal | gigacalorie |
| Hz | Hertz |

# Currency

Monetary unit: Macedonian Denar

Exchange rates: IMF does not provide exchange rate for the Denar prior to the 1995.

| Year | Denar/US$ | Denar/Euro |
|------|-----------|------------|
| 1995 | 37.88 | 49.55 |
| 1996 | 39.98 | 50.70 |
| 1997 | 50.00 | 56.71 |
| 1998 | 54.46 | 61.00 |
| 1999 | 56.90 | 60.70 |
| 2000 | 65.90 | 60.90 |
| 2001 | 68.03 | 60.93 |

Source: IMF. International Financial Statistics, June 2002.

*Note*: Values are annual averages

# INTRODUCTION

## I.1    The physical context

The former Yugoslav Republic of Macedonia is a landlocked country in the middle of the southern Balkan Peninsula. With a surface area of 25,713 km², the country is one of the smallest in Europe. It is bordered by Yugoslavia to the north (border length 232 km), Bulgaria to the east (165 km), Greece to the south (262 km), and Albania to the west (191 km).

Large and high mountain massifs characterize the country's topography. The average elevation is 850 metres above sea level and more than 30 per cent of the land area is above 1000 metres. The country has 14 mountain peaks higher than 2,000 metres. The highest peak, the 2,753-metre-high Golem Korab, is situated on the Albanian border. Amid the mountains are flat valleys and plains interconnected by passes or deep ravines. The Vardar River bisects the whole country. Of its total length of 388 kilometres, 301 kilometres are inside the country, passing through the capital Skopje before crossing to Greece and finally flowing to the Aegean Sea near Thessalonica. The rivers of the country belong to three basins: the Aegean Basin (covering 80 per cent of the country), the Adriatic Basin and the Black Sea Basin.

The country is located in a region of high seismic activity. In 1963, Skopje suffered a devastating earthquake that damaged or destroyed about 80 per cent of its buildings and killed more than 1000 inhabitants. Between 1970 and 1990, the Skopje Seismological Observatory (Sts. Kiril and Metodij University, Skopje) registered about 30 earthquakes with a magnitude exceeding 5 degrees on the Mercalli-Cancani-Sieberg (MCS) scale; approximately 4.8 on the Richter scale.

Almost the entire territory is a transitional region between Mediterranean and continental climates. Along the valleys of the Vardar and Strumica rivers the climate is temperate Mediterranean. The interior of the country has a moderate continental climate with warm, dry summers and cold, wet winters. The openness of the Aegean Sea river basin and the high mountains reaching 2,700 metres influence the Mediterranean and continental climates, resulting in an average rainfall of 500-700 mm annually. Precipitation is insufficient and unevenly distributed throughout the year. The mountainous western region receives over 1000 mm of rainfall a year, while the annual precipitation in the Vardar valley is less than 500 mm.

In general, summers and autumns are warm and dry, and winters are relatively cold with heavy snowfall. The temperature range is huge. The maximum summer temperature in most agricultural areas reaches 40°C, and the coldest winter temperature drops to as low as –30°C, while the average annual temperatures are above +10°C almost everywhere. The average temperature in July is 22°C and in January –3°C. The warmest region of the country is Demir Kapija, where temperatures in July and August exceed 40°C.

The country has three large tectonic lakes, fifteen artificial lakes and twenty-five glacial lakes located at high altitudes in the mountain ranges. The largest of the tectonic lakes, Lake Ohrid (altitude 693 m), has a total area of 349 km², of which one third (118.9 km²) lies in Albania. Lake Ohrid is 287 metres deep, its water has a special colour, and, in summer, the water temperature reaches 24°C. Its natural conditions have helped life forms from the Tertiary Period to survive.

Lake Prespa (altitude 853 m) is situated to the east of Lake Ohrid in a fertile valley at the junction of the borders of the former Yugoslav Republic of Macedonia with Albania and Greece. Of its total area of 274 km², 209 lie in the former Yugoslav Republic of Macedonia and the rest is divided between Albania and Greece. The smallest of the tectonic lakes, Lake Dojran, is situated in the south-east of the country and shared with Greece.

In addition to the three big tectonic lakes there are artificial lakes in almost every part of the country, and 25 small, shallow, clear water glacial lakes in the high mountains of Sar, Pelister, Jablanica and Jakupica.

**Figure I.1: Land use, 1999**

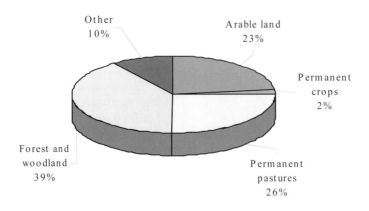

*Source*: http://www.fao.org. 2002.

**Figure I.2: GDP – composition by sector: 1990 and 2000 (per cent of the total)**

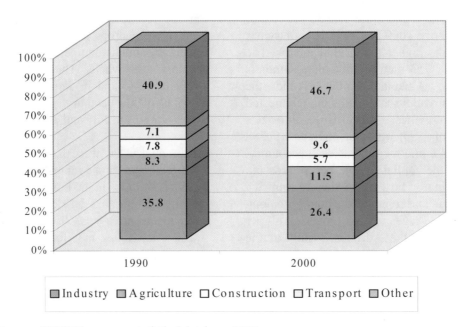

*Source*: UNECE common statistical database, 2001.

Forests and woodland cover 39 per cent of the country and 23 per cent is arable land. Two per cent is under permanent crops, 26 per cent is used as permanent pastures and the use of 10 per cent is undefined. Agricultural output is diversified, with half the arable land producing maize, livestock, tobacco, and fruit and vegetables. Dairy farming is also important.

The country has no domestic oil resources and most of its oil is imported from Thessalonica, Greece, by road. All the natural gas is imported and Skopje is connected to the Bulgarian natural gas network. The only domestic energy source is coal. In 1999,

the country produced 7.25 million tons of coal, mainly low-grade brown lignite. Most of the coal is consumed domestically, primarily to generate about 60 per cent of the electricity. Of the country's total electricity generating capacity of 1440 MW, 79 per cent is produced by thermal power and the rest by hydropower.

The country is relatively rich in mineral resources, including zinc, lead, silver, gold, antimony, manganese, nickel, chromium, copper, iron ore, and tungsten. Industrial output in 1999 included 26,000 tons of lead, 20,000 tons of zinc, 9,000 tons of copper, 9,000 tons of iron ore and 10 tons of silver.

## I.2    The human context

The country's fertility rate decreased from 2.3 per 1000 in 1991 to 1.9 in 2000, but it is still higher than the European average of 1.4. The birth rate also decreased from 16.6 per 1000 in 1990 to 14.5 in 2000. The current population is 2.027 million and was roughly the same throughout the 1990s.

About 62 per cent of the population lives in urban areas, mainly in the five largest cities: the capital Skopje (pop. 443,612), Bitola (pop. 86,049), Prilep (pop. 71,803), Kumanovo (pop. 94,333) and Tetovo (pop. 64,855). The average population density of 81 inhabitants/km$^2$ is lower than the EU average of 114 inhabitants/km$^2$.

There has been a significant decline in infant mortality. In the past ten years infant mortality decreased from 31.6 infant deaths per 1000 live births in 1990 to 11.8 in 2000. The average life expectancy at birth in 2001 was 74.0 years. Female life expectancy was 76.4 years and male life expectancy lower at 71.8 years.

The country's literacy rate in 1999 was 94 per cent, and the education attainment of post secondary or tertiary education for adults aged 25 years or more in 1990 was 8.9 per cent.

## I.3    The economic context and the transition to a market economy

### The legacy

In 1946 the former Yugoslav Republic of Macedonia was one of the six constituent republics of the Socialist Federal Republic of Yugoslavia. As Yugoslavia began to disintegrate at the beginning of the 1990s, a referendum was held in the then Republic of Macedonia of Yugoslavia. The referendum demonstrated massive support for independence and the Republic of Macedonia became the only republic to secede peacefully from Yugoslavia.

At independence in November 1991, the former Yugoslav Republic of Macedonia was the least developed of the Yugoslav republics, with a GDP per capita about one third that of Slovenia, the richest of the republics. The collapse of Yugoslavia ended transfer payments from the central government and put an end to the advantages of belonging to the Yugoslav internal "free" trade area. At the same time, between 50 and 60 per cent of its trade was with the other republics of Yugoslavia, and predominantly with Serbia.

The break-up of the federation and international sanctions against Yugoslavia in May 1992 had a disastrous effect on the country's economy. Sanctions hit agricultural exports to Yugoslavia particularly hard. The country suffered further in 1994 and 1995 from economic blockades by Greece. The blockade severed the Republic's trading links, causing fuel shortages and accelerating the economic downturn.

The decline in industrial production between 1990 and 1995 reached double-digit numbers, ranging from 10.5 per cent to 17.2 per cent. GDP decreased 30 per cent between 1989 and 1995. All other economic indicators pointed in the same direction, e.g. registered unemployment increased from 24.5 per cent in 1991 to 36.6 per cent in 1995. Inflation spiralled out of control in 1992, when the Consumer Price Index (CPI) rose 1511 per cent and the Producer Price Index (PPI) 2198 per cent. The whole economy was in tatters as GDP fell and inflation rose at the same time.

**Table I.1: Demography and health indicators, 1990-2001**

|  | 1990 | 1991 | 1992 | 1993 | 1994 | 1995 | 1996 | 1997 | 1998 | 1999 | 2000 | 2001 |
|---|---|---|---|---|---|---|---|---|---|---|---|---|
| Birth rate (per 1000) | 16.6 | 17.1 | 16.2 | 15.6 | 17.2 | 16.4 | 15.8 | 14.8 | 14.6 | 13.5 | 14.5 | .. |
| Fertility rate (per 1000) | 2.1 | 2.3 | 2.2 | 2.2 | 2.2 | 2.1 | 2.1 | 1.9 | 1.9 | 1.9 | 1.9 | .. |
| Mortality rate (per 1000) | 6.9 | 7.3 | 7.8 | 7.5 | 8.1 | 8.3 | 8.1 | 8.3 | 8.4 | 8.3 | 8.5 | .. |
| Infant mortality rate (per 1000) | 31.6 | 28.3 | 30.6 | 24.1 | 22.5 | 22.7 | 16.4 | 15.7 | 16.3 | 14.9 | 11.8 | .. |
| Female life expectancy at birth (years) | .. | 74.5 | 73.7 | 74.7 | 74.8 | 74.5 | 75.3 | 75.1 | 74.9 | 75.7 | 75.7 | 76.4 |
| Male life expectancy at birth (years) | .. | 69.9 | 69.0 | 69.5 | 69.9 | 70.0 | 70.6 | 70.5 | 70.5 | 70.7 | 71.2 | 71.8 |
| Life expectancy at birth (years) | .. | 72.1 | 71.3 | 72.0 | 72.3 | 72.2 | 72.9 | 72.8 | 72.7 | 73.1 | 73.4 | 74.0 |
| Population aged 1-14 out of total (%) | 26.2 | 24.5 | 24.3 | 25.2 | 24.9 | 24.6 | 24.2 | 23.8 | 23.3 | 22.8 | 22.3 | .. |
| Population aged 65 and over out of total (%) | 7.3 | 8.1 | 8.3 | 8.4 | 8.6 | 8.8 | 9.0 | 9.2 | 9.5 | 9.8 | 10.1 | .. |

*Sources*: UNECE. PAU 2002, World Bank 2001, CIA Factbook 2001, WHO. Health for all Database 2002.

**Table I.2: Living standard indicators, 1990-2001**

| | 1990 | 1991 | 1992 | 1993 | 1994 | 1995 | 1996 | 1997 | 1998 | 1999 | 2000 | 2001 |
|---|---|---|---|---|---|---|---|---|---|---|---|---|
| Passenger cars (per 1000 inhabitants) | .. | .. | .. | .. | .. | .. | 143 | 145 | 144 | 144 | 148 | .. |
| Telephone lines (per 1000 inhabitants) | 148 | 149 | 161 | 166 | 173 | 179 | 185 | 205 | 219 | 234 | .. | .. |
| Mobile telephone subscribers (per 1000 inhabitants) | .. | .. | .. | .. | .. | .. | 1 | 6 | 15 | 23 | .. | .. |
| Internet hosts | .. | .. | .. | .. | .. | 90 | 193 | 499 | 1,125 | 2,242 | .. | .. |
| Estimated Internet users | .. | .. | .. | .. | .. | 800 | 1,500 | 10,000 | 20,000 | 30,000 | .. | .. |

*Sources*: ITU. Yearbook of Statistics 2001and Macedonia. Statistical Yearbook 2001.

The United Nations recognized the former Yugoslav Republic of Macedonia in April 1993 and this enabled the country to become a member of the International Monetary Fund (IMF) and gain access to international markets. By 1994, the European Union had replaced Yugoslavia as the former Yugoslav Republic of Macedonia's main trading partner. At the same time closer economic ties with Albania absorbed some of the former trade with Greece.

**Transition to a market economy 1996**

The recession bottomed out in 1995; in 1996 and 1997, GDP grew 1.2 per cent and 1.4 per cent, respectively, and, in 1998, GDP growth accelerated to 3.4 per cent. Even with the Kosovo conflict, GDP continued to grow: 4.3 per cent in 1999 and 4.5 in 2000. However, in 2001, GDP shrank (-4.1 per cent), largely as a result of internal conflict. After increasing from -10.6 per cent in 1990 to 4.5 per cent in 1998, industrial output fell 2.6 per cent in 1999, recovered in 2000, but fell 3.1 per cent again in 2001.

In the Balkan context the country's economic performance has produced some astonishing results. It managed to achieve a 4 per cent budget surplus in 2000, as a combined result of the income from the newly introduced value-added tax and a windfall profit from the sale of the Macedonian telecom to the Hungarian telecom company MATAV. Successful privatization in 2000 boosted the country's reserves to over 700 million United States dollars (US$).

Years of economic hardship developed a grey economy operating outside the tax and social security systems, disregarding government regulations. It is estimated that in 1998 the grey economy was responsible for half the country's GDP. This might partially explain a situation where, despite increasing GDP, decreasing inflation and a stable currency, unemployment has continued to increase since 1991. According to an IMF estimate, only 53 per cent of the working-age population participated in the labour force in 1999. IMF also estimated that, in the same year, 32.4 per cent of the labour force was unemployed. Statistics of the Economic Commission for Europe put registered unemployment figures for 1999 even higher, at 43.8 per cent of the workforce. The country is experiencing very high unemployment but also "non-employment," with more than 700,000 people neither working in the formal sector nor seeking work.

*Privatization*

Privatization, crucial to the transition to a market economy, became a priority for the independent country. However, the first privatization concept was introduced in 1989, before independence, with the Law on the Social Capital of the former Yugoslav Federation. Internal shares were issued to all the employees of socially owned enterprises (SOEs), making employees shareholders in their companies. This process transformed over 600 enterprises in the Republic of Macedonia of Yugoslavia into joint-stock companies or limited-liability companies.

In June 1993 the country relaunched the process of privatization by the enactment of the new Law on Transformation of Enterprises with Social Capital. The results of the previous privatization with internal shares were generally recognized, but only after an audit by official supervisory institutions, authorized by the Law to control the privatization transactions made under the previous law.

In the new privatization model, every share acquired has to be traded, and every privatizing enterprise is considered as an individual case. There is no mass privatization, based on the distribution of vouchers.

Altogether approximately 1678 legal entities have been privatized, including almost 1300 commercial enterprises and 426 agricultural sector companies. Excluded from privatization are the enterprises and organizations that are essential to the national interest.

## I.4 The institutions

The former Yugoslav Republic of Macedonia is a multiparty democracy. There is universal suffrage for persons over 18. A new constitution in August 2001 gives greater rights to the country's ethnic Albanian population.

The President is the head of State, chosen by general, secret and direct election for a five-year term (previously the National Assembly elected the President), but limited to two terms. The President nominates the Prime Minister, whose appointment must be approved by the National Assembly. The President has a right of veto, but he cannot veto laws passed by a two-thirds majority in the Assembly.

The national parliament consists of a 120-member unicameral National Assembly (*Sobranie*). The Assembly is elected by popular vote for a four-year term. All members are elected by proportional representation.

The country's higher judicial system consists of a seven-member Judicial Court and a nine-judge Constitutional Court. There are also lower-level trial and appellate courts. The legal system is based on the civil law system and includes judicial review of parliamentary actions.

## I.5 Environmental context

The National Environmental Action Plan (NEAP), published in 1997, lists air pollution as the country's most serious environmental problem. Air pollution is mainly caused by industry and traffic. Poor air quality affects half the country's urban population, and studies have associated air pollution with the respiratory diseases suffered by large numbers of children in the cities.

The main sources of water pollution are the major cities and the more than 130 industrial facilities spread throughout the country. Waste-water treatment is almost non-existent, since there is only one official waste-water treatment plant in the whole country. The Vardar River, which supplies 75 per cent of the country's total water resources, is heavily polluted by untreated urban and industrial waste water.

Current ways of dealing with municipal solid waste are rudimentary. In addition to 25 known landfills, the country is littered with local waste-disposal sites. Almost all of them lack environmental safety features and pose a risk to the groundwater. Industrial and hazardous waste create an even more serious problem. There is no nationally organized system for the collection, treatment or disposal of industrial waste.

Water-level fluctuation due to irrigation and low rainfall has seriously affected the aquatic biodiversity of Lake Dojran, and overgrazing, deforestation and poor farming practices have damaged the soil. According to the NEAP, 38 per cent of the land of the former Yugoslav Republic of Macedonia is classified as "seriously eroded".

## Table I.3: Selected economic indicators, 1990-2001

| | 1990 | 1991 | 1992 | 1993 | 1994 | 1995 | 1996 | 1997 | 1998 | 1999 | 2000 | 2001 |
|---|---|---|---|---|---|---|---|---|---|---|---|---|
| **GDP in current prices** (NC billion M Den) | 0.5 | 0.9 | 11.8 | 59.2 | 146.4 | 169.5 | 176.4 | 186.0 | 195.0 | 209.0 | 235.5 | .. |
| **GDP in current prices** (US$, billion) | 4.5 | 4.7 | 2.3 | 2.5 | 3.4 | 4.5 | 4.4 | 3.7 | 3.6 | 3.7 | 3.6 | 3.5 |
| **GDP per capita** (US$ purchasing power parity per capita) | 4,421.8 | 4,276.8 | 4,059.5 | 3,827.8 | 4,075.6 | 4,076.0 | 4,168 | 4,304 | 4,483 | 4,723 | 5,003 | .. |
| **GDP** (change, 1989=100) | 89.8 | 84.3 | 78.7 | 72.8 | 71.6 | 70.8 | 71.6 | 72.6 | 75.1 | 78.4 | 81.9 | 78.5 |
| **GDP** (% change over previous year) | -10.2 | -6.2 | -6.6 | -7.5 | -1.8 | -1.1 | 1.2 | 1.4 | 3.4 | 4.3 | 4.5 | -4.1 |
| **Share of agriculture in GDP** (%) | 8.3 | 12.7 | 16.8 | 10.3 | 10.9 | 12.8 | 12.9 | 12.4 | 12.9 | 12.5 | 11.5 | .. |
| **Industrial output** (% change over previous year) | -10.6 | -17.2 | -15.8 | -13.9 | -10.5 | -10.7 | 3.2 | 1.6 | 4.5 | -2.6 | 3.5 | -3.1 |
| **Agricultural output** (% change over previous year) | -10.0 | 18.0 | 0.0 | -20.0 | 8.0 | 4.0 | -2.0 | 1.0 | 4.0 | 1.0 | .. | .. |
| **Labour productivity in industry** (% change over previous year) | -6.2 | -9.6 | -9.9 | -9.3 | -4.9 | 3.1 | 10.5 | 10.2 | 8.2 | -7.6 | 8.4 | .. |
| **CPI** (% change over previous year, annual average) | 596.6 | 110.8 | 1,511.3 | 362.0 | 128.3 | 15.7 | 2.3 | 2.6 | -0.1 | -0.7 | 5.8 | 5.5 |
| **PPI** (% change over previous year, annual average) | 394.0 | 112.0 | 2,198.2 | 258.3 | 88.9 | 4.7 | -0.3 | 4.2 | 4.0 | -0.1 | 8.9 | 2.0 |
| **Registered unemployment** (% of labour force, end of period) | .. | 24.5 | 26.2 | 27.7 | 30.0 | 36.6 | 38.8 | 41.7 | 41.4 | 43.8 | 44.9 | .. |
| **Balance of trade in goods and non-factor services** (million US$) | -418.0 | -225.0 | -7.0 | 43.0 | -185.0 | -219.8 | -317.0 | -386.2 | -418.3 | -393.4 | -556.4 | -460.0 |
| **Current account balance** (million US$) | -409.0 | -259.0 | -19.0 | 15.0 | -158.0 | -221.8 | -289.0 | -276.4 | -308.2 | -113.4 | -113.5 | -400.0 |
| **Current account balance** (as % of GDP) | -9.1 | -5.5 | -0.8 | 0.6 | -4.7 | -5.0 | -6.5 | -7.4 | -8.6 | -3.1 | -3.2 | .. |
| **Net FDI inflows** (million US$) | .. | .. | .. | .. | 24 | 10 | 11 | 16 | 118 | 32 | 170 | 420 |
| **Net FDI flows** (as % of GDP) | .. | .. | .. | .. | 0.7 | 0.2 | 0.2 | 0.4 | 3.3 | 0.9 | 4.7 | .. |
| **Cumulative FDI** (million US$) | .. | .. | .. | .. | 24 | 33 | 44 | 60 | 178 | 210 | 379 | 799 |
| **Foreign exchange reserves** (million US$) | 1 | 3 | 53 | 105 | 149 | 257 | 240 | 257 | 306 | 430 | 429 | 739 |
| **Total net external debt** (million US$) | 499 | 397 | 847 | 1,159 | 1,267 | 1,326 | 1,200 | 1,053 | 1,148 | 1,064 | 1,059 | .. |
| **Exports of goods** (million US$) | 1,113 | 1,150 | 1,199 | 1,055 | 1,086 | 1,205 | 1,147 | 1,237 | 1,292 | 1,190 | 1,319 | 1,155 |
| **Imports of goods** (million US$) | 1,531 | 1,375 | 1,206 | 1,012 | 1,271 | 1,425 | 1,464 | 1,623 | 1,711 | 1,584 | 1,875 | 1,615 |
| **Ratio of net debt to exports** (%) (calc) | 44.8 | 34.5 | 70.6 | 109.9 | 116.7 | 110.1 | 104.6 | 85.1 | 88.8 | 89.4 | 80.3 | .. |
| **Ratio of gross debt to GDP** (%) | 11.0 | 9.0 | 39.0 | 50.0 | 42.0 | 36.0 | 33.0 | 35.0 | 41.0 | 41.0 | 42.0 | .. |
| **Exchange rates: annual averages** (NC/ US$) | 11.3 | 19.7 | 5.1 | 23.3 | 43.3 | 38.0 | 39.9 | 50.0 | 54.5 | 56.9 | 65.9 | 68.0 |
| **Population** 1000 | 2,028 | 2,039 | 2,056 | 2,066 | 1,946 | 1,966 | 1,983 | 1,997 | 2,008 | 2,017 | 2,026 | 2,030 |

*Source*: UNECE Common statistical database 2002 and National Statistics 2002.
*Note*: NC = national currency

## Ministries of the former Yugoslav Republic of Macedonia

| | |
|---|---|
| Ministry of Defence | Ministry of Internal Affairs |
| Ministry of Justice | Ministry of Foreign Affairs |
| Ministry of Finance | Ministry of Economy |
| Ministry of Transport and Communications | Ministry of Agriculture, Forestry and Water Economy |
| Ministry of Labour and Social Policy | Ministry of Education and Science |
| Ministry of Culture | Ministry of Health |
| Ministry of Local Self-Government | Ministry of Environment and Physical Planning |

**Figure 1.3: Map of the former Yugoslav Republic of Macedonia**

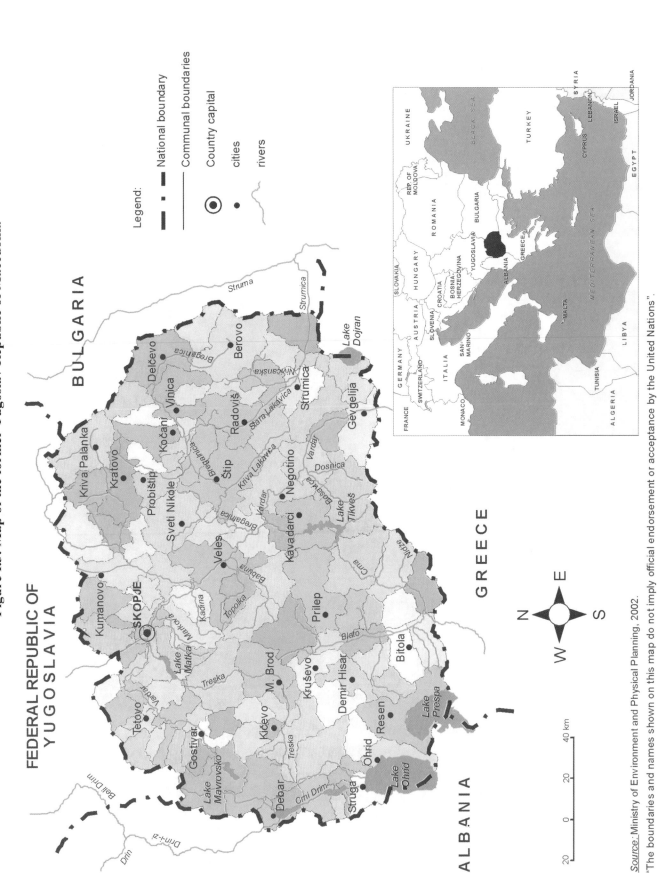

Legend:

- — · — National boundary
- —— Communal boundaries
- ⊙ Country capital
- • cities
- rivers

FEDERAL REPUBLIC OF YUGOSLAVIA

BULGARIA

GREECE

ALBANIA

SKOPJE

Kumanovo
Tetovo
Gostivar
Kičevo
Debar
Struga
Ohrid
Resen
Bitola
Demir Hisar
Kruševo
M. Brod
Prilep
Veles
Sveti Nikole
Probištip
Kratovo
Kriva Palanka
Delčevo
Vinica
Kočani
Štip
Radoviš
Negotino
Kavadarci
Berovo
Strumica
Gevgelija

Lake Mavrovsko
Lake Matka
Lake Prespa
Lake Ohrid
Lake Tikveš
Lake Dojran

Rivers: Beli Drim, Drim, Drim-zi, Vardar, Treska, Crni Drim, Topolka, Kadina, Markova, Babuna, Cma, Crna, Blato, Bregalnica, Kriva Lakavica, Stara Lakavica, Bošava, Dosnica, Nivicanska, Strumica, Struma

N
W — E
S

40 km
20    0    20    40 km

*Source:* Ministry of Environment and Physical Planning, 2002.

"The boundaries and names shown on this map do not imply official endorsement or acceptance by the United Nations".

UKRAINE, REP. OF MOLDOVA, ROMANIA, BULGARIA, SLOVAKIA, HUNGARY, CROATIA, SLOVENIA, BOSNIA-HERZEGOVINA, YUGOSLAVIA, GREECE, ALBANIA, AUSTRIA, SAN-MARINO, ITALIA, GERMANY, SWITZERLAND, FRANCE, MONACO, MALTA, LIBYA, TUNISIA, ALGERIA, EGYPT, TURKEY, CYPRUS, LEBANON, SYRIA, ISRAEL, JORDANIA, BLACK SEA, MEDITERRANEAN SEA

# PART I: THE FRAMEWORK FOR ENVIRONMENTAL POLICY AND MANAGEMENT

*Chapter 1*

# *LEGAL AND REGULATORY INSTRUMENTS*

## 1.1 Introduction

At its independence in the 1990s the former Yugoslav Republic of Macedonia, like other Central and East European countries in transition, started moving toward a market economy. The Government and its citizens are making an enormous effort to achieve economic growth based on the principles of sustainable development. Now the country is tackling the situation and trying to overcome the negative consequences of regional armed conflicts.

As part of its economic development programme, the Government is developing its environmental policy and identifying its priorities for environmental protection and the sustainable use of natural resources. The Constitution adopted by the Parliament in late 1991 provides the protection and promotion of the environment as one of its fundamental values (art. 8). Article 43 of the Constitution states: "Everyone is entitled to a healthy environment, and everyone is obliged to protect and improve the environment". This provision forms the basis of all environmental legislation and policy.

Certain recent decisions influence substantially the new approach to environmental protection:

(a) The first attempt at decentralization based on the Law on Local Self-Government, adopted in January 2002, the draft Law on Local Finance and the Law on the Territorial Division and on the Determination of Local Self-Government Units (Law on Municipal Boundaries) intended to give local authorities the means to implement the Law on Local-Self Government;
(b) The EU approximation process obliges the administration to transpose and implement the relevant directives of the "Environment" Chapter.

## 1.2 Environmental policies and strategies

The country is actively involved in the "Environment for Europe" ministerial process. As part of this process, in December 1996, the Government developed and adopted the National Environmental Action Plan (NEAP), which is still the country's main environmental strategy. Article 14 of the framework Law on the Environment and Nature Protection and Promotion of 1996 also requires a NEAP. Three criteria guided the NEAP: the protection of human health; the improvement of the environment to enhance the quality of life and the conservation of natural resources for sustainable development.

The preparation of the NEAP was the first step towards the integration of environmental policy into the country's economic and social development programmes because it concerns not only the relevant environmental authority but also other institutions with responsibilities for environmental protection. The NEAP was drafted with the participation of all relevant stakeholders in the country, including the non-governmental community. It was supported by the World Bank.

The NEAP was prepared for the five-year period from 1997 to 2001. However, in early 2002, it was still the operative plan. Its priorities are to:

- Improve air quality.
- Improve water quality.
- Conserve biodiversity, especially in Lakes Ohrid, Prespa and Dojran.
- Reforest and preserve existing forests.
- Strengthen the management capacity of institutions responsible for environmental monitoring and enforcing environmental legislation.

The NEAP was adopted more than five years ago and its implementation has been ongoing. Since certain system changes, such as decentralization and EU approximation, are under way, the NEAP needs to be revised and harmonized with the existing situation. Work on updating the NEAP of 1996 is being funded by the European Commission. It was approved under the 2001 CARDS Programme and started at the beginning of 2002.

The Ministry of Environment and Physical Planning intends to prepare a strategy for sustainable development based on the Action Plan. The conceptual approach to the strategy was prepared by the Institute for Social and Legal Research in 2000, with support from the Ministry of Environment and Physical Planning and the United Nations Development Programme (UNDP).

In line with the NEAP priorities, one of the planned activities is the preparation of local environmental action plans (LEAPs). There is also a legal obligation in the Law on the Environment and Nature Protection and Promotion (art. 14): "The National Environmental Action Plan requires local authorities and the city of Skopje to approve local environmental action plans for the environment and nature protection and promotion." Twenty-one local authorities have prepared LEAPs; seven have completed their plans; five are in an implementation phase; and the rest are preparing them. The Ministry of Environment and Physical Planning is coordinating this activity through an inter-institutional body established for this purpose. It is expected that the implementation of the LEAPs will be an integral part of municipal development programmes. Experience with the preparation and implementation of the LEAPs show that the local authorities lack financial resources, institutional capacity and managerial experience. There is also insufficient public awareness of the goals and the importance of the LEAPs because of inadequate publicity.

In 1999 the Government adopted its National Environment and Health Action Plan (NEHAP). Its preparation and implementation were coordinated by the Ministry of Health, in cooperation with the Ministry of Environment and Physical Planning. In September 2001 the World Bank organized a workshop to encourage the implementation of the NEHAP and, in particular, the preparation of Local Environmental Health Action Plans (LEHAP) in the local authorities.

The Spatial Plan is another very important strategic document in terms of environmental protection. The existing Plan dates from 1988 and is unenforceable because of the rapid changes in society with impacts on physical planning, e.g. the enormous expansion of the city of Skopje. Preparation of a new plan, started in 1995, has been completed and is currently before Parliament for adoption. (see Chapter 12 on Human health and the environment)

Several documents define specific aspects of the strategic development of the environment. In 1995 the Ministry of Agriculture, Forestry and Water Economy began preparation of a strategy for the development of agriculture, forestry and water management. The Strategy addresses environmental aspects of forest and water protection, taking into account the fact that the Ministry of Environment and Physical Planning is responsible for the protection of biodiversity, national parks and water, soil, flora and fauna.

The draft National Strategy for Waste-water and Solid Waste Management was completed at the end of 1999 but has not yet been adopted by the Government.

The Ministry of Agriculture, Forestry and Water Economy is working now on an updated Water Master Plan to replace the old plans, which are still valid. The goal is to create an adequate document to govern the management of all water resources in the country. Parallel to this, the updated Water Master Plan will address not only water use and supply issues, but also the impact of human activities on water quality. The Ministry plans to work closely with other relevant ministries, such as the Ministry of Environment and Physical Planning and the Ministry of Transport and Communications.

In July 2001, in collaboration with the Academy of Sciences and Arts, the Ministry of Agriculture, Forestry and Water Economy published its Agricultural Development Strategy up to 2005, which addresses all agricultural production sectors. (see Chapter 9 on Agriculture and forest management)

With funding from the Global Environment Facility (GEF), the Ministry of Environment and Physical Planning started to prepare a national biodiversity strategy in 2001 to strengthen the implementation of the Convention on Biological Diversity.

## 1.3    Legal framework

The legal system has three levels: the Constitution at the highest level, laws at the second, and sub-laws (normative acts such as decrees, regulations, decisions, instructions, orders) at the third.

The framework law on environmental protection is the Law on the Environment and Nature Protection and Promotion adopted in 1996 (Official Gazette No. 69/96), which follows the principles of the

1994 Model Law on the Environment of the Council of Europe. It regulates some of the basic rights and obligations of State administrative bodies with environmental responsibilities, such as those concerning the submission of environmental and nature protection data to the Ministry of Environment and Physical Planning (art. 9), as well as those of physical and legal entities, the funding of environmental and nature protection (from the national budget and from the Fund for Environmental and Nature Protection), the monitoring of the environment, the relevant bodies for the implementation and enforcement of environmental legislation, some general rules for environmental management instruments such as authorizations for industrial activities, approvals for the exploitation of mineral raw materials, eco-audits, eco-labelling, the development of the pollutants inventory, the assessment of environmental impacts, the supervision and control of environmental protection measures, and the penalties for violation of the Law. The Law seems very comprehensive, embracing nearly all aspects of environmental protection. On the other hand, it would be very difficult to implement and enforce because its provisions are too broad in terms of appropriate procedures. The Law is not consistent with the environmental legislation of the European Union.

Other basic laws regulating environmental policy are listed below.

- The Law on the Protection of Rare Species (Official Gazette No. 41/73);
- The Law on Meadow and Pasture Management (Official Gazette No. 20/74);
- The Law on the Protection of Lakes Ohrid, Prespa and Dojran (Official Gazette No. 45/77);
- The Law on the Conservation of National Parks (Official Gazette No. 33/80);
- The Law on Geological Research and Mineral Raw Material Exploitation (Official Gazette No. 18/88);
- The Law on Investment Structure Construction (Official Gazette No. 15/90);
- The Law on Hydro Meteorological Activities (Official Gazette No. 19/92);
- The Law on Fire Protection (Official Gazette Nos. 43/86; 37/87; 51/88; 36/90 and 12/93);
- The Law on the Prevention of Harmful Noise (Official Gazette Nos. 28/84; 10/90 and 62/93);
- The Law on Fishery (Official Gazette No. 62/93);

- The Law on Air Protection against Pollution (Official Gazette Nos. 20/74; 6/81; 10/90 and 63/93);
- The Law on Spatial and Urban Planning (Official Gazette No. 4/96);
- The Law on Hunting (Official Gazette No. 20/96);
- The Criminal Code (Official Gazette No. 37/96);
- The Law on Forests (Official Gazette No. 47/97);
- The Law on Waters (Official Gazette Nos. 4/98 and 19/2000);
- The Law on Waste (Official Gazette No. 37/98);
- The Law on Public Hygiene, and the Collection and Transport of Municipal Solid and Industrial Waste (Official Gazette No. 37/98);
- The Law on the Protection of Plants (Official Gazette Nos. 25/98 and 6/2000);
- The Law on the Organization and Work of the State Administration (Official Gazette No. 58/2000).

There are a number of regulations containing environmental standards and appropriate procedures taken from the regulations of the former Socialist Federal Republic of Yugoslavia, for instance:

- Regulations on the submission of monitoring reports, and on the control and recording of monitoring data on harmful substances discharged into the air (Official Gazette No. 9/76);
- Regulations on the methodology for monitoring and identifying harmful substances in the air (Official Gazette No. 9/76);
- Regulations on the classification of objects that can pollute the air in residential areas by discharging harmful substances and the formation of sanitary protection zones (Official Gazette No. 13/76;
- Regulations on the implementation of urban sanitation measures (Official Gazette No. 11/76);
- Regulations on the maximum allowed concentrations and quantities of harmful substances that can be released into the air from different sources of pollution (Official Gazette No. 3/90).

None of the regulations applies EU environmental standards. One of the biggest weaknesses in the implementation of environmental standards is the general nature of the regulations; i.e. there is no categorization of polluters according to type of industry, amount and type of pollution. Consequently, there are no emission limit values (e.g. for waste-water discharge) for individual sources of pollution as to their size and type.

The entire environmental legislation is currently under revision. New laws or amendments to existing laws on specialized areas of environmental protection are planned. The Law on the Protection of the Natural Heritage is before Parliament for adoption. It will replace two existing laws: the Law on the Protection of Rare Species and the Law on the Conservation of National Parks, and it will present an integrated approach in line with EU directives.

Although recently changed and amended, the Law on Waters is under revision. The intention of the Government is to harmonize water policy and water management issues with the relevant EU directives.

Some other environmental laws have been or are being prepared by the Ministry of Environment and Physical Planning. According to the Ministry's legislative programme in late 2001, the following draft laws were to be approved by the end of 2002:

- The draft law on environmental impact assessment;
- The draft law on air quality;
- The draft law on changes and amendments to the Law on Waste;
- The draft law on changes and amendments to the Law on Spatial and Urban Planning.

In mid-2002, however, the fate of these draft laws was unclear. The Ministry of Environment and Physical Planning had reconsidered whether to proceed with new laws or to adopt by-laws in order to allow for more flexibility and adaptability in the future.

A serious disadvantage in the environment law is the absence of measures to decentralize some responsibilities to the local level. However, a first step to change this situation was the adoption of the Law on Local Self-Government at the beginning of 2002. Its article 22, paragraph 1, item 2, clearly states that "municipalities shall be competent for the following actions: protection of the environment, nature and space regulation; measures for the protection and prevention of water, atmosphere and land pollution; protection against noise and ionizing radiation". Although very broad,

this allows the central authorities to delegate certain environmental protection, monitoring and control obligations to local self-government. The Law also states that all relevant legislation should be consequently revised and amended by the end of 2003.

*EU approximation of national environmental legislation*

On 12 April 2001 the former Yugoslav Republic of Macedonia and the European Community signed the Stabilization and Association Agreement. This Agreement is now the driving force behind environmental policy because it obliges the country to harmonize its environmental legislation with EU norms. Article 103 of the Agreement presents the priorities for achieving the goals laid down. The harmonization of environmental legislation, i.e. continuous approximation of the laws and regulations to the standards of the European Community, is an important mechanism for the efficient implementation of environmental policy.

The Sector for European Integration within the General Secretariat of the Government (Council of Ministers) has worked out the Government Strategy for Approximation of the Legislation. The basic documents of the Strategy are the Action Plan for the Implementation of the Stabilization and Association Agreement and the National Programme for Approximation of the Legislation. Section 7 of the Programme concerning the environment sets the deadlines for the harmonization of the different areas of environmental legislation with the respective EU legislation. Highest priority is given to horizontal legislation, including the Directive on Environment Impact Assessment, the Directive on Access to Environmental Information, the Directive on Information, and the Regulations of the European Environment Agency. The country is considering revising all deadlines contained in the "Environment" section of the Approximation Programme to make them more realistic.

Part of the PHARE Programme, Country Operational Programme 1999 (COP99), has given considerable support to the approximation of environmental legislation in several areas, such as water, waste and access to information. Under a German Technical Assistance (GTZ) project a draft law on air quality has been prepared and training has been provided for the Ministry's staff to prepare and implement legislation on air.

*Implementation of multilateral environmental agreements (MEAs)*

The former Yugoslav Republic of Macedonia has ratified 14 conventions by a special law on ratification for each. With their publication in the Official Gazette they become part of domestic law and cannot be changed or amended according to article 118 of the Constitution. They are implemented either through changes and amendments to existing national legislation or through new laws. In some cases sub-laws, such as regulations and instructions, have been prepared. (see Chapter 5 on International cooperation)

*Environmental Impact Assessment*

There is no legal procedure for environmental impact assessment (EIA). The basic Law on the Environment and Nature Protection and Promotion (art.15) specifies that physical and legal entities should, in their activities and investment and production projects, provide for the rational use of natural resources and should monitor the impacts of their activities on the environment and nature. An entrepreneur is obliged to ensure the protection of the environment and nature by preparing technical documentation containing, among other things, information about the environmental impacts of the proposed activity (called the "environmental-technological report") and its development. The Ministry of Environment and Physical Planning, through the Environment Office, approves the technical document and gives its consent to the proposed investment activity or facility on the basis of the ecological assessment. The Law on Investment Structure Construction specifies that, as part of the technical documentation needed to obtain a construction permit, besides the basic conditions, other conditions prescribed in other laws and acts, especially the Law on the Environment and Nature Protection and Promotion, need to be met.

The Ministry of Transport and Communications requires an environmental-technological report for facilities that are expected to have an impact on the environment. There is no legally binding list of activities (facilities) for mandatory assessment although article 15 of the Law on the Environment and Nature Protection and Promotion stipulates that: "the Minister of the Environment shall prescribe the kind of investment sites on which technical documentation assessing environment impact has to be prepared". Sometimes the Ministry

of Environment and Physical Planning decides on the need for such an assessment but this is not the rule. However, in practice the banking system requires developers applying for loans to submit their investment programmes to the Ministry for its opinion on the suitability of the facility from an environmental point of view.

The Ministry of Environment and Physical Planning, through the State Environment Inspectorate, takes part in the technical inspection of facilities that have polluting processes.

Depending on the circumstances, the assessment method followed in the environmental-technological reports was modelled on assessment methodologies in force either in an EU member country or in the former Yugoslavia. The lack of consistency has been a matter of concern for the Ministry, and the Environment Office within the Ministry has recently developed guidelines on the preparation of the "draft" on environmental impact assessment. The guidelines focus on the main elements of the assessment, including: a description of the location, a description of the object and the production processes; possible changes and impacts on the environment; and prescribed measures for the protection of the environment.

Although it has not yet adopted national legislation for environmental impact assessment, the former Yugoslav Republic of Macedonia ratified the UNECE Convention on Environmental Impact Assessment in a Transboundary Context (Espoo Convention) in August 1999. After ratification international agreements become part of national law and can therefore be implemented. There have, however, been no cases of implementation to date.

As indicated above, procedures for environmental impact assessment are not yet fully worked out, and they need to be harmonized with the EU Directives on Environment Impact Assessment. A draft law on EIA has been prepared, but its adoption is being questioned. The draft still needs a clear transposition of the provisions of the EU Directives referring to the screening and scoping of the EIA processes, the consultation process, access to information and public participation. According to the "Environment" Section of the Approximation Programme, the law on EIA, as part of the horizontal legislation, is a priority. More recent consideration is being given to developing a by-law for environmental impact assessment in place of the draft law.

*Permitting*

The legal and institutional frameworks for an adequate environmental permit and enforcement system are being developed. In late 2000, the Law on the Environment and Nature Protection and Promotion was amended to provide the legal basis for developing a permit system (art. 30). The country intends to transpose into national legislation the EU Directive on Integrated Pollution Prevention and Control (IPPC), which stipulates integrated environmental permitting.

Construction permits are issued by the Ministry of Transport and Communications on the basis of an application that briefly describes the proposed activity and its impacts on the environment. These applications are reviewed by the Ministry of Environment and Physical Planning.

Operation permits, however, require written opinions from all concerned inspectorates, including the State Environment Inspectorate. Depending on the Inspectorates' opinion, conditions may be imposed for the proposed activity. In general, new establishments and economic activities are authorized without limitation on their duration.

There is no system that regulates licences, such as pollution permits, for existing facilities, and thus no means to oblige a company to comply with the legal limits on pollution. This is one of the issues that need to be addressed in the new framework law in coordination with the relevant EU directive. The situation now requires facilities with pollution sources to prepare and submit environmental-technological reports to the State Environment Inspectorate in the Ministry of Environment and Physical Planning. These should include an analysis of the pollution sources and measures for the reduction of pollution so that the facility complies with the maximum allowable concentrations (MAC). Remediation should take place within five years. The transposition of the EU Directive on IPPC will introduce integrated permits for new and existing industrial installations.

There is provision, in article 19 of the Law on the Environment and Nature Protection and Promotion, for the Ministry of Environment to prescribe a procedure that would allow the voluntary participation of industrial enterprises in an environmental management scheme (eco-audit). This provision could help industries to organize an environmental management system closer to the ISO 14001 standard. However, the implementing regulation for this procedure has not yet been developed.

Article 20 of the same Law provides for the Ministry of Environment, in accordance with other ministries, to regulate the procedure and criteria for labelling "eco-products" for the market. As with article 19, no normative act required for implementation has been approved.

In order to regulate the transport of dangerous goods and chemicals through the national parks a joint commission from the Ministry of Transport and Communications, the Ministry of Environment and Physical Planning and other institutions has been established. Special emphasis has been placed on the Mavrovo National Park, crossed by a number of major cross-country roads. A regulation laying down the requirements for the said transport is expected to be adopted.

The Environment Office, through its Division for Biodiversity, issues import and export certificates for rare and endangered species of wild flora and fauna following the requirements of the Convention on International Trade in Endangered Species of Wild Fauna and Flora (CITES), which the former Yugoslav Republic of Macedonia ratified in July 2000. No quotas have yet been fixed for these certificates.

*Enforcement*

According to article 39 of the basic Law on the Environment and Nature Protection and Promotion, the Inspectorate should supervise the implementation of this Law. Environmental inspections are based on standards contained in laws and regulations, including maximum allowable concentrations of emissions. Existing MACs, however, are outdated and inadequate, which makes their enforcement even more problematic. When regulatory levels are exceeded, inspectors may prescribe measures to reduce the adverse impacts from pollution, such as improving the cleaning processes (e.g. waste-water treatment systems, filters) and installing pollution control equipment (self-monitoring equipment), or impose fines. Fines vary from 1,500 to 15,000 euro. In extreme cases, production facilities can be closed, a measure that has been taken on a few occasions (e.g. the "MHK Zletovo" lead and zinc smelter in Veles). The inspector's decision can be appealed in the courts. In 95 per cent of the cases the inspectors' orders have no positive results (fines are not paid): either the appeals are successful or the court fails to review the case within the two-year deadline.

Currently, the State Environment Inspectorate employs ten inspectors. All polluting enterprises are subject to inspection, irrespective of their capacity. Inspections are based on the environmental-technological reports presented by the enterprises to the State Inspectorate and cover air, water, ionizing and non-ionizing radiation, soil, protected nature and noise. Inspections of activities relating to municipal waste are unsystematic. The Inspectorate relies on sampling data from the inspected entities (self-monitoring data). On occasion samples are taken by the Division for Laboratory Research within the Environment Office.

The State Environment Inspectorate focuses on the most heavily polluting industry (roughly 100 companies). These companies are identified from data supplied by the State Agency for Statistics. The Ministry of Environment and Physical Planning is developing a comprehensive inventory of pollution sources (around 1000) that will enable it to target polluters more systematically. Enterprises are generally inspected four or five times a year, but much more frequently in special cases.

A number of other inspectorates exist at central and local levels. The Ministry of Agriculture, Forestry and Water Economy and the Ministry of Health have inspectorates. In addition, the State Communal Inspectorate, created in 1999, verifies the application of the laws at communal enterprises of national importance. Enterprises of municipal importance are subject to the authority of local inspectorates. Inspections are not properly coordinated among the different inspectorates; often overlapping or separate inspections, like the inspection on the health risk, which is of the competence of the Ministry of Health, are omitted. It is expected that the future delegation of some responsibilities for environmental monitoring and inspections to the local level, to local self-governments, will improve the enforcement of environmental legislation.

## 1.4 Conclusions and recommendations

The National Environmental Action Plan (NEAP) is the basic document for the development of the national environmental strategy. It has also contributed to the preparation of local environmental action plans (LEAPs), and therefore

contributed to decentralization and the delegation of environmental responsibilities to the local authorities. The recently approved work on the updating of the NEAP of 1996 gives another opportunity not only to reflect the changes that have occurred but also to stimulate the development of a national environmental strategy based on sustainable development.

*Recommendation 1.1:*
*The Ministry of Environment and Physical Planning should develop and implement NEAP 2 and a sustainable development strategy, and it should focus more on instruments for implementation, including, for example, strategic environmental assessment, environmental impact assessment, and integrated permitting.*

There are many other strategic documents in the form of environmental studies, reports, plans and strategies financed and prepared by international organizations. The National Strategy for Waste-Water and Solid Waste Management, the Study on the Monitoring of Air Pollution and the Integral Water Resources Development Study highlight different aspects of environmental protection and give substantial advanced direction to environmental management. However, they do not have legal status because they have not been formally adopted or incorporated into national legislation. At the same time, the Spatial Plan that has been presented to Parliament for adoption aims at the integration of many environmental issues into spatial planning, thus taking into consideration environmentally sound solutions for waste water and solid waste treatment, as well as water supply, throughout the country.

Parliament should give priority to the adoption of the Spatial Plan, acknowledging its leading role in the national physical planning system and indirectly also in environmental programmes and plans. The Plan should be consistent with all other strategic documents on the environment prepared with the financial support of international organizations (see recommendation 12.1).

Although there are many laws and regulations covering almost all aspects of environmental protection, most of them are old and inadequate for the current situation in the country. Another general weakness of environmental legislation is the lack of implementation due to the institutional separation of State bodies responsible for that implementation, insufficient professional staff in the administration and the weakness of the controlling authorities.

The EU approximation process is the trigger for the revision of all acts concerning the environment. The existing legislative framework on environmental protection needs to be updated and aligned with EU environmental directives. This enormous work is at its very beginning. There is still discussion as to how the requirements of the priority horizontal legislation will be transposed. There is no final decision as to whether instruments for environmental management, such as environmental impact assessment (EIA), permits and economic instruments, should be included within the new framework law for the environment or should be reflected in separate acts.

*Recommendation 1.2:*
*(a)  The Ministry of Environment and Physical Planning in cooperation with other Ministries and institutions should develop and implement a new law on environmental protection as a framework for environmental legislation which includes instruments for environmental management such as an environmental information system and access to it, economic instruments, an environmental impact assessment procedure, strategic environmental assessment and an environmental monitoring system.*

*(b)  The Ministry should also complete stand-alone acts for air, water, protected areas and biodiversity, underground resources, transport, waste and noise, giving the opportunity to bring the legislation in conformity with the relevant European Union directives*

Among the regulatory instruments for environmental protection, environmental impact assessment is one of the most important tools for the whole investment process. This instrument is not developed in the country. This causes difficulties in the approval of large-scale projects of national and international importance and will continue to so. There are a few cases where EIA has been carried out by foreign consultants, but there is still no specific legal procedure that requires the involvement of all concerned and interested parties in the assessment.

*Recommendation 1.3:*
*The Ministry of Environment and Physical Planning should give special attention to the full transposition of the European Union's EIA Directives in national environmental legislation. On the basis of the new framework law, a by-law for environmental impact assessment should be drawn up, defining clearly all important steps of the EIA process: screening, scoping, consultations, access to information, decision-making and access to justice. The by-law should decentralize the assessment process in a rational manner, e.g. delegate competencies to local self-government for small-scale activities.*

As the former Yugoslav Republic of Macedonia adapts its legislation to make it consistent with the requirements of the European Union, more attention needs to be given to the implementation and enforcement of legislation, official strategies and plans. Strengthening the Ministry of Environment and Physical Planning and particularly such enforcement mechanisms as the State inspectorates are important for this purpose.

*Chapter 2*

# *INSTITUTIONAL ARRANGEMENTS*

## 2.1    Introduction

Since independence in the early 1990s, the former Yugoslav Republic of Macedonia has taken important steps towards strengthening its institutions for environmental protection, though the process is still not completed. The 1996 Law on the Environment and Nature Protection and Promotion – (arts.19 and 20) and its amendments designate the main environmental authority (the Ministry of Environment and Physical Planning), and other central authorities with environmental responsibilities, such as the Ministry of Agriculture, Forestry and Water Economy, the Ministry of Health, the Ministry of Economy, the Ministry of Internal Affairs, and the Ministry of Transport and Communications. The principal role in environmental matters and in the coordination between different organizations and departments belongs to the Ministry of Environment and Physical Planning.

The Law on the Organization and Work of the State Administration, adopted in 2000, establishes the functions and responsibilities of all the State administration bodies, including the ministries.

## 2.2    Institutions with responsibilities for environmental protection at the national level

*Ministry of Environment and Physical Planning*

The most important body with a direct role in the development of environmental policy is the Ministry of Environment and Physical Planning, established as a separate ministry in 1998. It was previously a department of the former Ministry of Construction, Urban Planning and Environment. The Physical Planning Department was incorporated into the Ministry of Environment in June 2000. The remaining responsibilities of the former Ministry of Construction, Urban Planning and Environment were transferred to the Ministry of Transport and Communications.

The creation of the Ministry of Environment and Physical Planning, though it is seen as a milestone in the unification of environmental institutional arrangements, has not solved the fragmentation of responsibilities for environmental monitoring, the management of cross-sectoral issues and the setting of standards. The environmental responsibilities of other ministries, notably the Ministry of Agriculture, Forestry and Water Economy, the Ministry of Health and the Ministry of Transport and Communications, combined with the comparatively weak position of the Ministry of Environment, explain to a large extent the present inadequate legislative framework and low level of enforcement.

Article 28 of the Law on the Organization and Work of the State Administration defines the responsibilities of the Ministry of Environment and Physical Planning as follows:

- Monitoring the state of the environment;
- Protecting waters, soil, air and the ozone layer;
- Protecting against noise and radiation; and protecting biodiversity, mineral resources, national parks and protected areas;
- Rehabilitating polluted areas;
- Proposing measures for the treatment of hazardous waste;
- Physical planning;
- Operating the physical information system; and
- Carrying out inspections and supervision within its scope of activity.

There are some discrepancies in the structure of the Ministry as laid down in the Law on the Environment and Nature Protection and Promotion and as stipulated in the Law on the Organization and Work of the State Administration. For example, the Law on the Environment and Nature Protection and Promotion provides for an "agency" for the environment within the Ministry, a fund for the environment and nature protection and promotion with the status of a legal entity, and an inspectorate for the environment and nature protection and promotion as a special body within the Ministry. The Law on the Organization and Work of the State Administration refers to an environment "office", not to an "agency;" it makes no mention of a fund and it does not refer to a State environment inspectorate as a "special body within the Ministry". The Ministry's structure in figure 2.1 follows the provisions of the Law on the Organization and Work of the State Administration.

The Ministry currently has approximately 80 full-time employees and 15 people working on a special contractual basis. According to the attached scheme the Ministry is organized into five departments and four bodies, as follows:

- The Department for Regulation and Standardization
- The Department for European Integration
- The Department for Sustainable Development
- The Department for Physical Planning
- The Environmental Information Centre
- The State Environment Inspectorate
- The Environment Office
- The Office for the Spatial Information System
- The Fund for the Environment and Nature Protection and Promotion.

The Department for Regulation and Standardization is responsible for the development of all laws and other regulations on environmental matters; it manages the relevant multilateral agreements and conventions with regard to the issues within its scope. One of its most important functions is linked to the analysis of EU directives, regulations and recommendations, the transposition of the environmental legislation of the European Union and the coordination of international technical assistance for legislative approximation. This is an area of heightening importance and increasing work, and the office responsible is seriously understaffed.

The Department for European Integration was established to develop the EU integration policy. It coordinates activities with the Department for European Integration of the Government and the relevant departments of the Ministry of Foreign Affairs. The need for additional staff to cope with the bulk of the work entailed in EU approximation is well understood. It is accepted that the implementation of EU policy is still not fully integrated into the responsibilities of this Department, e.g. the development of a division for project preparation and overall coordination of international cooperation projects. The respective responsibilities of the Department for Regulation and Standardization and the Department for European Integration in the approximation process are not sufficiently clear. Better integration and streamlining may be crucial here.

The Department for Sustainable Development is responsible for the implementation of environmental policy in accordance with the concept of sustainable development. This implies that the core work of this Department should be the preparation and coordination of environmental strategies, programmes and plans, and the development of economic instruments. However, the Department is currently split into four separate divisions: (i) the Division for Project Preparation; (ii) the Division for Intersectoral Cooperation; (iii) the Division for Lake Ohrid Project Implementation; and (iv) the Division for Lake Dojran Project Implementation. At present this structure does not respond to expectations of what sustainable development should be. It needs to be considerably restructured and oriented more towards the development of environmental strategies and programmes and economic instruments.

The Department for Physical Planning is responsible for the development and implementation of the Spatial Plan, so it is involved in the coordination of physical planning on a national level. Currently the Plan is before Parliament for adoption.

The Environmental Information Centre collects, processes and provides information on the environment to the public, the Ministry and other international institutions. It has a Public Relations Office with a library. The Centre has the authority to control the ambient air quality monitoring network. It may well be expanded and tasked with monitoring all environmental media and so become the national environmental monitoring centre.

The State Environment Inspectorate carries out inspections to check compliance with environmental standards and prescribe measures against pollution, both regularly and as required in accordance with the Law on the Environment and Nature Protection and Promotion. Out of a total of eleven staff, the Inspectorate currently has seven inspectors who cover inspections throughout the country. The Inspectorate itself is centralized, but most of the national inspectors are located in sensitive areas (heavily industrialized areas or protected areas), such as Veles and Bitola. Bearing in mind the overall need for better implementation and enforcement of legislation, regulations and standards, there is an urgent need to strengthen the staff of the State Inspectorate at all levels and particularly at the local level.

The Environment Office ("Agency") was set up in the Ministry with a view to separating the responsibility for the development of policies and legislation (Ministry) from their implementation and monitoring (Office). The Office has four divisions: Monitoring and Environmental Impact Assessment; Laboratory Research; Natural Heritage Protection; and Biodiversity. The Office has the potential of an agency. At present it is restricted to environmental permitting for nature protection. Environmental impact assessment is still not developed. Effective executive authority in the Ministry demands a fully empowered agency. This will first require a change in the Law on the Organization and Work of the State Administration.

The Office for the Spatial Information System keeps all relevant information (maps, plans) for physical planning in the country. It provides data upon request to interested institutions and to other physical and legal persons.

The Fund for the Environment and Nature Protection and Promotion (Environment Fund) is responsible for overall investment in the implementation of environmental projects. Originally established in 1998, the Fund was provided the basis for transformation into an independent agency by virtue of the Law on the Organization and Work of the State Administration (Official Gazette no. 58/2002). There is currently a draft law on the environment fund that, if passed by Parliament, would make the Fund fully independent from the Ministry but supportive of its goals and policies (see Chapter 3 on Economic instruments and privatization).

*Other national institutions with environmental responsibilities*

Parliament has the duty to influence environmental policy and legislation through its Commission for Environment, Youth and Sport. The members of the Commission review documents and legal acts related to the environment and submit suggestions and positions to Parliament before the adoption of the laws.

There is another permanent body within the Government: the Commission for the Economic System, Sustainable Development and Current Economic Policy. The Commission is composed of Government Ministers and deals with issues encouraging sustainable economic development, spatial and regional development, scientific and technological development; and the rational use of materials, energy and other resources. It is a consultative body to the Government, facilitating its work on intersectoral issues at policy level.

The institutional frame responsible for functions, measures and tasks related to environmental protection is supported by the activities of other State administrative bodies. The Ministry of Agriculture, Forestry and Water Economy has the most closely related activities and competence with the Ministry of Environment and Physical Planning. The most important issue treated by these two ministries is water management. The Ministry of Agriculture, Forestry and Water Economy is also responsible for matters concerning the use of agricultural land, forests and other natural resources, the protection of livestock and plants against diseases and pests, the monitoring and examination of the state of waters, the maintenance and improvement of the water regime, permitting for water use and waste-water discharge, hydromelioration systems, hydrological and agro-meteorological measurement, and studying and researching meteorological, hydrological and bio-meteorological phenomena and processes.

The Ministry of Health, including the State Sanitary and Health Care Inspectorate, deals with a number of issues related to environment protection, such as: monitoring the pollution of air, water, soil and foodstuffs; monitoring and protecting the population against the harmful effects of gases, radiation, noise, and air, water and soil pollution; controlling the quality of food and monitoring the whole hygiene-epidemiological situation. The Ministry of Health is obliged to submit regularly the data that it collects on the environment to the Environmental Information Centre at the Ministry of Environment and Physical Planning. The Ministry of Health was also involved in the drafting group for the law on air quality within the Ministry of Environment. However, both ministries expressed the need for stronger cooperation and coordination of environmental activities.

**Figure 2.1: Ministry of Environment and Physical Planning**

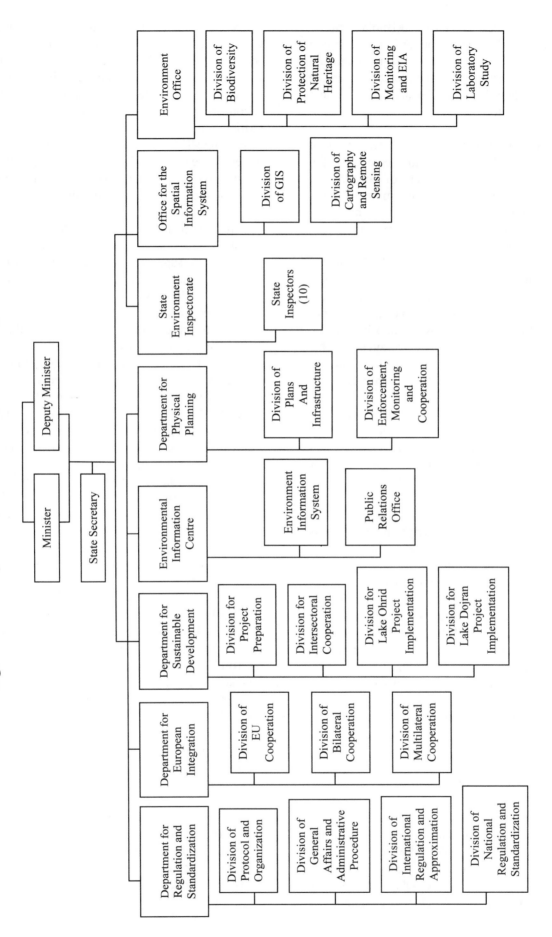

The Ministry of Transport and Communications has competence in the area of transport and communal affairs and certain environmental responsibilities, especially through the State Communal Inspectorate. This Ministry was created through the restructuring of the Government (1998), in which the former Ministry of Construction, Urban Planning and Environment was split into the Ministry of Transport and Communications and the Ministry of Environment and Physical Planning. However, there remains some ambiguity in their respective competences. For example, the Ministry of Transport and Communications is responsible for the construction and maintenance of water-supply facilities, for communal activities (waste water, solid waste), for urban planning and for transport (source of pollution). The State Communal Inspectorate monitors the construction and maintenance of the infrastructure, including water-supply facilities, sewerage systems and landfills and ensures that legal and physical entities consistently apply all legal requirements. The Ministry of Environment and Physical Planning is supposed to monitor almost all of the above activities, from the environmental protection viewpoint.

The Ministry of Economy is responsible for the exploitation of mineral raw materials and the application of common technical norms and standards in commercial and industrial activities. The Commission of Standardization is the Ministry of Economy's environmental body, coordinating the standard-setting action of governmental bodies.

The Ministry of Internal Affairs helps other bodies with inspections to check implementation of the environmental legislation by physical and legal entities. This State organ is responsible for controlling the production, trade, storage and safety of inflammable liquids, gases, explosives and other hazardous substances and their transport.

A Cleaner Production Centre has started work (training staff, with assistance from the Czech Republic and the United Nations Industrial Development Organization (UNIDO)) and is preparing demonstration projects. The Centre is based at the Chamber of Commerce and the intention is that it should operate as a non-governmental organization facilitating the introduction of cleaner technologies in industry. (see also Chapter 8 on Waste management)

*Regional and local administration with environmental responsibilities*

Although there is no regional level public administration in the former Yugoslav Republic of Macedonia, individual ministries and public services do sometimes operate in "regional" units responsible for several villages or local authorities. For example, the State Communal Inspectorate controls the application of the law in communal enterprises of national importance, while enterprises of local importance are subject to inspection by local inspectorates.

The State Inspectorate for Construction and Urban Planning within the Ministry of Transport and Communications issues construction permits regionally through 34 Inspectorates. Inspectorates of the Ministry of Agriculture, Forestry and Water Economy and the Ministry of Health are also involved in environmental matters in their particular fields of competence. Communication between the inspectorates of different ministries, and between the State and municipal inspectorates, where it exists, appears to be unsystematic. There is an obvious need to streamline coordination between the different inspectorates, especially where they share responsibilities, e.g. responsibility for the enforcement of the Basel Convention lies with the Ministry of Environment and Physical Planning (Environment Office), whereas the enforcement of solid waste management is the responsibility of the State Communal Inspectorate.

The country has a "local self-government system" that includes the city of Skopje and 123 local authorities. Local authorities (usually through communal enterprises) may manage drinking-water supplies, green areas and solid waste disposal, and they also have some responsibilities in the areas of construction, land-use planning and zoning. Local authorities, however, are financially dependent on the national Government, as their own sources of revenue are inadequate. There are no specialized units for environmental protection.

At the beginning of 2002, a new Law on Local Self-Government was adopted. It defines the functions of local self-government units in the former Yugoslav Republic of Macedonia and gives local authorities competence in the field of environmental protection. Article 22 makes local authorities responsible for taking measures to protect water, the atmosphere and land from pollution, to protect nature and to ensure protection against noise and ionizing radiation. It also includes another group of measures linked to environmental protection and communal activities for which they are responsible, such as water supply and waste-water drainage, public hygiene, the disposal of municipal waste, public transport, and the maintenance of green areas. However, the Law gives the local authorities neither enough funds nor financing instruments to accomplish these functions. According to the transitional provisions of the Law on Local Self–Government, all relevant legislation, including environmental acts, should be revised before the end of December 2003 so as to delegate more rights to local government and to clarify the financing of local government tasks. The new Law on Local Self-Government will be complemented by a new Law on Local Revenues and Finances, which is being discussed.

Local authorities lack competence and, therefore, play only a minor role in environmental planning, decision-making, environmental monitoring and enforcement. The entire institutional framework should be enriched with a strong public information system, capable of mobilizing a great number of entities in the achievement of an environmental protection policy. Significant results have already been achieved, especially through institutions financed by international organizations, which have contributed to the raising of awareness of the importance of environmental protection action. The best example is the current method of preparing and discussing the Local Environmental Action Plans (LEAPs), which are playing the role of local environmental strategy.

## 2.3    Conclusions and recommendations

The Ministry of Environment and Physical Planning is committed to adopting a policy of environmental management relying for the present on a mixture of administrative and market-based instruments. At the same time the question of capacity inside the Ministry remains a major obstacle to exercising its responsibility. The structure of the Ministry was adopted in May 2001 following the requirements of the Law on the Organization and Work of the State Administration and seems to be complete, but is so only in formal terms. The recommendations of the PHARE project on capacity-building and strengthening the Ministry have not yet been implemented. In fact, major parts of the Departments' activities overlap, while the Ministry urgently needs competent staff to

coordinate and lead work on the transposition and implementation of the environmental body of law of the EU and the development and use of economic instruments in the environmental management.

*Recommendation 2.1:*
*The Ministry of Environment and Physical Planning should undertake the necessary steps, which could include internal restructuring, to correspond better to the needs of the European Union integration process:*

*(a) The Department for Sustainable Development should be reinforced. Particular attention should be given to strengthening capacity to prepare policies and strategies, to facilitate intersectoral coordination with relevant ministries, and to coordinate with local authorities in the preparation and implementation of Local Environmental Action Plans and the development of economic instruments.*

*(b) The Department for European Integration should be strengthened.*

*(c) Coordination and cooperation between the Department for Legislation and Standardization and the Department for European Integration is of critical importance.*

As mentioned above, the Ministry of Environment and Physical Planning is determined to adopt and develop an advanced environmental policy and environmental management in the near future. Appropriate organization and staffing for this challenging task is important for the Departments within the Ministry and will also play a decisive role in the implementation of the strategies and regulations, and in the functions of the Environment Office (Agency) and the State Environment Inspectorate.

*Recommendation 2.2:*
*The Ministry of Environment and Physical Planning should give the highest priority to strengthening its implementation bodies - the Environment Office and the State Environment Inspectorate:*

*(a) The Environment Office should be strengthened and reorganized into an executive environment agency for the implementation and enforcement of environmental legislation and fully oriented to the requirements of environmental*

*management. In this regard the agency should, as a minimum, consist of an environmental monitoring centre (providing monitoring of all environmental media), an EIA and permitting division (dealing with single permits: air, waste water, waste, as well as with integrated permits), and a division for laboratory research. (see also recommendation 4.2)*

*(b) The State Environment Inspectorate should be strengthened at local levels with small units of two or three specialists and appropriate equipment. Coordination among the different inspectorates, especially where they share responsibilities in environmental protection should be streamlined through a better exchange of information and joint site visits or*

*site inspections. (see also recommendations 12.4 and 14.5)*

To fulfil its obligations as the competent body for environmental protection, the Ministry of Environment and Physical Planning needs clear definitions of its responsibility and its mandate regarding the environmental aspects of legislation, monitoring, data management and enforcement. This will probably take a long time and a number of legislative changes. At the same time, some action is possible now, where there is a clear common understanding among ministries of the functions of the Ministry of Environment as a national body for the environmental monitoring system. (see recommendations 4.2 and 4.3)

*Chapter 3*

# ECONOMIC INSTRUMENTS AND PRIVATIZATION

## 3.1 Macro-economic background

The country's economy has made a strong and sustained recovery since the Kosovo crisis in 1999, with GDP growth of over 4.5 per cent in 2000, the country's highest since the start of transition. Positive achievements in the past year include sustained economic recovery and stabilization, some important privatization and structural reforms, new agreements with the IMF and World Bank, a significant trade agreement with the EU, new infrastructure projects under the Stability Pact and a new government programme to address poverty and further structural reform. Outstanding challenges include the need to make further progress with the privatization or closure of large loss-making enterprises, the sale of key public monopolies in strategic sectors (such as the electricity utility), and the rationalization of the financial sector through further privatization and consolidation. Table 3.1 illustrates the period of economic development.

## 3.2 Economic instruments for environmental protection

*Background and policy objectives*

The former Yugoslav Republic of Macedonia appears to be at an early stage in the creation and application of proper environmental economic instruments. However, the official documents defining the country's environmental policy and the newly created Environment Fund ('Fund for the Environment and Nature Protection and Promotion') seem to be significant steps towards the development of such instruments.

The economic instruments in force today in the former Yugoslav Republic of Macedonia include:

- Taxes on the extraction and use of natural resources, e.g. taxes on water, land, minerals, flora and fauna;

- User charges for municipal services, e.g. charges for water supply, sewage treatment, and waste collection and disposal;
- Product charges, e.g. charges related to transport;
- Penalties and fines for non-compliance;
- Financial incentives such as grants and soft loans.

In addition to these environmental taxes, several environmentally motivated tax allowances and exemptions from VAT, excise tax, income and profit taxes have been enacted.

The Law on the Environment and Nature Protection and Promotion provides a basis for the further development of environmental policy, for the present environmental management, and for the strengthening of institutional capacity. The Law sets overall objectives for environmental protection, and gives the guiding principles and instruments to be used in pursuing them. But the Law does not clearly stipulate one of the core principles of environmental management, the user and polluter pays principle. Neither does the Law provide any basis for a system of charges for environmental pollution. Article 38 does state that "Polluters shall provide funds to protect and promote the environment and nature, in the form of a so-called eco-deduction", But this "eco-deduction" is not specified by law, and cannot be interpreted as the user and polluter pays principle.

The National Environmental Action Plan (NEAP) constitutes a core document in that it sets the aims and approach of the future framework of the country. It recommends a set of priority projects and a number of institutional and regulatory measures, including the need to restructure economic incentives so as to encourage more efficient resource use and, in particular, to develop a system of pollution and user charges. This system can be developed only when the user and polluter pays principle is adopted and followed at all levels of government.

**Table 3.1: Macro-economic indicators, 1992-2000**

| | 1992 | 1993 | 1994 | 1995 | 1996 | 1997 | 1998 | 1999 | 2000 |
|---|---|---|---|---|---|---|---|---|---|
| GDP (% change) | -6.6 | -7.5 | -1.8 | -1.1 | 1.2 | 1.4 | 3.4 | 4.3 | 4.5 |
| Consumer prices (annual average % change) | 1,511.3 | 362.0 | 128.3 | 15.7 | 2.3 | 2.6 | -0.1 | -0.7 | 5.8 |
| Inflation* (%) | .. | 229.6 | 55.4 | 9.2 | 3.0 | 4.4 | 0.8 | -1.1 | 5.8 |
| Unemployment (% of labour force) | 26.2 | 27.7 | 30.0 | 36.6 | 38.8 | 41.7 | 41.4 | 43.8 | 44.9 |
| Total FDI (in million US$, cash receipts, net) | 0.0 | 0.0 | 24.0 | 10.0 | 11.0 | 15.8 | 117.7 | 31.8 | 169.5 |

*Source*: UNECE. Common Statistical database, 2002.

*Source**: National Bank of the former Yugoslav Republic of Macedonia, 2001.

An effective system of pollution charges is based on identifying specific sources and levels of pollution, and establishing a monitoring and enforcement network. The Ministry of Environment and Physical Planning has made a first attempt to develop an inventory and a computer database of major industrial polluters. The next step is the evaluation of the financial impact of pollution charges and the gradual introduction of a set of pollution charges. The staff of the Environment Fund is drafting a law on environmental pollution charges that, when adopted, could serve as an 'interim' ('standby') law, until the user and polluter pays principle is incorporated in other environment-related laws.

*Economic     instruments     for     pollution management*

Instruments for air pollution management

Air management is based on the 1974 Law on Air Protection, which has been amended several times. The Government is currently preparing a new law to approximate relevant EU legislation and update the country's air quality standards, which were established in 1990. The existing standards relate to concentrations of pollutants in exhaust gases and emissions, and are enforced through environmental inspections. Penalties and fines can be levied on the basis of the Law on the Environment and Nature Protection and Promotion for not delivering the necessary data to the cadastre of air pollutants, and on the basis of the Law on Air Protection when air emissions exceed the allowed concentrations. (see also Chapter 7 on Air Management)

Instruments related to transport

Several transport-related taxes have been introduced. These are non-environmental economic instruments but, since they affect transport, they also affect the environment. These are excise tax and value-added tax (VAT) on fuels and vehicles, road user charges (road toll), and a registration tax on vehicles. The taxes are collected by the Public Revenue Office.

The 1996 Law on Public Roads introduced a road user tax, or road toll. The road toll is based on distance and the category of the vehicle. Vehicles are divided in four categories and the rate ranges from 1.7 denars per kilometre for the lightest category to 10.2 denars per kilometre for the heaviest category. Total revenue from road tolls in 1999 was 540 million denars. Revenue is channelled into the Road Fund and will be used for the maintenance, building and reconstruction of the country's roads.

The registration tax for motor vehicles was introduced through the Law on the Environment and Nature Protection and Promotion, and the revenue from these charges is channelled into the Environment Fund. The fee amounts to 4 per cent of the registration price for vehicles without catalytic converters and 2 per cent for vehicles with catalytic converters.

The Law on Excise Tax (Official Gazette Nos. 32/2001 and 50/2001) established excise taxes for oil derivatives and passenger vehicles. The excise tax on petrol differentiates slightly between leaded and unleaded petrol. The excise tax on leaded petrol is 62 per cent, on unleaded petrol 59 per cent and on diesel 50 per cent of the retail prices. The excise tax on passenger vehicles is calculated on the basis of engine capacity, and amounts to 25 per cent on vehicles with engines of up to 2 litres and 55 per cent on vehicles with engines of over 2 litres. Retail prices of diesel are lower than those of leaded and unleaded petrol. Furthermore, a VAT of 19 per cent was introduced in 2000 to replace the former Law on Sales Tax on Products and Services. (see also Chapter 13 on Transport and the environment)

**Table 3.2: Excise taxes on fuels**

| Crude oil | Tax rate |
|---|---|
| Leaded petrol M B 86 | 62% |
| Leaded petrol M B 98 | 62% |
| Unleaded petrol BM B | 59% |
| Diesel | 50% |
| Kerosene | 17% |
| Petroleum and heavy oils | 10% |
| Crude oil | 11% |

*Source*: The former Yugoslav Republic of Macedonia. Law on Excise Tax, 2001.

Instruments for water resource management

Instruments for water resource management include abstraction charges, user charges for water supply and consumption, sewage and waste-water charges, and non-compliance fees. There are no charges on effluent discharges. The Law on Waters governs the conditions of water allocation and use, water pollution, and water finance.

The supply of water and the collection and treatment of waste water are the responsibility of the public water companies. According to the Law on Waters, water prices are set by the water companies and finally approved by the communal authorities. In practice, the Government sets nationwide maximum water prices that are in line with its anti-inflation policies. The water tariffs barely meet the water companies' operating and maintenance costs and do not allow them to upgrade the distribution networks which have significant leaks.

In most households, the water is not metered, which does not encourage users to save water. The price of drinking water differs from municipality to municipality. The average price in 1999 across the State was 9.40 denars/m$^3$ (US$ 0.20/m$^3$).

The Law on Waters defines a number of violations. The fines range from 150,000 to 300,000 denars for legal entities and from 10,000 to 50,000 denars for individuals.

There are only three waste-water treatment stations in the country so untreated waste water is discharged into rivers in most places. The sewage and waste-water charge for households amounted to 4.97 denars/m$^3$ (US$ 0.10/m$^3$) in 1999.

The Law on Waters lays down fines for discharging untreated waste waters into groundwater and surface water. However, enforcement is weak and based on low penalties, which are not often paid. As a result only 6 per cent of all industrial waste water is treated. Water pollution is expected to get worse as the economy revives and industrial production increases. (see Chapter 6 on Water Management)

Instruments for waste management

Municipal waste management is required by several laws, such as the Law on Waste, the Law on Municipal Services (Official Gazette No. 45/97), and the Law on Public Hygiene, and the Collection and Transport of Municipal Solid and Industrial Waste.

The only economic instrument related to waste management is the user charge for municipal waste services. Based on present regulations, the solid waste charges are set by each municipal service company and approved by the city council. The waste collection and disposal charge is based on the area of floor space per household and ranges from 0.44 to 3.07 denars per square metre per month. Companies pay a charge that ranges from 0.44 to 6.00 denars per square metre if their waste is collected by municipal services. Most of the larger industries have their own industrial waste sites. Only 20 to 40 per cent of households pay their waste charge. The low tariffs and collection rates do not create true market conditions, and social considerations still dominate when establishing the rates for waste charges. The decreasing collection rates in the course of recent years have led to the introduction of a proviso to the Law on Municipal Services that no municipal service will be provided unless paid for (i.e. the user will be disconnected). In practice, this regulation has never been enforced for social reasons.

The Law on Public Hygiene, and the Collection and Transport of Municipal Solid and Industrial Waste gives users the possibility of paying a reduced charge in exchange for sorting and recycling different types of waste. For this purpose, the municipality must provide separate containers for the different waste types. This provision could clearly provide an incentive for waste reduction and internal recycling, but has not yet been implemented.

Revenue generated is sufficient to cover the cost of operations and sometimes maintenance, but for new equipment and investments public enterprises have to depend on additional resources from other activities. In addition, the rate is far from sufficient to provide proper incentives for waste reduction and separation.

The Law on Municipal Services and the Law on Waste set maximum fines for legal entities and individuals – service providers and beneficiaries – that do not comply with their provisions. The communal inspectorates are responsible for ensuring compliance. (see also Chapter 8 on Waste Management.)

*Economic instruments for natural resource management*

Economic instruments for natural resource management are widely used in the former Yugoslav Republic of Macedonia. The taxes and payments are mainly related to water abstraction and use, the use of land and forests, the extraction and use of minerals, and fishing and hunting. The taxes and payments have more a command-and-control than an economic incentive character, and are used to enforce nature protection legislation. The procedures for using natural resources are laid down in several laws and regulations. The main responsibility for natural resource management lies with the Ministry of Agriculture, Forestry and Water Economy. The Ministry of Economy is in charge of the management of mineral resources.

Enforcement incentives (fines and non-compliance fees)

Fines and penalties can be imposed if evidence is found of violation of environmental legislation. Fines vary from 3,000 to 300,000 denars per violation. The Criminal Code also envisages legal provisions related to the environment. It defines 16 different criminal acts against the environment; the penalties vary from fines to imprisonment of up to ten years. It should be mentioned that the implementation of these articles leaves much to be desired. According to article 218 of the Criminal Code, for example, significant pollution of air, soil or water, which may endanger human life and health, is punishable by up to three years' imprisonment. These sentences are rarely executed due to a lack of cooperation between the legal bodies and the police.

When violations against environmental legislation are proved, the State Environment Inspectorate may impose fines or lower production levels, or require the installation of pollution control equipment. In extreme cases, facilities can be closed, a measure that has been taken on only a few occasions.

Ninety per cent of the lawsuits instituted by the Environment Inspectorate will never be resolved because a statute of limitations imposes a two–year deadline. Only 10 per cent will actually reach the court, of which an even smaller percentage is settled in favour of the Ministry of Environment.

## 3.3    Environmental    financing    and expenditures

*National sources of finance*

In the past three years, environmental spending has been very limited and has not exceeded 0.5 per cent of the gross national product. The main sources of financing are the central and local budgets, an extrabudgetary fund, and foreign financing. Budgetary funds are also allocated for implementing programmes in other infrastructure activities which are indirectly connected to the environment.

State Budget

The Public Investment Programme was set up to reflect government priorities and is in line with the country's State budget. The Public Investment Programme for the period 2001-2003 consists of 172 investment projects, with a total estimated cost of US$ 1,030.77 million. The projects are grouped in different sectors; energy, transport, water management, communal services and housing, environment, other economic sectors, education and science, health, and non-economic sectors. According to the Public Investment Programme, little financing is available for environmental investments (1.25 per cent of total investment for 2001-2003). However, environment-related investment projects are also indirectly grouped under other sectors in the Programme. In allocating funds to the environment, the Programme follows the investment priorities identified in the NEAP and the LEAPs.

The amount of the total State budget allocated to the Ministry of Environment was 170.7 million denars in 2000 and 187.2 million denars in 2001. This was sufficient to cover salaries, social insurance, administration and maintenance. The budget for 2002 will be decreased to approximately 137 million denars, due to government spending restrictions following the recent armed conflict.

**Table 3.3: Planned Public Investment Programme expenditures by sector**

in million US$

| Sector | 2001 | 2002 | 2003 | total |
|---|---|---|---|---|
| Total | 392.2 | 364.4 | 274.2 | 1030.8 |
| Energy | 71.6 | 53.6 | 46.3 | 171.5 |
| Transport | 122.2 | 139.6 | 131.7 | 393.5 |
| Water management | 11.3 | 8.1 | 7.6 | 26.9 |
| Municipal services & housing | 51.5 | 81.5 | 35.5 | 168.4 |
| Environment | 6.3 | 5.8 | 0.8 | 12.9 |
| Other economic sectors | 20.2 | 19.5 | 14.8 | 54.5 |
| Education & science | 19.7 | 10.6 | 3.9 | 34.1 |
| Health | 30.5 | 11.4 | 3.9 | 45.8 |
| Non-economic sectors | 59.1 | 34.5 | 29.7 | 123.2 |

*Source*: The former Yugoslav Republic of Macedonia. Public Investment Programme 2001-2003.

Additional resources for environmental projects came from foreign donors and the income from privatization of the State telecommunication sector.

At the local level, the municipalities are responsible for various public services, some of which are directly related to environmental protection. The municipalities have authority over the natural resources in their area and have to ensure a good-quality service for water supply, waste water and municipal waste management. In this context, the adoption of the new Law on Local Self-Government is an important step for environmental decisions taken locally. The Law provides for the transfer of certain competencies for environmental matters from the central Government to the municipalities. The law that will establish the financing of local government is still being drafted. Municipalities will become self-financing and have the right to set tariffs for municipal services. At the moment, the municipalities are financially dependent on State budget allocations, which cover only salaries and related expenditures. Additional sources of revenue under the control of municipalities are property taxes, communal fees and incomes from municipal services.

Extrabudgetary funds

The establishment of an environmental fund was first considered in the 1996-1997 Law on the Environment and Nature Protection and Promotion. Three articles in the Law contemplated a source of funding for environmental projects. The Environment Fund was created in April 1998 within the Ministry of Environment. The legal basis for the establishment of an independent fund is provided in article 66 of the Law on the Organization and Work of the State Administration;

however, implementation requires a separate law, establishing the structure and activities of the Fund, and this law has not yet been passed. The Fund therefore remains under the auspices and responsibility of the Ministry.

According to the Law on the Environment and Nature Protection and Promotion, the basic aim of the Fund is to provide finance for encouraging preventive and remedial measures for the environment and natural resources. The Fund's assets are spent in accordance with a programme based on NEAP and LEAP priorities. The draft programme is prepared by the Fund's staff and, through the Ministry of Environment, submitted for approval to the Government. At the end of the year, the Fund submits a report on the programme's implementation to the Government. The Fund has recently prepared a list of priority projects, taken from among project applications from local governments. To improve this process, the Fund has been sending questionnaires to municipalities and visiting municipalities and local government officials to identify potential environmental investment projects.

According to the Law on the Environment and Nature Protection and Promotion, financial resources for the Fund should be provided by the State budget, donations and fines paid by polluters. However, these sources have never reached the Fund. Basic revenue is generated from the registration of motor vehicles and boats (see above). With this income, the Fund has an annual inflow of approximately 50 million denars, or US$ 720,000. Expenditures have taken the form of grants, and co-financing arrangements (often with the United States Agency for International Development (USAID)) have been frequent.

A draft law on the Environment Fund is under preparation. Should it be adopted, the Fund would need to be reorganized under a new board of directors and a new investment policy would have to be decided. The law, as currently drafted, would establish the rules and functions of the Fund, determine its institutional status and create new sources of finance. Early proposals to derive revenue from taxes on various oil derivatives and on tobacco products may not survive the redrafting process, although they could be introduced at a later stage. Anticipated revenue from these taxes was expected to provide approximately US$ 3 million per year. More generally, the law is expected to introduce the polluter pays principle, which would enable future developments in environmental fiscal instruments. The new Environment Fund would make available both grants and loans to industry and government for environmental investments. The project selection process would be public, with final decisions made by a nine-member board of directors. The board would be composed of four representatives from the Ministries of Environment, Agriculture, Transport And Finance, and five subject-matter experts. Cooperation with commercial banks would be explored as a means of facilitating the Fund's new types of banking activities.

The Fund is exploring the possibilities of debt-for-environment swaps to finance environmental investments. A debt-for-environment swap gives the country an opportunity to reduce its external debt in exchange for mobilizing domestic resources for environmental investment and protection.

The long-term strategy for the Fund envisions the introduction of pollution charges in accordance with the polluter pays principle as a future source of revenue and an incentive to industry to reduce pollution.

Most extrabudgetary resources for environmental projects are provided by multilateral aid agencies, international financial institutions and individual foreign governments. Major donor organizations providing assistance are the EU, World Bank, USAID, UNDP and GTZ. The Public Investment Programme for 2001-2003 has indicated environment projects for a total amount of US$ 12.9 million, of which US$ 10.77 million financed by foreign donors.

## 3.4    Privatization and the impacts on environmental protection

*Background and current status of the privatization process*

The central legal document governing the privatization of State-owned enterprises is the Law on Transformation of Enterprises with Social Capital enacted in June 1993. However, enterprises started privatizing four years earlier, in 1989, after the passage of the Law on Social Capital (Official Gazette No. 84/89). Immediately after independence in September 1991, the Government of the former Yugoslav Republic of Macedonia announced that the federal law was no longer in force and that a new law would soon be promulgated. The new law was enacted after extensive debate two years later. The practical implementation of the law started with the establishment of the Agency for the Transformation of Enterprises with Social Capital in October 1993 (Official Gazette No. 38/93).

The main method for privatization in the country is the sale of enterprises case by case, rather than by vouchers or some other non-cash system. The management employee buy-out system has been used the most, and the bulk of the shares is in the hands of employees and management.

The Privatization Agency is the key institution responsible for the administration and support of the privatization process. The Agency's mission is associated with the final goal of ownership transformation: to improve the efficiency of the country's economy by establishing well-managed companies which can successfully compete in the international markets.

By 31 December 2001, 1,678 enterprises had been privatized (out of the 1,767 enterprises included in the privatization process that started in 1993). The total estimated value of the transformed capital was over €2.3 billion, and the total number of employees involved in this process was 229,151. The total amount of foreign investments both through privatization and post-privatization sales was around US$ 260 million (€300 million) in January 2002, according to the Privatization Agency.

According to the Law on Transformation of Enterprises with Social Capital, many enterprises were excluded from privatization. These are mainly agricultural, forestry, water-supply enterprises, industries of special social interest, and enterprises that have monopoly status by law. However, the transformation of some enterprises that were excluded from privatization at the beginning has been made possible by the Law on Public Enterprises and several separate laws for special industries and resources (e.g. Law on Mining, Law on Forestry, Law on Waters). Agricultural enterprises and cooperatives can be privatized under the 1996 Law for the Transformation of Agricultural Enterprises and Cooperatives with Social Capital

*Impact of privatization on the environment*

Privatization legislation demands no environmental assessment during the privatization process, and environmental concerns are not taken into consideration. Currently, there are no other regulations on environmental impact assessment either.

The Government has adopted an action plan for the restructuring of 40 loss-making State-owned companies. For this purpose, it has established the Enterprise Restructuring and Privatization Committee, consisting of representatives of different ministries, including the Ministry of Environment and Physical Planning. The World Bank's Financial and Enterprise Sector Adjustment Loan (FESAL-II) process has helped to strengthen the environmental management review during the restructuring of these companies. In the initial phase of the restructuring process, the Government will obtain independent external advice, consisting of a financial and economic cost-benefit analysis taking into account the cost of any contingent liabilities, such as environmental clean-up costs. Upon conclusion of the analysis, the Government will evaluate the most viable option and determine whether the enterprise should be fully privatized or closed down. The privatization contract requires the owner to prepare a detailed environmental plan, including clean-up action, as part of the business development plan, which would move the company towards EU environmental standards. This plan should be in compliance with existing environmental protection legislation. It is not clear to what extent these environmental requirements are put in practice, nor does the contract include procedures for preparing an environmental plan or

indicate a solution for environmental liability for past pollution.

## 3.5   Conclusions and recommendations

Economic instruments for environmental protection are not well developed in the former Yugoslav Republic of Macedonia. Only a few economic instruments are in place, and these are conceived mainly as user charges for water and waste with a revenue raising purpose.

An effective system of pollution charges is based on identifying specific sources and levels of pollution, designing and implementing a reasonable system of pollution charges, and establishing a monitoring and enforcement network led by the State Environment Inspectorate. The Ministry of Environment and Physical Planning has made a first attempt to develop an inventory and a computer database of major industrial polluters. The next step is the evaluation of the financial impact of pollution charges and the gradual introduction of a set of pollution charges. Currently, the staff of the Environment Fund is drafting a law on environmental pollution charges. This law, when adopted, will serve as an 'interim' ('standby') law, until the user and polluter pays principle is incorporated into other environment-related laws.

*Recommendation 3.1:*
*The Ministry of Environment and Physical Planning should develop an effective system of pollution charges, in cooperation with other ministries and stakeholders. A first attempt should be made by further elaborating the legally binding provisions of this system. (see also recommendations 6.6)*

*Recommendation 3.2:*
*The Ministry of Environment and Physical Planning, should strengthen its competence to develop economic instruments for environmental protection. The respective staff should have access to training in environmental economics and the principles of economic instruments and their implementation. (see also recommendation 2.1.a)*

In 1998 the Environment Fund was established within the (then) Ministry of Construction, Urban Planning and Environment, now the Ministry of Environment and Physical Planning. The legal basis for the establishment of an independent Fund can be found in article 66 of the Law on the Organization and Work of the State Administration; however, implementation requires a separate law, establishing the structure and activities of the Fund, and this law has not yet been passed. The Fund, therefore, remains under the auspices and responsibility of the Ministry.

Establishing an independent fund could help to ensure its operation as an independent entity, that is, as a financial intermediary through which funding would be channelled for activities related to environmental protection. One of the main reasons for passing the proposed law is to replace the Fund's budgetary revenues with new sources of funding for environmental protection, as a key prerequisite for the implementation of the National Environmental Action Plan.

The finances of the Environment Fund are used in accordance with a programme based on NEAP and LEAP priorities. This programme is prepared by the Fund's staff and, through the Ministry of Environment, submitted for approval to the Government. To date, only 12 of the country's 123 municipalities (self-government units) have created LEAPs. The Fund has also developed a set of procedures and application forms to be used by municipalities and private companies applying for financing for their environmental projects. To improve this process, the Fund has been visiting municipalities and local government officials to identify potential environmental investment projects. The Fund has recently prepared a list of priority projects on the basis of applications. This long list of possible projects provides little guidance on how to allocate the limited resources of the Fund among the wide variety of projects.

The financing strategy of the Fund should describe the objectives and set priorities among the different environmental issues. Once the areas eligible for funding have been identified, a list of priorities should be set for each area. This should draw heavily upon the national environmental action plan and should identify the most urgent environmental threats. In other words, the strategy should not be a 'shopping list' of projects to receive financing, but should specify appraisal criteria that projects must meet, including requirements such as environmental effectiveness and cost-effectiveness.

*Recommendation 3.3:*
*(a) The Government should, as soon as possible, clarify the status of the Environmental Fund as an independent financing institution for environmental protection with clear and transparent management and independent supervision.*

*(b) The Environment Fund, in cooperation with the Ministry of Environment and Physical Planning, should develop a financing strategy that describes objectives and sets priorities among the different environmental projects, consistent with the national environmental policy goals, particularly those contained in the NEAP.*

According to the privatization legislation, no environmental assessment is required during privatization and environmental concerns are not taken into consideration. Currently, there are no regulations on environmental impact assessment either.

The Government has recently adopted an action plan for the restructuring of 40 loss-making State-owned companies. A first attempt has been made to incorporate environmental concerns in the privatization of these companies. The privatization contracts require the owner to prepare a detailed environmental plan as part of the business development plan, which should be in compliance with existing environmental protection legislation. But the contract does not include procedures for preparing an environmental plan, nor does it indicate a solution for environmental liability for past pollution.

*Recommendation 3.4:*
*The Government should increase the role of the Ministry of Environment and Physical Planning in privatization and insist on the introduction of environmental audits or environmental impact assessments for industrial enterprises undergoing privatization. The Privatization Agency should include environmental clauses in the sales contracts for the privatization of enterprises. (see also recommendation 11.3)*

*Chapter 4*

# ENVIRONMENTAL INFORMATION AND PUBLIC PARTICIPATION

## 4.1    Demand for information

Environmental information is essential to the work of the Ministry of Environment and Physical Planning, and it serves as a particularly important input to the preparation of the National Environmental Action Plan, Local Environmental Action Plans, the National Environmental Health Action Plan and all other plans and strategies under its purview. Environmental information is also needed by the ministries that are responsible for matters with environmental concerns, such as the Ministry of Health, the Ministry of Agriculture, Forestry and Water Economy, the Ministry of Transport and Communications, and the Ministry of Economy. While most environmental policies and laws are formulated nationally, municipal government has a fundamental need for environmental information at the local level in order to implement existing policies i.e. Local Environmental Action Plans, and to develop environmental policy in the future.

It is not only the Government that needs information. The business sector is a user of environmental information, and this will become increasingly important as the country moves toward EU accession.

There is also considerable interest by the public in environmental information. The Public Relations Office, established by the Ministry of Environment and Physical Planning in 2001, received 264 visits (one visit may include more than 1 person) in 2001. The general public accounted for 33 per cent of visits; NGOs, 24 per cent; members of the public concerned with specific issues, e.g. construction, pollution, 19 per cent; schoolchildren, 12 per cent; and international visitors, 10 per cent. The Public Relations Office receives around 10 to 15 phone calls per week. There are about 150 readers a year who used the library of the Public Relations Office searching for environmental information. There are about 150 environmental NGOs of which 20 are very active. They are among the major consumers of environment-related information.

## 4.2    Environmental    Information    and Education

Environmental information is also needed by the education sector, where it should be an integral part of curricula at all levels. In 1998, the former Yugoslav Republic of Macedonia joined the GLOBE Program (Global Learning and Observations to Benefit the Environment) and introduced environmental education activities in four primary and five secondary schools. The country has also been a part of the Healthy School Network of the United Nations Children's Fund (UNICEF) and the World Health Organization (WHO) since 1995. The institution responsible for implementing the Network is the Bureau for Education Development of the Ministry of Education and Science in cooperation with the Institute of Psychology of the Faculty of Philosophy-Skopje.

Environmental issues are also introduced indirectly through the official curriculum. Effective in 2002, ecological issues are included in the geography curriculum for the $6^{th}$ and $8^{th}$ grades. This includes such issues as pollution of natural resources (air, water, soil), biosphere, impact of human activities, and local environment, where inputs of environmental information are of high importance. The high-school curriculum incorporates topics on health and the environment. The Bureau for Education Development develops these curriculum programmes.

The Faculty of Mechanical Engineering at the St. Cyril and Methodius University offers a four-year Bachelor of Interdisciplinary Studies in Environmental Engineering that focuses on environmental monitoring, the protection of ecosystems and environmental legislation. Since 1996, 15 students have earned their degrees in this field and two have continued their studies abroad. Unfortunately, there is no clear cooperation between the Ministry of Environment and Physical Planning and the University, which could secure sustainable capacity building for environmental management in the future. Although some books were published with funding from Eco Fund, the lack of teaching materials and the lack of communication with the Ministry of Environment and Physical Planning remain an obstacle to interdisciplinary studies.

## 4.3    Data sources

### Monitoring

The monitoring of environmental parameters such as air, water, soil and radioactivity falls under the jurisdiction of many institutions and is poorly coordinated. Monitoring is primarily conducted by the Hydrometeorological Institute, the Ministry of Environment and Physical Planning, the Ministry of Health through the State Institute for Health Protection, and the Ministry of Transport.

There is no comprehensive environmental monitoring programme in the country. So far, all monitoring activities have been established and conducted independently of each other, and have not always followed the same goals and objectives. Newly established monitoring programmes, e.g. the air monitoring network in Bitola, the automatic monitoring stations on the River Vardar supported by the Phare Cross-Border Cooperation programme and the ongoing Lake Ohrid project, are project-based activities and driven by external funding. The result is monitoring activities that are dispersed rather than integrated on the basis of entire ecosystems. The former Yugoslav Republic of Macedonia is aware of this problem and is currently developing a monitoring programme for one ecosystem, i.e. waters.

In general, the number of monitoring stations has decreased since the early 1980s. At the moment monitoring is based on a comparatively small number of measurements points. The Ministry of Environment and Physical Planning, which monitors air quality, has four stations in Skopje and one mobile monitoring station. It measures 12 parameters: $SO_2$, CO, NO, $NO_2$, $NO_x$, suspended particulate matter (SPM), wind direction and speed, temperature, $O_3$, solar radiation, and humidity. There are two air-monitoring stations in Veles that belong to the "MHK Zletovo" Lead and Zinc Smelting Company. The State Institute for Health Protection conducts measurements of $SO_2$ and smoke only in places where they may affect human health. Another air monitoring network is managed by the Hydrometeorological Institute, which

operates 19 urban stations, 11 of which are in Skopje. They measure $SO_2$ and "black smoke".

The station in Lazaropole was established within the UNECE Cooperative Programme for Monitoring and Evaluation of the Long-range Transmission of Air Pollutants in Europe (EMEP), and is managed by the Ministry of Agriculture, Forestry and Water Economy (Administration of Hydrometeorological Affairs). However, it has not been functioning properly since 1992, due to a lack of appropriate equipment for the required measurements. The station is performing measurements of rainfall, and should soon be able to provide data on this for the period 1992-97.

The Hydrometeorological Institute monitors surface water quality from 60 measurement points throughout the country. For financial reasons, the Institute stopped monitoring groundwater and soil quality in 1981. Four basic parameters – dissolved oxygen, biological oxygen demand, pH, and chemical oxygen demand – are measured in leaches from the Skopje waste site once a month. The State Institute for Health Protection monitors drinking and bathing water quality. The Institute has 10 centres throughout the country located in Skopje, Bitola, Kochani, Kumanovo, Ohrid, Prilep, Strumica, Tetovo, Veles and Shtip.

In general, monitoring standards like maximum allowable concentration date back to the 1970s and 1980s, and some of the measurements, e.g. noise pollution, do not apply to pollution limits at all. However, it should be noted that harmonization of the country's legislation with the EU is currently under way. Only a few of the current standards are in line with EU legislation, such as drinking water quality standards, which are also consistent with WHO standards. Air monitoring data from the four monitoring stations in Skopje are comparable with the limit values prescribed by the relevant EU directives. Current monitoring often does not include such important parameters as heavy metals and persistent organic pollutants, and appears to be inadequately linked to public health monitoring.

There are differences between the laboratories in the capital and those in the countryside. The State Institute for Health Protection in Skopje, for instance, operates adequately with modern equipment, which is regularly calibrated and maintained, but the equipment in country laboratories does not permit continuous monitoring.

Poorly maintained and calibrated monitoring equipment results in inadequate and poor-quality data. For example, $SO_2$ and $NO_x$ concentration measurements in Skopje sometimes appear negative, which clearly shows an equipment error. In such cases, the monitoring equipment requires urgent maintenance. However, few organizations such as the State Institute for Health Protection participate in inter-calibration programmes.

*Statistical data*

There are data gaps on air and water discharges resulting from a lack of systematic data collection. Basically the State Environmental Inspectorate and the Environmental Information Centre collect measurements of discharges from the industrial waste-water treatment plants and air polluters. The Environmental Information Centre receives air emission data from only 18 to 22 major polluters. The Inspectorate focuses on the country's approximately 100 heavily polluting companies.

The State Statistical Office collects social and economic data directly from entities through surveys and gathers data from different ministries. It also collects limited environmental information like geographical data on lakes, rivers, mountains, natural sites of importance, and hydro-meteorological parameters. The statisticians pay special attention to improvements in the services offered to users. One good example is the Statistical Year Book 2001, which was designed on the basis of user feedback surveys. The surveys showed that there was a high demand for business-related information and that users wanted better visual presentation including graphics.

According to the State Statistical Office, researchers and students are the most likely to request environment-related information. Although currently the demand for environmental statistics is high, the environmental indicators presented in the Statistical Year Book published annually are limited. The Ministry of Environment and Physical Planning has made several attempts to establish a mechanism for the dissemination of environmental information through statistical year books, but so far without success. An informal working group has been established with experts from both the Ministry and the State Statistical Office to discuss air and water statistics.

*Data processing*

According to the Law on the Environment and Nature Protection and Promotion, public administration bodies, scientific organizations and institutions that monitor the environment and nature are obliged to submit their environmental data to the Ministry of Environment and Physical Planning. Within the Ministry, the Environmental Information Centre, established in 1998, manages environmental data. The vision of the Centre is to become the main environmental databank in the country through the establishment of a comprehensive base of relevant, accurate and publicly accessible information on the quality of the environment.

The Environmental Information Centre is adequately equipped to process environmental data. Within the framework of the Country Operational Programme 1997 (COP97), the PHARE project, the European Environment Agency's EIONET project and others, the Centre will receive computer equipment, although not all of it has yet arrived. The Centre has also not yet established the dial-up services envisaged in the COP97 project for experts in the Ministry, field researchers and other data providers. However, this project should be completed by the end of 2002, and other projects will continue to develop the technical capacities of the Centre.

With the exception of the air monitoring data, the Centre's data compilations can hardly be defined as databases since the data are stored in Excel format and cannot be retrieved quickly and efficiently.

In spite of its adequate equipment and very competent staff, the Centre operates inefficiently and in a time-consuming manner. For instance, most of the environmental data from the State Institute for Health Protection and the Hydrometeorological Institute are received on paper and manually keyed into Excel files. Some data are received in Excel and Word format.

## 4.4 Access and dissemination

*Access to environmental information*

The Constitution does not explicitly refer to environmental information, but it does guarantee free access to information in general. There are a number of laws by which access to environmental information is secured, including the Law on the Environment and Nature Protection and Promotion, and the Law on the Social System of Information and the Information System of the Socialist Republic of Macedonia (Official Gazette No. 14/84).

Current legislation does not clearly state what concrete environmental information particular entities have to provide. Even if it is clear that information on the state of the environment and nature protection needs to be made available to the public, there are no specifications in terms of its form and the frequency (annual or biannual) of reporting.

The Aarhus Convention, to which the former Yugoslav Republic of Macedonia is a Party, requires transparency and the accessibility of environmental information available in electronic databases. Although the country's legislation does not contain provisions for this, the database on air quality is publicly available. The Catalogue of Data Sources, which includes meta-information on existing sources of environmental information, institutional information and activities, is publicly available as well. Even if the database is up and running, it requires more substantial inputs. The current number of records is not satisfactory. The Environmental Information Centre is establishing a pollutant release and transfers register. It is expected to be ready by the end of 2002. There are no electronic databases on policies, plans and programmes in the country.

The Constitution guarantees the right of citizens to submit a request or to complain to the State authorities if they feel that public information is not satisfactory. Additionally, article 7 of the Law on Environment and Nature Protection and Promotion states that environmental information has to be publicly "available upon request". However, the mechanism to implement this is not specified in national legislation. There are no provisions on time limits for public authorities to respond to requests or complaints, nor on conditions when the request can be refused, nor on how to make information available, nor on the form and nature of the information to be provided. Over the past two years the Ministry of Environment and Physical Planning has received on average four or five requests for information a day, all of which were answered. Information is not available on the response rate of other public authorities. In general,

information is free of charge, but individuals cannot copy or make printouts of published documents free of charge.

The applicable legal regulations (the Law on the Organization and Work of the State Administration and the Law on Personal Data Protection) provide clear guidelines concerning the non-disclosure of information, especially in cases of data related to national security, official and business secrets, the protection of citizens, personal data and the protection of intellectual property. Article 7 of the Law on Environment and Nature Protection and Promotion clearly states that information about both "actual risk" and "potential risk" to the environment should be disclosed to the public.

The lack of appropriate legislation makes it difficult for the public to gain access to information, especially information on sensitive issues that is not available in the Ministry of Environment and Physical Planning but in other public administration bodies. There are also cases when the information released is misleading and contradictory. Examples include information on the release of water from Lake Ohrid in 2000 and the pollution resulting from the lead and zinc smelter in Veles.

*Dissemination of environmental information*

The Ministry of Environment and Physical Planning is responsible for the dissemination of environmental information, e.g. state of the environment reporting. All other institutions that monitor the environment and nature are obliged to submit environmental data to it. The weakness in the present legislation lies in specifying how the information should be disseminated and how the public should be informed about the potential risk or danger to human health or the environment. There are also no provisions on the frequency of reporting.

Up-to-date information and press releases concerning the Ministry's activities are available on its web site,                              . State-of-the-Environment (SoE) reports were produced in 1998 and 2000, but these are available only in electronic format. In 2001 only 4.9 per cent of the population in the country was connected to the Internet. The work plan of the Environmental Information Centre for 2002 indicates that electronic SoE reporting will continue in the future.

The Environmental Information Centre established a Public Relations Office in 2001 in the city of

Skopje to secure physical accessibility and active communication. This Office is a good example of the dissemination of environmental information that should be shared with other environmental information providers internationally. There are, however, still significant constraints to optimal operation. For example, there is no efficient technical communication between the two units of the Centre. The lack of Internet and Intranet communication does not allow the release of such publicly available "hot" environmental information as daily air quality measurements. If maximum allowable concentrations of $SO_2$ and $NO_x$ are exceeded, information is released through other channels.

In addition, while the Public Relations Office operates a library that provides easy access to a number of books, magazines and digital materials, qualitative and target-oriented printed environmental information remains poor at national level. Within the PHARE COP97 project the library is expected to expand its collection of foreign printed materials on environmental issues. Both governmental and non-governmental organizations are actively involved in disseminating information through the printed media.

With support from the Environment Fund and external donors, many municipalities have already taken significant steps towards improving environmental information management. For example, within the activities of the Local Environmental Action Plans, eight municipalities have created citizen information centres, and another two centres are planned. The Association of Municipalities has also been established to serve as a municipal lobby group and forum for sharing experiences and information on good practices.

Environmental information is also disseminated by other means. For instance, hourly air quality data taken directly from measurement sources are publicly displayed in graphical and numerical formats in the automatic air monitoring centre in the city of Skopje. The Ministry of Environment and Physical Planning actively distributes information of vital importance to the public through the mass media, press conferences, events promoting publications, and other public presentations. The Ministry also actively runs advertisements on television and campaigns such as the protection of the UNESCO natural and cultural heritage sites "Save Lake Ohrid", and in Skopje the "In Town Without My Car" campaign.

In general, the flow of environmental information to the public through the mass media has increased during the past two years. There are on average two or three environment-related articles published in daily newspapers. An NGO, the Environmental Press Centre, was established in 1999 to serve the journalists and the media in South Eastern Europe with potential news stories, background environmental information and access to independent expert advice. Even if the Centre is experiencing some difficulties, a considerable number of journalism-related activities have been carried out since its establishment. Examples of these are the Campaign for the Protection of the Ozone Layer, the Black and White Eco List, and voting through newspapers on environmental issues. One big step forward is the Eco-Caravan project, which promotes the use of the country's ecological areas, such as Mariovo, Porece, Malesevija, for ecologically sound activities such as eco-tourism and eco-agriculture. Importance is given not only to short-term campaigns but also to activities that are designed to secure a sustainable future, such as educating environmental journalists. Since environmental journalism is relatively new, there is a strong need for capacity-building.

## 4.5 Public participation and awareness-raising

An environmental NGO community has developed since independence. Today, there are 150 NGOs concerned with different kinds of environmental issues, but only some 20 are active. In general, public awareness about NGOs remains low, partly because of the strong centralization that existed in the country. The NGOs do not talk enough to each other.

There are several NGOs that have a considerable influence on people's general attitudes towards environmental issues. One of the biggest umbrella NGOs, with about 10,000 members, is the Environmental Movement (DEM). It includes 29 local environmental NGOs as full members and 17 other organizations and institutions as associate members. Important regional networks of NGOs, such as the Regional Environmental Center's Regional Office in Skopje (REC), have been established. The former Yugoslav Republic of Macedonia is also part of the South-Eastern European Environmental NGO network, which represents a first effort to develop the cooperation of environmental NGOs on a regional level. Most of the NGOs are active not only in the capital but also locally.

Many of these NGOs operate under difficult conditions caused by chronic underfunding and, consequently, tend to be driven by the priorities of external donors. Some support is made available through the REC-Skopje, which initiates projects and distributes small grants of approximately €3,000. Last year it financed 30 such small projects. Support is also provided by the European Commission, bilateral donors, the Stability Pact (under the Regional Environmental Reconstruction Programme for South-Eastern Europe) and the national government, for example, through the Ministry of Environment and Physical Planning. A few NGOs are starting to move away from donor-driven agendas and are beginning to adopt strategic interest areas, with concrete goals and objectives.

NGOs often compete with each other for limited funding and this can lead to poor collaboration, increased competition among them, and a lack of solidarity in approaching the same environmental problems. Most of the projects do not extend beyond a period of one year. This not only makes it difficult for NGOs to pursue strategic goals, but it also increases the likelihood of projects being disjointed and having a limited long-term value.

In spite of these obstacles, NGOs have undertaken a number of tangible activities focused on public participation since the 1990s. These include campaigns ("Save Lake Ohrid"), the distribution of leaflets and brochures, and the organization of public round tables (on the production of healthy food and organic farming).

NGOs have become key players in the implementation of a wide range of environmental policies and projects, notably through the Local Environmental Action Plan process. In general, the development of environmental laws occurs out of public sight and there is serious lack of transparency in enforcement procedures. Exceptions where NGOs were involved in drafting legislation include the Law on the Environment and Nature Protection and Promotion drafted in 1995 and the Law on Access to Information drafted in 2001. The NGO community influenced the decision to establish the Ministry of Environment and Physical Planning in 1998. The Journalists' Legal Environmental Centre was established to increase awareness and participate in the preparation of new environmental legislation. However, this practice of including the public in decision-making processes is found only in the Ministry of Environment and Physical Planning and not in the other ministries that have competence in the protection and improvement of the environment.

The NGO community is also hindered by its poor knowledge of legislative and institutional frameworks and legal procedures. Sometimes there is lack of public interest when NGO members are not personally affected by a problem, and this may result in "crisis participation".

An effort is being made to introduce the Aarhus Convention to a broad range of entities, including local governments, the business sector and NGOs, and to define the main barriers to its implementation. NGOs also developed an action plan for the implementation of the Aarhus Convention in 2000 and, on the initiative of REC-Skopje, set up an NGO Lobby Group to follow up the action plan and lobby State administrative bodies to take action. The action plan was presented and discussed at a round table among the Lobby Group and fourteen representatives from nine State institutions. A meeting with members of Parliament was scheduled, but, unfortunately, due to the country's political and security problems priorities were temporarily changed. Although the document has no legal status, NGOs began to implement it. Certain activities included in the action plan still remain to be implemented, but it is expected to be completed by the end of 2003. REC-Skopje is providing secretariat services for the Lobby Group to help them establish closer cooperation with State administrative bodies.

The Ministry of Environment and Physical Planning has also carried out a number of public campaigns aimed at increasing the public's awareness of the environment, including, for example, "Protection of Our Environment", "In Town Without My Car", "Spring Time-Environment Time" and "Save water so that there will be enough for all".

*Access to justice*

Although access to justice is an obligation under the Aarhus Convention, daily practice in the country is not very promising. Up to 80 per cent of environmental violations are not heard within two years of filing, resulting in the cases automatically being dismissed. Of those cases that have gone forward, around half have resulted in a warning only, while the other 50 per cent involved penalties that have often been very small and inadequate to compensate for environmental losses or damage to human health.

## 4.6 Policies, strategies, institutions

The management of environmental data is governed by the Law on the Environment and Nature Protection and Promotion and the National Environmental Action Plan (being updated), which should be the basis of Local Environmental Action Plans. These laws support the most important steps in environmental data management, namely, environmental data collection and processing, and the dissemination of environmental information. Other relevant legislation for environmental data management includes the Law on Health Protection, the Law on Statistics, and the Law on the Organization and Work of the State Administration.

Among the many public institutions that are involved in the gathering and analysis of environmental data are the Ministry of Environment and Physical Planning, the Hydrometeorological Institute, the State Institute for Health Protection, the Ministry of Transport and Communications, and the Ministry of Agriculture, Forestry and Water Economy.

The coordination, systematization and standardization of all relevant environmental information and its delivery to the end-users are included in the tasks of the Environmental Information Centre, but execution is not possible under the present set-up. The exchange of information among the different institutions is critical, but there is very little of it at present. One exception is the exchange of data between the State Institute for Health Protection and the Hydrometeorological Institute and the Ministry of Environment and Physical Planning.

Monitoring environmental parameters is highly fragmented among the Hydrometeorological Institute, the Ministry of Environment and Physical Planning, the State Institute for Health Protection and the Ministry of Transport. The lack of a monitoring programme has caused gaps in important measurements. Additionally, the legal mandate for monitoring is rather weak. For instance, the monitoring of groundwaters and surface waters is not explicitly required by the Law on Waters. There are four different laws covering noise issues in general, but there is no legislation that specifically covers sound levels and the exhaust systems of motor vehicles.

By signing the Stabilisation and Association Agreement with the EU, the former Yugoslav Republic of Macedonia is obliged to harmonize its legislation with EU legislation. Implementation of the new legislation will require more information to be collected and analysed, made accessible and disseminated broadly. The country is also a Party to a number of relevant international conventions, e.g. the Convention on Access to Information, Public Participation in Decision-making and Access to Justice in Environmental Matters (Aarhus Convention), the Convention on Biological Diversity and the United Nations Framework Convention on Climate Change, where information dissemination is one of the components of compliance. Among these, the Aarhus Convention is the most relevant to information management.

However, the concepts of public participation and citizens' rights have not yet been sufficiently rooted in national law. Present environmental legislation does not contain the necessary provisions to ensure access to information and justice. The absence of both a law on environmental impact assessment and an integrated pollution and prevention control system further exacerbate the problem.

The only law of relevance to the environment that calls for a transparent decision-making process is the Law on Spatial and Urban Planning. As provided by this Law, expert discussions on drafts of national, regional, urban and municipal spatial plans as well as plans for national parks should be held with the participation of representatives of bodies and organizations from the areas concerned. Furthermore, a public hearing on the draft of detailed urban plans and urban plan documentation should be conducted for a period of at least ten days.

As part of a Stability Pact project that covers six South Eastern European countries, the Ministry of Environment and Physical Planning, REC and other NGOs conducted a comprehensive analysis of the needs and priorities for the development of an implementation strategy for the Aarhus Convention in the country, and this analysis has been circulated to the ministries and other governmental institutions that deal with environmental matters.

Upon its finalization, the document "Needs and Priorities for the Development of an Implementation Strategy for the Aarhus Convention in the former Yugoslav Republic of Macedonia" will be used by an inter-ministerial working group as the basis for the development of a strategy for the implementation of the Aarhus Convention. The first inter-ministerial meeting was organized by the

Ministry of Environment and Physical Planning at the beginning of 2002.

## 4.7 Conclusions and recommendations

There are several laws that govern the most important steps for the management of environmental information; there are, however, gaps in both monitoring policy and access to environmental information. The collection, processing and dissemination of environmental information are dispersed among a number of institutions, and there is no national environmental information system. The result is an inefficient exchange of out-of-date information.

The country is a Party to the Convention on Access to Information, Public Participation in Decision-making and Access to Justice in Environmental Matters (Aarhus Convention). The Convention's implementation is a challenging task for the country. In general, environmental laws are prepared out of public sight. There is serious lack of transparency in the application of the enforcement and justice mechanism.

*Recommendation 4.1:*
*(a) A new law on access to environmental information in accordance with the Aarhus Convention should be prepared by the Ministry of Environment and Physical Planning and adopted by Parliament. It should include a clear description of the rights of the public to have access to environmental information.*

*(b) The Ministry of Environment and Physical Planning, in close cooperation with other public authorities, should prepare a strategy for the implementation of the Aarhus Convention. It should require certain legislative changes and strengthen the capacities of government officials at all levels and local non-governmental organisations to enable broad public access to information and public participation in decision-making processes.*

There is no comprehensive national monitoring programme that would serve policy objectives. The current monitoring network is driven by sporadic and irregular demand. Monitoring data are not very reliable, and the maximum allowable concentrations (standards) of pollutants are out of date. Certain parameters, such as heavy metals and persistent organic pollutants, are not covered at present. Important data gaps, e.g. discharges into air and water, appear in the collection and dissemination of statistical environmental information.

*Recommendation 4.2:*
*The Ministry of Environment and Physical Planning, in cooperation with relevant institutions, should develop a centralized, strategic monitoring programme capable of delivering the environmental information needed by all decision makers. Such a programme should harmonize the disparate methods, standards and indicators currently in use by various monitoring authorities and ensure a closer alignment of monitoring data and environmental policy objectives. (see also recommendation 7.3)*

The Environmental Information Centre was established to provide decision makers and the general public with relevant, accurate and publicly available environmental information. Work has begun, but the information flow from government ministries and institutes to the Environmental Information Centre is not satisfactory. Data exchange is still mostly done on paper, and in most cases it is manually transferred to Excel files. The information flow within the Ministry of Environment and Physical Planning is also unsatisfactory.

*Recommendation 4.3:*
*The Ministry of Environment and Physical Planning should improve the flow of environmental information between the Ministry and other entities involved in environmental data and information by further developing a national environmental information system.*

There are important data gaps in the collection and dissemination of statistical environmental information, particularly with regard to discharges of air and water pollutants. Currently, the Environmental Information Centre is receiving air emission data from only 18 to 22 major polluters.

*Recommendation 4.4:*
*The Environmental Information Centre should collaborate with the State Statistical Office on the collection of data on the discharges of pollutants, taking into account the ongoing negotiations on the PRTR protocol, under the Aarhus Convention. The State Statistical Office should incorporate relevant environmental indicators in the Statistical Year Book. (see also recommendation 14.1)*

The activities of the Public Relations Office in the city of Skopje and the eight citizen information centres in other municipalities may be regarded as a best practice in the dissemination of environmental information. Although the Public Relations Office provides access to international and national printed materials, user-friendly and easily understandable environmental information is lacking. The State-of-the-Environment reports are available only on the Internet, which obviously affects access to information not only by the general public but also by decision makers.

*Recommendation 4.5:*
*The Public Relations Office of the Environmental Information Centre should be linked with the citizen information centres established in the municipalities. The Ministry of Environment and Physical Planning should focus on a strategy for the dissemination of environmental information. Within this strategy the Environmental Information Centre should consider publishing State-of-the-Environment Reports both in print and on the Internet, as well as executive environmental information i.e. headline indicators.*

*Chapter 5*

# *INTERNATIONAL COOPERATION*

## 5.1 Introduction – the International Framework

Two major factors influence the current international cooperation of the former Yugoslav Republic of Macedonia. The first is the ongoing support by the international community, not only by the European Union and its member States, but also by the United States of America, Canada and Japan. The second factor is the perspective of further European integration, meaning closer cooperation and association with the European Union, as well as increased regional cooperation among the countries of South-East Europe, including regional cooperation in the framework of the Stability Pact.

Whereas some other South-Eastern European countries are already in the process of accession to the European Union, other States in the Balkan region, including the former Yugoslav Republic of Macedonia, are concentrating on their Stabilisation and Association Agreements with the European Union. The former Yugoslav Republic of Macedonia signed its Stabilisation and Association Agreement in April 2001. One of the main goals of these agreements is to prepare the partner countries for accession to the European Union.

Another important factor relevant to environmental governance in the country is the Framework Peace Agreement (the so-called Ohrid agreement), signed by representatives of the communities of the former Yugoslav Republic of Macedonia, under the auspices of the European Union and the United States of America, in summer 2001. Amongst other points, the Framework Agreement called for the further development of a decentralized government by the revision of the Law on Local Self-Government (January 2002), and invited the international community to assist in and support this process.

## 5.2 Global and Regional Environmental Cooperation

Environmental cooperation at global and pan-European levels takes place mainly within the framework of international organizations, such as the United Nations Economic Commission for Europe (UNECE), the United Nations Environment Programme (UNEP), the Global Environment Facility (GEF), the United Nations Development Programme (UNDP), international financing institutions (IFIs), such as the World Bank, the European Investment Bank (EIB) and the European Bank for Reconstruction and Development (EBRD), the Council of Europe, and the Organization for Security and Cooperation in Europe (OSCE), amongst others. The participation of the country in multilateral environmental agreements (MEAs) on a global, regional or subregional scale is another stimulus to legal and policy reforms, and offers a framework for cooperation, technical assistance and capacity-building.

Within the United Nations system, UNDP is an important partner which, through its resident office, provides support, including capacity-building, strengthening of the Ministry of Environment and Physical Planning, training of staff in project management, implementing various projects, and as a GEF implementing agency (e.g. the first national communication on climate change).

GEF is a major international source of funding for environmental projects, such as the Lake Ohrid project (implemented through the World Bank), the national biodiversity strategy (World Bank), or the development of the national implementation plan for the Stockholm Convention on Persistent Organic Pollutants (with UNEP).

The first National Environmental Action Plan (NEAP) was developed with assistance of the World Bank. The OSCE economic forum frequently organizes regional seminars on environmental issues. The main role of the Council of Europe is in biodiversity-related matters, such as the country's participation in the Pan-European Biological and Landscape Diversity Strategy (PEBLDS) or the Emerald network.

The World Bank is an important environmental actor, mainly as a GEF implementing agency, and it supported the development of the first NEAP. The Bank's Financial and Enterprise Sector Adjustment Loan (FESAL II) has helped to strengthen the environmental management of companies that have been restructured during privatization.

The Regional Environmental Center (REC) established a Country Office in Skopje in 1993. REC is conducting numerous activities in the country, such as public information and participation campaigns, NGO capacity-building, assistance to municipalities, and support for the development of environmental legislation and the implementation of MEAs.

Part of the Stability Pact is the Regional Environmental Reconstruction Programme (REReP), also strengthening subregional environmental cooperation, making environmental cooperation a bridge between countries and communities in the region. The main regional REReP projects in which the former Yugoslav Republic of Macedonia is the lead country are the development and enhancing effectiveness of economic instruments (REReP 1.5.1), the regional strategy for hazardous waste management (REReP 1.10) and the development of a regional environmental press centre (REReP 2.1). There is also a project on capacity-building for cleaner production in the country, implemented through the United Nations Industrial Development Organization (UNIDO) and funded by the Czech Republic. (see also Chapter 11 on Industry, energy and the environment)

In the framework of its post-conflict assessment activities in the Balkan region, UNEP carried out an environmental assessment in the former Yugoslav Republic of Macedonia in autumn 2000. The report concluded that the refugee influx had led to minimal long-term environmental degradation and that national priorities should focus on the rehabilitation and clean-up of five industrial hot spots posing immediate threats to human health and the environment. (see also Chapter 11 on Industry, energy and the environment)

In 2001, at the request of UNDP, UNEP conducted a strategic environmental policy assessment, providing strategic recommendations for governments, civil society, United Nations bodies and the international donor community.

For the environment, Stabilisation and Association Agreements typically stipulate approximation to the EU body of law on environmental policies, resource management and pollution control, amongst others. An analysis of the approximation process, schedules and timetables is contained in Chapter 1. An important EU funding programme supporting activities undertaken under the Stabilisation and Association Agreements is the Community Assistance for Reconstruction, Development and Stabilisation (CARDS) (former PHARE I and II). Currently, in the framework of the CARDS programme, assistance is provided to the Ministry of Environment and Physical Planning to strengthen its capacity in legal reform and approximation. This will lead to the revision of several pieces of legislation and to approximation to the EU body of law.

Increased cooperation with Europe started in 1995, when the country became eligible for PHARE and was granted support in the critical aid programme. In 1996, environmental protection was included in the PHARE cross-border programme, e.g. setting up monitoring stations for the River Vardar. The CARDS 2001 support included three components: a feasibility study of the regional solid waste strategy, the preparation of the second NEAP, which will be shaped according to European integration priorities, and support in equipment, e.g. for air pollution monitoring. Recently, the European Commission has presented its CARDS strategy for 2002 – 2006 with "environment and natural resources" as one of its priorities for cooperation. It includes institutional capacity-building for strong and independent institutions, approximation and enforcement. Water quality, air quality and waste management are considered priorities to increase health protection.

In January 2002, the European Agency for Reconstruction was given the task of managing the €26 million EU Emergency Assistance Programme for the country. The Agency opened an operational centre in Skopje, and will assume management responsibility for all other EU assistance programmes, as from March 2002. There is no specific portfolio for environmental projects in the country.

## 5.3 Bi- and Trilateral Cooperation

Bilateral cooperation is important in several respects. It includes general environmental cooperation agreements with neighbouring or nearby countries, such as Albania, Bulgaria and Greece. An agreement with Yugoslavia is being finalized, and the ones with Croatia and Slovenia are being updated. These agreements typically aim at promoting sustainable development and the protection of the environment by developing legislative and administrative mechanisms in accordance with international agreements and EU law, undertaking joint research, monitoring and information exchange, and cooperating in the management of transboundary natural resources and pollution prevention, amongst other areas.

A particularly important subject of bi- and trilateral cooperation is the management and use of transboundary natural resources and ecosystems, such as major transboundary rivers and lakes shared by the former Yugoslav Republic of Macedonia with its neighbouring countries (Lakes Ohrid, Prespa, Dojran, and river Vardar). Cooperation with Albania is advanced in relation to the basin management and the protection of Lake Ohrid. The bilateral Lake Ohrid Conservation Project was initiated with support from Switzerland and the World Bank by the signature of a memorandum of understanding in 1996, and from 1998 onwards the project has been supported by GEF, through the World Bank as implementing agency. In 2000, Albania and the former Yugoslav Republic of Macedonia established watershed management committees for Lake Ohrid, and these have been cooperating since then.

In February 2000, the Prime Ministers of Greece, the former Yugoslav Republic of Macedonia and Albania agreed on the Declaration on the Creation of the Prespa Park and the Environmental Protection and Sustainable Development of the Prespa Lakes and their Surroundings, so creating the first trilateral transboundary protected area in South-East Europe. The Coordination Committee of the Prespa Park, composed of representatives from Albania, Greece and the former Yugoslav Republic of Macedonia, met for the first time at the beginning of 2001. Also, cooperation concerning Lake Dojran is ongoing: a bilateral meeting with Greece was held, and a specific memorandum of understanding for Lake Dojran is being drafted.

The bilateral technical cooperation of the former Yugoslav Republic of Macedonia with various donor countries should also be mentioned. The main partners involved include Austria, Germany, Italy, Japan, Sweden, Switzerland, the United States and the European Union.

## 5.4 Institutional Arrangements for International Environmental Cooperation

There are several State institutions involved in international environmental cooperation in the country. First to mention is the Ministry of Environment and Physical Planning. It was established at the beginning of 1998, in order to implement the Law on the Environment and Nature Protection and Promotion and the National Environmental Action Plan (NEAP). Clearly, international cooperation has also been a driving force behind the establishment of the Ministry, and today this is an increasingly important part of the Ministry's activities, from the perspective of technical cooperation and project management, bilateral cooperation, and participation in international agreements and processes.

Other ministries seriously involved in environmental matters include: the Ministry of Agriculture, Forestry and Water Economy, which is competent for water management and use, and hydrological regimes; the Ministry of Transport and Communications, which is in charge of public works in relation to water management; and the Ministry of Health. The existing fragmentation of competences at national level finds its continuation in the competing interests of the ministries in international environmental cooperation within their competences.

An important actor in international cooperation is the Environment Fund, set up with the support of USAID, and currently developing into an important co-financing partner for projects. The Environment Fund has signed two memoranda of cooperation for development and institution-building with the United States. As a co-financing partner, the Fund has carried out several air and water protection projects. So far, the Fund has also played an important role in improving donor coordination, by organizing periodic meetings with its main donors (United States, Germany, Switzerland), assessing a list of priority projects and exploring co-financing arrangements. The Environment Fund is currently used as an example of best practice for the establishment of an environmental fund in Serbia, and is providing technical assistance to the Serbian authorities involved.

The main departments within the Ministry of Environment and Physical Planning dealing with international issues are the Department for European Integration, the Department for Regulation and Standardization, and the Department for Sustainable Development, each with various, sometimes overlapping, responsibilities in international cooperation. In early 2002, the Department for Sustainable Development was preparing for the World Summit on Sustainable Development (Johannesburg, 2002), and it can be expected that this event will help to further develop and finalize the national strategy on sustainable development, including the establishment of the (inter-ministerial) national council for sustainable development.

National relations with foreign donors are within the competence of the Government, which defines the overall policy and decides on issues that are of national interest or for which a consensus in decision-making is necessary. The National Coordinator of Foreign Aid (the Deputy Prime Minister) is responsible for national coordination and chairs the Committee of Ministers for the Coordination of Foreign Aid.

Besides the Minister of Environment and Physical Planning, the Committee of Ministers is composed of the Minister of Foreign Affairs, the Minister of Finance, the Minister of Economy, the Minister of Agriculture, Forestry and Water Economy, and the Minister of Transport and Communications. The Committee decides on the allocation of aid according to sectoral strategies and priorities, and collects information for programme implementation. A technical coordination group for the support of the Committee of Ministers has also been created.

The Sector for European Integration was set up as the operational service of the National Coordinator of Foreign Aid. It acts as the permanent secretariat of the Committee of Ministers, ensures the synergy of various projects and channels foreign aid for European integration. Finally, the Ministries, including the Ministry of Environment and Physical Planning, are in charge of the preparation of sectoral strategies, the definition of sectoral priorities and the coordination of implementation in their respective domains.

In the decentralization process, the municipalities are playing an increasingly important role in the definition and implementation of environmental policies, not only in air, waste and water management, but also in ensuring the participation of local communities in environmental decision-making. The international donor community has long since recognized the importance of municipalities as the level of State organization that is nearest to the people, and focused much attention on it.

From the beginning of its operations in the former Yugoslav Republic of Macedonia, USAID has supported municipal capacity-building activities, such as the establishment of citizen information centres in several municipalities. The Environment Fund, established with the support of USAID, focuses its activities to a large extent on co-financing measures for infrastructure improvements at municipal level. UNDP has implemented its "Green and Clean" project in numerous municipalities, including waste collection and management and clean-up measures. The preparation of Local Environmental Action Plans (LEAPs) has also been supported by several donors, such as the Institute for Sustainable Communities (ISC), the Regional Environmental Center (REC) and German Technical Assistance (GTZ), currently supporting the development of the LEAP for the city of Skopje.

The LEAP provides for investments in the construction, rehabilitation and extension of water and waste-water infrastructure in five water utilities serving the municipalities of Kumanovo, Ohrid/Struga, Stip, Strumica, and Veles. The total budget was over €50 million, composed half by grants from European countries, half by a credit line from EBRD.

## 5.5 Cooperation in Multilateral Environmental Agreements

The former Yugoslav Republic of Macedonia is a Party to several MEAs, concluded at the global, pan-European or regional scale, which are an important factor for environmental policy development, harmonization and implementation.

*Convention on Long-range Transboundary Air Pollution*

Yugoslavia ratified the Convention in 1986, and the former Yugoslav Republic of Macedonia became a Party by succession on 30 December 1997 with effect from 17 November 1991. The former Yugoslav Republic of Macedonia has not yet ratified any of the eight Protocols to the Convention. Most of the implementing legislation originates in Yugoslav laws and regulations and is outdated. Currently, a law on air quality is being drafted with GTZ assistance. It is expected to fulfil relevant EU legislation and the requirements of the Convention (see Chapter 7 on Air management) and allow for the ratification of (some of) its Protocols. Implementation may also be assisted by the Japan International Cooperation Agency (JICA), which, since 1997, has funded the installation of four automatic air quality monitoring stations with plans to establish a monitoring network covering the entire country. Support for the installation of five further monitoring stations has been announced through CARDS and through JICA.

Air pollution is a high priority, which should be addressed in cooperation by all the stakeholders. These include international organizations and donors, the national administration (e.g. Ministries of Environment, of Health and of Finance), municipalities and the private sector. As air pollution is widely recognized as one of the main environmental problems at the domestic level, the implementation of this Convention will also remain a major challenge for the future.

*Convention on Access to information, Public Participation in Decision-making and Access to Justice in Environmental Matters (Aarhus Convention)*

The former Yugoslav Republic of Macedonia demonstrated the importance it attaches to the Aarhus Convention when it became the first country to ratify it on 1 July 1999. The main legislation implementing the Convention is the Law on the Environment and Nature Protection and Promotion. No specific implementing legislation has been adopted for the areas of access to information, public participation in decision-making or access to justice in environmental matters. As a main achievement, the Ministry of Environment and Physical Planning has established the Environmental Information Centre, which has been actively disseminating information to the public and to NGOs since it began operations several years ago. (see Chapter 4 on Environmental information and public participation)

*Convention on Environmental Impact Assessment in a Transboundary Context (Espoo, 1991)*

The former Yugoslav Republic of Macedonia ratified the Convention in August 1999. The Ministry of Environment and Physical Planning is responsible for its implementation, and a Unit for Monitoring and Environmental Impact Assessment has been created within the Environment Office, which is also in charge of coordinating all activities related to the Convention's implementation.

In order to implement the Espoo Convention, the Ministry of Environment and Physical Planning has included the appropriate provisions in the draft law on environmental impact assessment. The draft law is still being prepared; its finalization can be expected as part of the approximation to EU legislation.

*Convention on Biological Diversity and other biodiversity-related treaties*

The former Yugoslav Republic of Macedonia is a Party to major global and regional conventions related to the conservation and sustainable use of biological diversity, as well as to the protection of nature and of the natural heritage. The country acceded to the Convention on Biological Diversity in December 1997.

The responsible institution for implementation is the Ministry of Environment and Physical Planning, through its Environment Office – Division of Biodiversity (see Chapter 10 Nature and biodiversity management). The Ministry has set up a National Committee on Biological Diversity, including relevant governmental institutions and parliamentary commissions, scientific institutions and NGOs. The former Yugoslav Republic of Macedonia started developing its National Biodiversity Strategy and Action Plan in 2001, as part of a project for enabling activities funded by GEF and implemented through the World Bank.

The country has been a Party to the Ramsar Convention on Wetlands of International Importance Especially as Waterfowl Habitat since 1991, by way of succession to this treaty, which Yugoslavia had ratified. In 1995, Lake Prespa was designated as a Wetland of International Importance, currently the only one in the country. In 1979, Lake Ohrid was listed as a UNESCO

World Heritage site. For further information on cooperation for the protection of transboundary lakes, see section 5.3, on Bi- and Trilateral Cooperation" above.

Furthermore, the former Yugoslav Republic of Macedonia is a Party to the Bonn Convention on the Conservation of Migratory Species of Wild Animals, the Agreement on the Conservation of African – Eurasian Migratory Waterbirds, and the Bern Convention on the Conservation of European Wildlife and Natural Habitats.

### United Nations Framework Convention on Climate Change

The former Yugoslav Republic of Macedonia acceded to the United Nations Framework Convention on Climate Change in January 1998. It has not yet signed nor ratified the Kyoto Protocol, but is considering doing so in the near future. In January 2000, with the support of GEF/UNDP, the Ministry of Environment and Physical Planning established a project unit for the preparation of the first national communication to the Convention, which is currently being developed by the relevant national working groups, and which will be submitted in 2002. The Government set up a National Committee on Climate Change. The first national inventory of greenhouse gas emissions was completed in January 2002.

### Vienna Convention for the Protection of the Ozone Layer

The former Yugoslav Republic of Macedonia has been a Party to the Vienna Convention since 1994 through succession, and has ratified the Montreal Protocol as well as the London, Copenhagen and Montreal Amendments to the Convention. The law on the ratification of the Beijing amendment is currently before Parliament. In 1997, the Ministry of Environment and Physical Planning established the Office for Ozone Layer Protection (Ozone Unit) to coordinate project development and implementation, to monitor and control the trade in ozone-depleting substances, and to provide public information.

Several projects have been successfully implemented with the support of the Montreal Protocol's Multilateral Fund. According to its national reports, the former Yugoslav Republic of Macedonia succeeded in complying with the obligations set out in the Montreal Protocol in advance of the schedule applying to developing

countries (article 5 of the Montreal Protocol) by reducing its total consumption of ozone-depleting substances by more than 80 per cent.

### Convention on International Trade in Endangered Species of Wild Fauna and Flora (CITES)

The former Yugoslav Republic of Macedonia acceded to the Convention on 4 July 2000. The Government designated the Ministry of Environment and Physical Planning as the management authority issuing CITES permits and certificates for import or export. Within the structure of the Ministry, the Environment Office is in charge of implementing CITES procedures. Similarly, several scientific authorities have been designated by the Government. Currently, the country is establishing a national committee for the Convention. Also, some amendments to the Law on Customs have already been approved.

### Basel Convention on the Transboundary Movements of Hazardous Wastes and their Disposal

The former Yugoslav Republic of Macedonia acceded to the Basel Convention in February 1997. Currently, the Law on Waste and the Law on Public Hygiene, and the Collection and Transport of Municipal Solid and Industrial Waste are in force. However, no specific implementing legislation or regulations have been adopted. Regulations on the treatment of specific types of wastes have been drafted, but not yet enacted. The Ministry of Environment and Physical Planning, and in particular the Environment Office, has been designated as the competent authority for the Basel Convention.

The Environment Office manages procedures for the control of transboundary movements, which have been successfully applied to waste exports and transit. Small quantities of domestic hazardous wastes, mainly lead-containing batteries, are being exported. The country is experiencing serious problems with stockpiles of industrial waste (see Chapter 8 on Waste management).

Under REReP, the former Yugoslav Republic of Macedonia is the lead country for the development of the regional strategy for solid waste management. In this context, a feasibility study for the construction of a specialized landfill for hazardous wastes was prepared. The country has been taking an active part in the meetings of the

Basel Convention, as well as in the capacity-building activities organized by the Regional Environment Centre for Training and Technology Transfer, in Bratislava, Slovakia.

## 5.6 Conclusions and Recommendations

Since its independence in 1991, the former Yugoslav Republic of Macedonia has made considerable efforts and progress in its international environmental cooperation at bilateral, regional, European and global levels. However, there are still important environmental protection challenges to be met at home, of which the most important are in air pollution, water pollution and management, as well as in the management of hazardous and industrial waste. Several of these challenges can be of transboundary or regional importance and are being considered by the Ministry of Environment and Physical Planning as issues of national priority, within the limits of the State budget and administrative capacity.

The national priorities identified by the Ministry should also be considered issues of international importance. These include the reduction of air pollution, water pollution and management, as well as hazardous waste management.

*Recommendation 5.1:*
*The Ministry of Environment and Physical Planning should develop a strategy for international environmental cooperation, by taking the lead in initiating a consultative process at the national level, involving related Ministries and institutions.*

*The strategy should clearly identify major challenges, present national achievements, and main needs for technical cooperation, co-financing and foreign investment in the environment.*

*The Strategy should be developed by ensuring the maximum degree of public participation, and by promoting international environmental cooperation and agreements in media and public awareness campaigns.*

*The strategy should be used to promote the international cooperation priorities within the coordination mechanism set up by the Sector of European Integration at government level, and presented to and considered by the Committee of Ministers for the Coordination of Foreign Aid.*

In a few years, the country has achieved an impressive track record in addressing important transboundary environmental issues by regional and bilateral cooperation and agreements. These efforts have yielded considerable results in bi- and trilateral agreements, transboundary projects and management approaches. The Ministry of Environment and Physical Planning should continue these promising efforts as a matter of priority.

The Ministry should further promote and seek comprehensive solutions, such as further agreements and transboundary management plans for transboundary natural resources, including the management and reduction of pollution, and the restoration and conservation of its important water bodies shared with other countries in the region. These efforts should be based on a regional and basin-wide approach and prepare the country for compliance with the EU body of law. The regional approach should also be used in developing further projects for submission to international donors.

*Recommendation 5.2:*
*The Ministry of Environment and Physical Planning should:*
- *Prepare management plans in compliance with the European Water Framework Directive at the national level, and bilateral agreements for the major transboundary natural resources and water bodies;*
- *Accede to and implement the UNECE Helsinki Convention on the Protection and Use of Transboundary Watercourses and International Lakes;*
- *Take measures to support bilateral and multilateral agreements to implement the UNECE Espoo Convention on Environmental Impact Assessment in a Transboundary Context;*
- *The Government of the former Yugoslav Republic of Macedonia should ratify as soon as possible those protocols to the UNECE Convention on Long-range Transboundary Air Pollution Protocols to which it is still not a Party.*

In recent years, the former Yugoslav Republic of Macedonia and its Ministry of Environment and Physical Planning have made reasonable progress in participation in multilateral environmental agreements (MEAs). The country has ratified or acceded to most of the major MEAs, and the

Ministry's staff is actively represented in numerous international forums. However, an overall assessment of the level of implementation of MEAs shows that there is still a lot to be done in practical implementation and enforcement.

*Recommendation 5.3:*
*The Government of the former Yugoslav Republic of Macedonia should undertake more concrete measures for complying with those conventions to which it is already a Party.*

The ongoing process of State reform and decentralization might also influence decisions or donor preferences in a spirit of subsidiarity and decentralization. A number of very successful projects with international support have been implemented at municipal level, recognizing that municipalities have key responsibilities in protecting the health of their populations, as well as the environment that they inhabit. However, many municipalities still require capacity–building in various fields, ranging from project management, public information and participation, to policy

implementation. The lack of financial resources for communal infrastructure investments in water, waste and air management is severe and chronic.

*Recommendation 5.4:*
*The Ministry of Environment and Physical Planning should continue its support for capacity-building in municipalities' environmental management, and seek the cooperation of the international donor community in the development of LEAPs and programmes to support public participation, information and project development at local level.*

In a continuing process of stabilization and accelerated regional and international integration, the former Yugoslav Republic of Macedonia will be able to continue to rely on the support of the international community, including in international environmental cooperation. It can be expected that important cooperation programmes will continue and new ones be created, in particular in the context of cooperation with the European Community.

# PART II: MANAGEMENT OF POLLUTION AND OF NATURAL RESOURCES

*Chapter 6*

# WATER MANAGEMENT, INCLUDING PROTECTION OF LAKES

## 6.1    Water resources

### *Climatic and geographic features*

The country's topography is characterized by its mountain relief crossed by vast valleys and numerous long and narrow ravines. The country is under the combined influence of (i) a Mediterranean climate, (ii) a middle-European dry continental climate, and (iii) a mountain climate resulting from its mountainous (80 per cent of the territory) and high (up to 2700m) relief. Its climatic parameters, such as rainfall, temperature, atmospheric pressure, wind and moisture, vary greatly and all have a significant impact on its water regime.

Rainfall across the country is uneven and sporadic and small in quantity. Average annual rainfall is approximately 733 mm (i.e. 19 billion $m^3$). Dry and hot periods are long (summer-autumn) and cold periods short (winter). Rain is heavy from October to December, and lighter from March to May. Sudden short and intensive rainfall is also a characteristic of a Mediterranean climate. It produces intensive erosion and local floods that can destroy infrastructure and cause landslides.

The west receives heavy rain while dry spells sometimes lasting over 100 days mainly during the summer (July-September) are characteristic of the central part of the country. The smallest yearly rainfalls are registered in the centre and east of the country, in Gradsko (380 mm), Veles (470 mm), Kavadarci (489 mm) and Sveti Nikole (500 mm); the heaviest rain is registered in the west on the Shara and Baba Mountains (1400 mm and 1300 mm). The former Yugoslav Republic of Macedonia is classified as a semi-arid area. Its agriculture is limited by the availability of water.

### *Water reserves and availability*

The country's yearly average water availability from surface resources is approximately 5.5 to 6.5 billion $m^3$ (4.5 for a medium dry year), of which 0.4

to 0.6 billion from springs. The yearly volume of groundwater is about 0.3-0.5 billion $m^3$, an estimate that is considered to be low (Figure 6.1). Most of these resources are found in the Vardar basin (72 per cent) and, to a lesser extent, in the Crni Drim (25 per cent) and Strumica basins (3 per cent).

According to 1995-1996 data, 1.5 to 1.7 billion $m^3$ are used per year, 84 per cent from surface water and 16 per cent from groundwater and natural springs. Therefore, about one third of the water resources are used, which is indicative of a country with rather scarce water resources.

## 6.2    Natural hydrographic network

### *Surface Waters*

#### Rivers

There are four hydrographic catchment areas: Vardar, Crni Drim, Strumica and Juzna Morava. The key characteristics of the main rivers and their tributaries are shown in table 6.1.

- The River Vardar catchment area covers 20,661km$^2$, or 80.4 per cent of the country. It receives four major tributaries, the Treska, Pchinja, Bregalnica and Crna, and includes the Dojran Lake catchment area. It rises at 683 m above sea level (m.a.s.l.), and runs 301 km down to the Aegean Sea. The total yearly average of available water in this catchment area is about 4.6 billion $m^3$.

- The Crni Drim catchment area in the west covers the catchment areas of Lakes Prespa and Ohrid and that of the Crni Drim with its tributaries. The catchment area of the River Crni Drim covers 3,359 km$^2$, or 13.1 per cent of the former Yugoslav Republic of Macedonia. This region is the richest in water resources. The River Crni Drim flows from Lake Ohrid, at the town of Struga, at an altitude of 693 m.a.s.l and runs north along the Jablanica Mountains.

The total yearly average of available water in this catchment area is 1.64 billion m³.

- The Strumica catchment area in the south-east extends over the catchment areas of the Strumitsa, Cironska and Lebnitca Rivers to the Bulgarian border. It covers 1,649 km², or 6.4 per cent of the country's territory. The main tributaries of the Strumica River are the Vodotcha, Touriya, Radovishka Reka and Podareshka Reka. This area is the poorest in water resources and the lack of water affects all segments of human activities: water supply to the population (especially in the rural areas), industry and irrigation. This also aggravates the water quality situation and flow rates are often below the biological minimum in the periods when the rivers dry up. The total yearly average of available water in this catchment area is approximately 132 million m³.

- The catchment area of the Juzna Morava is on the territories of both Yugoslavia and the former Yugoslav Republic of Macedonia. In the latter, it covers an insignificant area of 44 km², and therefore it does not have a major impact on the water resources available in the country. The River Binacka Morava rises in the former Yugoslav Republic of Macedonia's territory and continues its flow into neighbouring Yugoslavia.

Lakes

The two biggest natural lakes in the former Yugoslav Republic of Macedonia are Ohrid and Prespa. They both belong to the Vardar catchment area.

- Lake Ohrid has endemic characteristics very similar to those of Lake Baykal and Lake Tanganyika. Its total volume is 50.68 billion m³, with a water surface of 357 km², a maximum length of 29.5 km, a width of 14.7 km and a maximum depth of 269.8 m. The Lake surface is at an average altitude of 693 m.a.s.l. This Lake is transboundary with Albania. About 70 per cent of its surface area (i.e. 250 km²) belongs to the former Yugoslav Republic of Macedonia. Of the total catchment area, 843km² belong to the former Yugoslav Republic of Macedonia and 308 km² to Albania. The Lake has been designated by UNESCO as a world natural heritage site for its crystal water and scenic beauty. It is a major tourist asset for the country.

- Lake Prespa has a total volume of 4.78 billion m³, with a water surface of 328 km², a total length of 43.3 km, a width of 16.4 km, and maximum depth of 55.55 m. The former Yugoslav Republic of Macedonia shares the lake with Albania and Greece, so that 197 km² of its water surface belongs to the former Yugoslav Republic of Macedonia, 48.4 km² to Albania and 82.3 km² to Greece. Its catchment area is 1,046.25 km², of which 571 km² belong to the former Yugoslav Republic of Macedonia. During the past 15 years the Lake's water level has declined significantly.

- Located in the south-east of the country, Lake Dojran, third in importance but the smallest natural lake in the former Yugoslav Republic of Macedonia, also belongs to the catchment area of the Vardar River. It, too, is shared with Greece. Its total water surface is 43 km², of which 25.62 km² belong to the former Yugoslav Republic of Macedonia and 17.07 km² to Greece. During the past 15 years its water table has fallen because of natural hydrologic phenomena, dry climate cycles and human uses. Lake Dojran is an isolated ecosystem with very specific flora and fauna, which are threatened. For a couple of years now the level of the Lake has risen, as a result of the improved hydrological situation, but it is still below its original level.

The Galitchica Mountain separates Lakes Prespa and Ohrid. A number of scientific observations show that the water from Lake Prespa situated at 854 m.a.s.l., or about 150 m above the Ohrid water table, runs off into Lake Ohrid through the karstic mountain grounds, and re-appears as surface springs at St Naum and as underground springs at the bottom of Lake Ohrid.

*Underground waters and springs*

The underground waters are primarily located under the main river valleys. There are not sufficient data on the quality and quantity of available underground waters. Some, albeit limited, information is available about the underground water level fluctuations in the Polog Valley, Skopje Valley, Ovche Pole, Kotchani Valley, Strumica Pole, the Bitola part of Pelagonija and the Struga Pole.

## Figure 6.1: Water resources

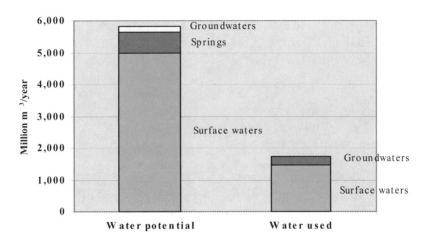

*Source:* Integrated Water resources Development and Management Master Plan, May 1999.

## Table 6.1: Characteristics of the main rivers

| River | River catchment | Catchment area (km$^2$) | River length (km) | Average annual flow (m$^3$/s) | Average annual volume (billion m$^3$) | Specific run-off (l/s/km$^2$) |
|---|---|---|---|---|---|---|
| Vardar | Vardar | 20,661 | 301 | 63-145 (a) | 4.600 | 7.0 |
| Treska | Vardar | 2,068 | 139 | 24.2 (b) | 0.764 | 12.9 |
| Lepenets | Vardar | 770 | 75 | 8.7 | 0.271 | 11.2 |
| Pchinja | Vardar | 2,841 | 137 | 12.6 (c) | 0.400 | 4.6 |
| Bregalnitca | Vardar | 4,344 | .. | 12.2 (d) | .. | 4.1 |
| Csrna Reka | Vardar | 4,985 | 228 | 29.3 | .. | 5.1 |
| Boshava | Vardar | 468 | 52 | 23.4 (e) | .. | .. |
| Crni Drim | Crni Drim | 3,359 | 45 | 52.0 (f) | 1.640 | 12.3 |
| Radika | Crni Drim | .. | .. | 19.3 | .. | .. |
| Strumica | Strumica | 1,649 | .. | 4.2 (g) | 0.132 | 3.1 |
| Binacka Morava | Juzna Morava | 44 | .. | .. | .. | .. |

*Source*: Protection and utilization of water and water economy infrastructure, 1998.

*Notes*:

(a) 63 in Skopje; 145 in Gergelija

(b) at its confluence with the River Vardar

(c) at Katlanovska Banja

(d) in Shtip

(e) at Rasimbegov Most

(f) at Shpilje hydro power station

(g) at Novo Selo

The registered number of springs totals 4,414, of which 58 have a capacity of 100 litres per second or more. A specific feature of the spring waters is their fluctuating outflow during the year. They reach their maximum during May-June and after heavy autumn rainfall. The total flow of these springs is estimated at over 20 m$^3$/s.

Of these springs, three are located in the middle course of the River Vardar, while the others are in the western regions. In the Treska catchment area, there are 18 springs; in the River Vardar catchment area, there are 19, of which the most important is the Rashche spring with an average capacity of 3.5 m$^3$/s (its maximum is over 6.0 m$^3$/s). This spring is very important as it supplies the city of Skopje and its surroundings (over 600,000 inhabitants and industry). In the catchment area of the River Crna Reka there are four springs, seven in the catchment area of the Crni Drim, including Lake Ohrid, of which the biggest is St. Naum, with a capacity exceeding 10 $m^3/s$.

The main geothermal zones with thermal waters are located in the regions of Volkovo-Skopje-Katlanovo, Kumanovo-Kratovo, Istibanja-Kotchani-Shtip, Strunitsa, Smokvitsa-Hegorci-Gevgelija and Kosovrasti-Debar-Banishte. Because they are few and their chemical composition particular, their use is limited to very specific purposes. Their waters are mainly used for balneological and spa therapy, and for bottled mineral drinking water, while some small quantities, as in Kochani for example, are used for heating greenhouses and other buildings.

### Water Quality and Trends

Water resources, i.e. ground and surface waters, are relatively clean in their upper course, and rapidly worsen along their middle and lower courses. This situation is the result of unpurified waste water discharged chiefly by human settlements, but also by industry and agriculture. In some places, for instance downstream of Skopje and Veles on the Vardar River, water quality even breaches the maximum limits for class IV. Often, the water bodies do not comply with the quality class objectives set for them.

The major polluters of surface and groundwaters are the municipal sewerage systems that collect household and industrial waste water (in many settlements rainfall drainage, too) and the industrial sewerage systems. In the agricultural northeast, there is significant pollution from livestock waste, farms, slaughterhouses, milk processing, meat and canned food industries. In general, polluted waters are directly discharged into receiving water bodies without any treatment. Some rivers are actually turned into collectors of waste water (dead rivers) by enormous pollution discharges. This is the case of the Vardar in Skopje after the urban waste-water discharges, in Veles after the waste-water discharge from the smelter plant and the fertilizer plant; and also with the Dragor near Bitola and the Kumanovka near Kumanovo. The water quality of the Vardar, Crna Reka, Strumesnica and Bregalnica rivers, after receiving household and industrial waste waters from the towns of Tetovo, Skopje, Veles (Vardar), Prilep, Bitola (Crna Reka), Kocani, Stip (Bregalnica) and Strumica (Strumesnica), is below regulation standard and in poor hydrobiological condition. In recent years the situation has somewhat improved because of the industrial decline. (see Chapter Introduction)

### Surface waters

The surface water quality situation in 1997 is represented in Figure 6.2. It reflects the quality classes as defined in the Decree on the Categorization of Waters (Official Gazette, No. 18/99) shown in Table 6.2 (a) and (b). There are no more recent comprehensive data available about surface water quality.

Surface water quality is unsatisfactory in the former Yugoslav Republic of Macedonia. A series of components indicates pollution from both households and agriculture. For instance, the content of nitrites has increased dramatically since the period 1978-1997 - especially in Bregalnica and Crna Reka. The same is true of the $BOD_5$ content in the same waterways. The level of dissolved oxygen is very low in Crna Reka at the Novaci and Skocivir measuring points, as well as in the Kumanovska and Dragor rivers after the waste-water discharges from Kumanovo and Bitola respectively. The nitrates in the waterways examined are within regulation limits.

Other elements indicating pollution from industrial sources are detected in a few specific places. Lead, zinc and cadmium are recorded in the River Vardar downstream of the smelter facility in the town of Veles. Cadmium is also present in concentrations above the norms in the measuring points of the upper course of the Bregalnica River and in Lake Tikves, which belongs to the Crna Reka basin. Chromium is found in the Vardar River after the Jugohrom production site upstream of the city of Skopje, although the standard value is not exceeded. Phosphorus and nitrates are present in the Vardar downstream of the fertilizer production facility of Veles. However, while the amount of these elements discharged by industrial facilities is high, there is no regular monitoring indicating exact levels.

---

**Box 6.1:     Lake Ohrid Conservation Project**

Lake Ohrid is a transboundary lake in the southwest of the former Yugoslav Republic of Macedonia and is transboundary with Albania on its western bank. It covers 349 km$^2$, of which 230 km$^2$ (66 per cent) belong to the former Yugoslav Republic of Macedonia. UNESCO classified it as a world natural heritage site in 1979. It is a natural, cultural and historical monument and the cradle of very ancient civilizations (Neolithic). The Lake is one of the oldest in Europe. Because of its oligotrophic state, it is one of the largest biological reserves in Europe, sheltering unique flora and fauna that are extinct elsewhere. Due to its age, many of Lake Ohrid's aquatic species are endemic, including 10 of its 17 fish species. The quality and hydrological conditions of Lake Ohrid are tied to those of Lake Prespa, as half of Lake Ohrid's water comes from Lake Prespa through an underground aquifer and natural siphon mechanism.

Lake Ohrid is an important cultural and tourist asset for the former Yugoslav Republic of Macedonia as the country has no access to the sea. For some time, the development of human settlements and tourist infrastructures have been putting a strain on the Lake. At present, more than 100,000 people live and work along its banks, and exert environmental pressure (domestic activities; tourism; textile, metal, electrical industries; and agriculture and fishing). A sewage collection ring has been built to collect discharges from Elsani to Struga (one third of the lake shore) and bring the waste water to treatment plants in Ohrid and Struga. However, a few villages and industrial facilities are not yet connected to it and pollution from agriculture is still uncontrolled. An additional pollution surplus is generated by tourism during the high season.  Different pieces of legislation specific to the Lake aim at controlling the human activities that could endanger it, such as fishing, the use of phosphate-containing detergent, the  introduction of allochtonous fish species. However, there is no harmonization in the objectives and legislation regarding the Lake and its management between the two border countries. This seriously impairs its sustainable management.

In 1996, in an attempt to protect the Lake from anthropogenic pressures, both border countries adopted the Lake Ohrid Conservation Project financed by GEF and implemented by the World Bank. The three-year project started in 1998 at a total cost of US$ 4.4 million, of which 2.4 million for the former Yugoslav Republic of Macedonia.  Its main objectives are to:
- Develop a basis for the joint management and protection of the Lake by the two border countries,
- Create conditions for promoting environmentally friendly solutions for the management of natural resources and the economic development of the watershed.

The first step consisted in developing a participatory watershed management approach. The project has involved all the local stakeholders, including many NGOs. A water management committee was set up, which is a good example for the establishment of river basin management committees in the rest of the country. A memorandum of understanding has been concluded between the two countries for harmonizing the Lake's monitoring programme. Still under debate is the sustainable management and control of fish stocks.  Pilot projects in forestry, tourism, spatial planning, sewage, waste management and the use of phosphate-free detergents are being developed in cooperation with NGOs. Since GEF support will come to an end in 2003, the success of the project may be jeopardized unless the Government mobilizes all its efforts and political will to consolidate this transboundary watershed management approach.

---

### Underground waters

Underground waters from karstic springs and from aquifers (over 80 per cent of the waters used for the settlements' water supply) have their watersheds (wide protection zone) usually in high mountain areas, where there are no industrial polluters and few people. The potential bacterial pollution can come only from extensive cattle breeding in the summer. While these waters have not been regularly monitored since 1981, spot checks show that most are quality class I or II. (see table 6.3)

For the underground waters used for drinking water and that are monitored by the Ministry of Health, the indicators of pollution of organic origin, such as COD, BOD, nitrogen compounds (ammonia, nitrates, nitrites) do not indicate any potential sanitary-hygienic problem, except for a small number of water-supply facilities in a few villages.

(see Chapter 14 on Human health and the environment)

### 6.3   Built   infrastructure   for   waterflow management

*Flood Control*

Because of its geomorphology and climate, the former Yugoslav Republic of Macedonia is very prone to flood damage. Recent examples of the destructive effects of such short-lasting rainfall were the floods in Negotino, Kavadarci, Valandovo and Strumitsa in 1995. For some time, waterflow regulation has been a basic water management activity. Measures have been taken in the river basins and in the riverbeds to improve their water flow and protect their immediate surroundings. The flood control systems include:

- The local regulation of riverbeds in urban areas;
- The systematic regulation of rivers over longer sections; and
- Control embankments and dikes.

The regulation of the Vardar River in Skopje dates back to after the big floods of 1895 and 1897. Since then, quay walls and control embankments were constructed and continuously expanded, in particular after the 1935 floods and during the 1950s. At the same time, the "Skopje Pole" drainage system of the city surroundings was also built up.

The 1950s and 1960s marked the construction of large hydro irrigation schemes (see below): extensive regulation works were undertaken to drain the Pelagonija region through the regulation of the rivers Tsrna, Dragor, Shemnitca, Blato and of a great number of streams; the Strumica region through the regulation of the River Strumica, the Monospitov Canal and some small streams; the Struga region through the melioration of the River Crni Drim and many small streams. Overall, outstanding regulation works have been undertaken on the River Vardar (in Gostivar, Tetovo, Skopje, Veles, Negotino, Kavadarci and Bogdanci), on the Treska (in Kichevo and Makedonski Brod), on the Pchinja (in Kriva Palanka and Kratovo), on the Bregalnica (in Berovo, Delchevo, Vinica, Kochani, Shtip), on the Tsrna Reka (in Prilep, Bitola and the Pelagonija system) and on the Crni Drim (in Resen, Tzarev Dvor, Struga, Sateska).

### Dams and Reservoirs

The uneven distribution of the surface waters in location, time and quality largely prevents the optimized use of water resources. Therefore, the construction of dams and the creation of reservoirs that modify the water regime and make it more manageable were essential. These infrastructures enable a full and efficient use of waters both in the water management (electricity production, irrigation, water supply) and the protection of the human environment from water harmful effects. The former Yugoslav Republic of Macedonia has two types of dams.

Large dams together with their auxiliary facilities enable the multipurpose use of water resources. The stored water is used for the water supply for the population, industry, irrigation, the production of electric power, flood control, for maintaining the biological minimum water flow, and for sports,

recreation and tourism. Started in 1938, construction became more active in the late 1950s and especially in the 1960s, resulting today in about 20 large dams. Thirteen big dams were built in the Vardar catchment area, three in the Strumica and three in the Crni Drim catchment areas. Most (13) of the dams were built as embankment dams with local material: clay, sand, gravel and crushed rock, for instance in Tikvesh (113.5 m) and Shpilje (112 m). The others are concrete arches and dams. At present, two high dams are under construction: the Kozjak Dam on the River Treska and the Lisitche Dam on the River Topolka. Total water storage capacity is 1.85 billion $m^3$ and 1.11 billion $m^3$ available capacity (compared to the capacity of Lakes Dojran of 0.43 billion $m^3$, Prespa 4.78 billion $m^3$ and Ohrid 50.68 billion $m^3$).

Over 120 small dams and reservoirs provide water for the irrigation of smaller areas, the water supply of rural settlements and local industries, and fish farming. The level of the small dams ranges from a few metres to 28 metres, while the volume of stored waters varies from 10,000 to 1 million $m^3$ depending on the dam. Total capacity is 10 million $m^3$. The total area that can potentially be irrigated from these small dams is approximately 58 thousand hectares, of which 42 thousand hectares were actually irrigated in 2000. A large part of the corresponding irrigation network has not been built owing to a lack of funds. Plans for building new reservoirs and completing the existing irrigation network of small reservoirs do exist and would aim at a more efficient use of the water from the small rivers. The construction of dams would have the usual environmental impacts: modification of the hydrological regime of rivers, modifications of river and terrestrial ecosystems, relocation of human settlements and human activities.

### Irrigation schemes and the drainage network

The climate and pedological conditions of the country are suitable for intensive and effective agricultural production, but only if water is efficiently provided through irrigation. The arable agricultural area totals approximately 667 thousand hectares, essentially located in valleys. Potentially, 400,000 hectares, i.e. 60 per cent of the total arable land, could be irrigated. A wide network of irrigation schemes has existed for some time in the country. About 160 smaller and bigger irrigation schemes have been built, covering an area of 163,692 hectares of fertile arable land, i.e. 40.9 per cent of the area that can be irrigated.

## Figure 6.2: Surface waters

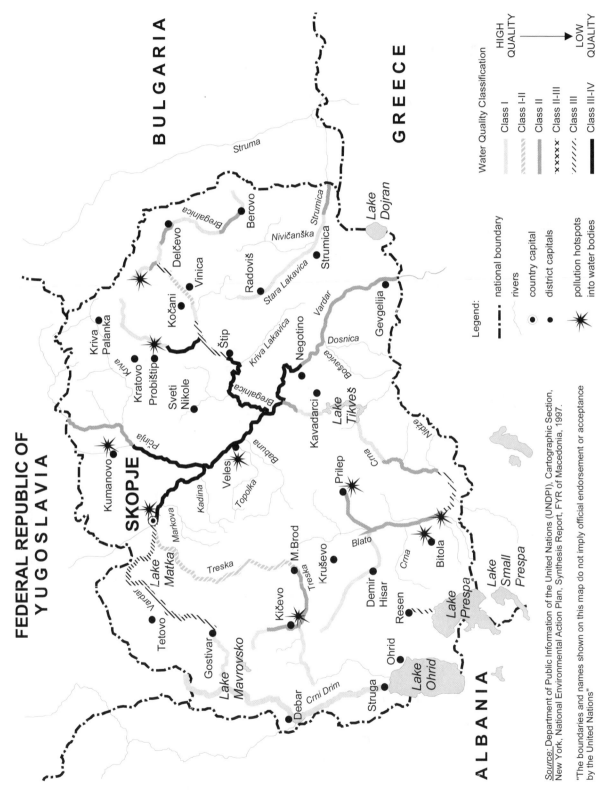

*Source:* Department of Public Information of the United Nations (UNDPI), Cartographic Section, New York, National Environmental Action Plan, Synthesis Report, FYR of Macedonia, 1997.

"The boundaries and names shown on this map do not imply official endorsement or acceptance by the United Nations"

**Table 6.2: (a): Ambient standards for global parameters in the different classes of water quality**

| Substances | Unit | Maximum allowable concentration (MAC) | |
| --- | --- | --- | --- |
| | | Class I* | Class III* |
| Dissolved oxygen | mg O$_2$/l | 8 | 4 |
| Saturation in oxygen | % | 90-105 | 50-75 |
| Biological oxygen demand (BOD) | mg O$_2$/l | 2 | 7 |
| Chemical oxygen demand (COD) | mg O$_2$/l | 10 | 20 |
| Total suspended matter | mg/l | 10 | 80 |
| Total dissolved matter | mg/l | 350 | 1500 |
| pH | pH units | 6.8-8.5 | 6.0-9.0 |
| Total coliforms | bacteria | 200 | 200,000 |

*Source*: The former Yugoslav Republic of Macedonia. Official Gazette No. 4/84.
*Note:* Based on the old classification system.

**Table 6.2: (b) Ambient standards for specific parameters in the different classes of water quality**

| Dangerous substances | Unit | Classes I and II* | Classes III and IV* |
| --- | --- | --- | --- |
| Ammonia | MgN/l | 0.10 | 0.5 |
| Ammonium | MgN/l | 1.00 | 10.0 |
| Nitrate | MgN/l | 1.00 | 15.0 |
| Nitrite | MgN/l | 0.05 | 0.5 |
| Hydrogen sulphide | mg/l | .. | 0.1 |
| Arsenic | mg/l | 0.05 | 0.05 |
| Antimony | mg/l | 0.05 | 0.05 |
| Copper | mg/l | 0.10 | 0.1 |
| Iron | mg/l | 0.30 | 1.0 |
| Mercury | mg/l | 0.001 | 0.001 |
| Cadmium | mg/l | 0.005 | 0.01 |
| Cobalt | mg/l | 0.20 | 2.0 |
| Molybden | mg/l | 0.50 | 0.5 |
| Nickel | mg/l | 0.05 | 0.1 |
| Lead | mg/l | 0.05 | 0.1 |
| Silver | mg/l | 0.01 | 0.02 |
| Chromium Cr-III | mg/l | 0.10 | 0.5 |
| Chromium Cr-VI | mg/l | 0.05 | 0.1 |
| Zinc | mg/l | 0.2 | 1.0 |
| Phenols | mg/l | 0.001 | 0.3 |
| Cyanide | mg/l | 0.01 | 0.1 |

*Source*: The former Yugoslav Republic of Macedonia. Official Gazette No. 7/87.
*Note:* Based on the old classification system.

**Table 6.3: Pollution load from waste waters discharged into rivers, 1996**

| Unit | Waste-water volume m$^3$/day | Suspended matter kg/day | BOD5 kg/day | Nitrogen kg/day | Phosphorus kg/day |
| --- | --- | --- | --- | --- | --- |
| **Total** | **293,394** | **218,309** | **62,048** | **14,702** | **2,642** |
| *of which* | | | | | |
| Vardar | 265,557 | 193,974 | 55,130 | 13,064 | 2,347 |
| Strumica | 10,616 | 9,168 | 2,606 | 618 | 111 |
| Crni Drim | 17,221 | 15,167 | 4,312 | 1,022 | 184 |

*Source*: REC. Final Country Report, Macedonia. June 2000.

Because the irrigation infrastructure has not been regularly maintained, is unequally managed, and is not complete, only 77 per cent, or 126 thousand hectares, are properly irrigated. Of this area, 61 per cent is irrigated by sprinklers and 39 per cent with other types of surface irrigation. The total water quantity required for the irrigated area is approximately 900 million m³, which represents 25 per cent of the total water quantity available from the river network during an average dry year (one sixth in a normal year). Irrigation is seen as a basis for the restoration of the country's agricultural potential. (see Chapter 10 on Nature and biodiversity management) To maximize the economic effects in the future, priority is currently being given to the rehabilitation and reconstruction of the obsolete infrastructure. (figure 6.3)

Drainage systems cover a total area of 82,195 hectares. This extensive drainage system was started in the 1930s to drain the frequent floods, and its construction continued till the 1960s. Drainage was necessary in many areas (or 'poles'), such as the Skopje Pole (6,600 hectares drained), Pelagonija (54,150 total), the Struga Pole (2,680 hectares), the Strumica Pole (9 thousand hectares), the Kochani Pole, the Bregalnica Pole (6 thousand hectares) the Ovche Pole (6 thousand hectares) and the Prespa Pole (1,900 hectares). Today, the existing drainage systems need to be maintained, reconstructed and rehabilitated, and the construction of the detailed drainage network has to be completed.

Currently, 40 thousand hectares of irrigation systems are being rehabilitated in three regions,

Tikveš, Bregalnica and Polog. The project will cost $32.5 million, of which $12.5 million is a credit and loan from the World Bank, $12 million a grant from the Netherlands Government and $8 million from the country itself. The project is conducted through the Ministry of Agriculture, Forestry and Water Economy. The biggest part of the resources is allocated to investments in infrastructures (71.5 per cent of total investment) and a smaller part for institutional development, i.e. finding ways to use and manage the irrigation systems more efficiently through pilot programmes, and research.

## 6.4 Pressures on water resources

*Overview of water consumption and discharges*

The most recent data on water consumption are from 1996. They certainly do not accurately reflect the present situation. Although both irrigation and the needs of the population were comparable between 1996 and 2000, industrial consumption might have decreased due to the economic crisis. In 1996, overall annual water consumption was about 1.72 million m³, of which 82 per cent for irrigation, 11 per cent for the public and 7 per cent for industry.

In general, domestic and industrial waste waters are directly discharged into water bodies. Only 6 per cent are treated first. Table 6.3 shows the pollution loads discharged by point sources into the rivers; nothing is known about diffuse emission sources.

**Figure 6.3: Trends in actual use of the installed irrigation network**

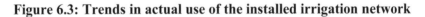

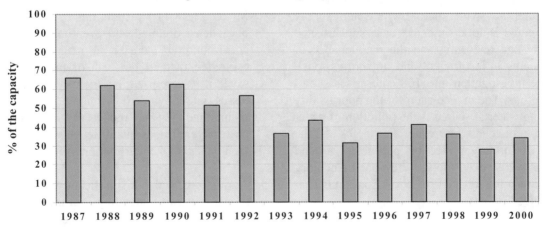

*Source*: Public Water Management Enterprise. 2002.
*Note*: Nominal capacity of the irrigation system = 163 thousand ha.

*Domestic use*

Some 0.2 billion m3 of water is abstracted annually for the population's needs (see Figure 6.4). Some 60 per cent of the inhabitants receive water from karstic springs, 20 per cent from wells and 20 per cent from surface waters. Surface water is also supplied from storage reservoirs such as the Strežević, Glaznja and Lipkovo, Turija, Ratevska Reka (River Ratevska), Gradče, Mantovo and Mavrovica reservoirs. Water consumption averages 250 to 350 litres per capita per day. That is higher than in Western countries, which have a water consumption average of 180 to 200 litres per capita per day. In most households the water is not metered for billing, which does not encourage water saving.

About 70 per cent of the population is connected to municipal water supply facilities (all urban settlements, including villages attached to them, i.e. 1,440,000 inhabitants), while the remaining 31 per cent rural population has local or individual water supply systems. In 2000, an analysis of the data on the water supply to 30 urban settlements with a total of 1.2 million inhabitants showed that the sanitary conditions of the facilities and the hygienic quality of the analysed water samples were generally satisfactory, i.e. ranged within the WHO drinking water standard limits. The most frequent reason for negative results was the lack of residual chlorine, and a certain number of parameters of organoleptic importance (manganese, iron, and sediment). The situation is not as good in rural areas. According to a similar analysis of rural settlements connected to a public water supply or to local facilities (individual wells, pumps, village fountains, springs), a relatively high number of samples (over 5 per cent) fail to meet the quality limits. In holiday resorts, hotels, catering and tourist facilities with their own water supply systems, water is not disinfected, or it is disinfected irregularly and unevenly, and the maintenance of these systems is insufficient and not professional. The same investigation into 108 enterprises shows similar results. The main reason for the poor quality of drinking water at source is the pollution of water bodies by untreated waste-water discharges and the absence of sanitary protection perimeters around the water wells, even though they are mandatory (Regulations on Sanitary Protection Zones, Official Gazette No. 17/83).

A key problem is the seasonal drinking-water shortages experienced by many cities and villages all over the country during the dry season (of which

Skopje, Kumanovo, Prilep, Kratova, Prila Palanka, Kichevo are the best known), during the cold season (Tetovo) or even all year around (Veles). A recent example is the city of Prilep in the summer of 2001, when hospitals, schools and kindergartens were not supplied with water and drinking water was distributed by tankers. In general the reason is the lack of sufficient water-storing capacity (reservoirs) and the poor management of supply equipment. It seems also that, although the Law on Waters explicitly spells out priorities for water users during a water shortage (population supply is the first priority), economic interests still prevail too often.

Regarding domestic waste-water discharges, only a few towns, namely Ohrid, Struga, Resen and Dojran, have a sewage system with a waste-water treatment plant. Elsewhere, domestic waste water is simply discharged without treatment into the rivers, with an adverse impact on the water quality downstream (Figure 6.2). There are projects for building waste-water treatment plants in Skopje, Bitola, Strumica and Prilep, but due to a lack of funds they are still just blueprints.

*Agriculture*

Agriculture is the main water consumer. Climatic conditions are favourable to agriculture, but irrigation is necessary (see Chapter 9 on Agriculture and forest management). Higher yields can be obtained by irrigation, for instance gardening yields can be increased threefold, vine and fruit plants eightfold, rice threefold, cereal cultures threefold, sugar beet two-and-a-half to threefold, alfalfa fivefold. As mentioned above, huge irrigation facilities have long existed, but they are not currently used to their full potential (Figure 6.3). According to the Agricultural Development Strategy (2001), by 2020, this irrigated area should be at least doubled and eventually tripled, with a corresponding increase in irrigation water. It is estimated that 50 per cent of the water could be saved if it were used in a more sustainable way and losses were avoided (irrigation systems properly maintained). The reduction in losses would preserve enormous quantifies of water, which could then be used for the irrigation of new surfaces.

Agriculture is also a significant water polluter. Big industrial cattle-breeding farms in the north (Kumanovo region), especially industrial pig farms, discharge their effluents into water bodies. They are the major polluter of the Vardar and its tributaries upstream of Skopje. Slaughterhouses and meat-canning factories in the same area are also big water polluters.

*Mining and Industry*

In spite of the economic recession of the past years, industry certainly remains the main polluter as far as toxic and eutrophic components are concerned. The chemical industry, leather manufacturing, food production, the meta- processing industry, lead and zinc smelting companies are the main industrial polluting branches (Chapter 11 on Industry, energy and the environment). Only a small number of industrial facilities (about 20) are equipped with waste-water pre-treatment stations on their premises, and few of them are operating at present. Depending on their size and location, industries discharge their waste waters either into municipal collectors or directly into surface waters. According to the UNEP Post Conflict Environmental Assessment (2000), the major potential water polluters are the copper mine in Radovis (Buchim S.C.) releasing copper; the metal resurfacing factory in Kicevo (Tane Caleski) releasing heavy metals, oils and other components; the copper-ore flotation plant in Bucim; the ferro-alloy plant releasing chromium in Jegunovce (HEK Jugohrom); the lead-zinc smelter in Veles releasing lead, zinc and cadmium; the lead-zinc mines in

Kamenica, Probistip and Toranica discharging cyanide, cadmium and other heavy metals; the organic chemicals plant releasing HCH isomers in Skopje (OHIS A.D.); the thermopower plant (REK Bitola) in Bitola discharging oils and heavy metals; the fertilizer factory in Veles (MHK Zletovo) discharging huge quantities of phosphate (4.6 million population equivalent) and nitrogen (0.4 million population equivalent); and many other sources of less importance (Figure 6.2). The Environment Inspectorate has drawn up a list (cadastre) of the most important polluters. However, at present, this list has not been completed with detailed environmental information. (see also Chapter 11 on Industry, energy and the environment)

*Hydroenergy*

In 2000, 18 per cent of the electricity was from hydropower. The annual hydroelectric potential of the rivers is vast (according to various reports, it could range from 5500 to 6500 GWh) and only exploited at 20 per cent of its capacity. The rehabilitation of old dams and projects for new dams are being considered (see above the description of existing infrastructure and the strategy for the future in Chapter 11 on Industry, energy and the environment)

**Figure 6.4: Water use, 1996**

**Total water consumption 1720 million m³/year**

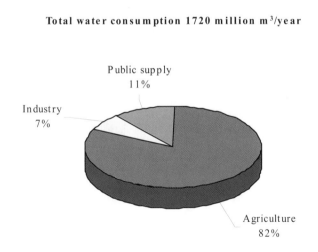

*Source*: Integrated Water Resources Development and Management Master Plan, May 1999.

## 6.5  Framework for water management

*Policies and strategies*

Because of the scarce water resources and their variability in time and space, the policy for water management has been geared toward a multipurpose use of water resources. Priority has been given to flood protection, managing the water to produce hydroenergy, building irrigation infrastructure for agriculture and supplying water to the population. The protection of the quality of the water bodies has never been tackled seriously. Moreover, most of the water bodies have a transboundary character and impact on the countries downstream. The country has water use and protection obligations toward its neighbours, an issue now sensitive since most of the bilateral agreements were concluded before the former Yugoslav Republic of Macedonia became independent. Whether these agreements are up to date in the present geopolitical situation is questionable. It is therefore important that they should be reviewed and updated. (see Chapter 5 on International cooperation and recommendation 5.3).

This complex use of water demands clear water management strategies, as has long been recognised. But since too many key players are involved in water management, it has proved difficult to agree on a strategy. This can be seen in the fact that several strategies have been drawn up but never implemented. In the meantime, the measures and actions taken do not cover water management in an integrated manner. Among the different projects, the following are the most important:

- The Water Management Plan of the Ministry of Agriculture, Forestry and Water Economy represents a long-term plan for the management and development of water resources. It has been implemented since 1975 and is to be replaced in 2004 by a new water master plan that is currently being prepared by the Water Fund for the Ministry of Agriculture, Forestry and Water Economy with the help of Germany (GTZ) and PHARE. It seems that so far the accent is to be placed much more on water supply than on water quality protection.

- In 1990, an initial programme for the integrated development of the Vardar Valley was adopted by Parliament. In 1994, this programme was updated and the importance of the valley as a main axis of communication (all means

including waterways) within the framework of the European spatial planning forecast by the European Council was highlighted. The building of hydropower plants, including a number of new dams (17) and storage reservoirs, is the backbone of the project. It opens up the possibility of increasing electricity production, of irrigating 70,000 ha more, of improving the water supply to municipalities and industry and flood and erosion protection, and of developing fishing and tourism. A first dam in Koziak on the Treska is under construction. The programme is at a standstill because of economic difficulties. Through the Public Investment Programme (2001-2003), the country is trying to find international financial institutions to co-finance these infrastructures (estimated at US$ 501.5 million).

- The 1996 NEAP recommended improving the management of water resources in particular by developing a water resources plan; improving water resources and effluent discharge monitoring; introducing standards for industrial effluent discharges, and introducing and enforcing the corresponding permits; improving the management of irrigation systems; improving the protection of the three big lakes; and building the necessary waste-water treatment facilities for municipalities and industry.

- Also, a draft national strategy for waste-water and solid waste management was completed in 1999 as part of a PHARE transboundary cooperation programme. The beneficiaries are the Ministry of Environment and Physical Planning and the Ministry of Transport and Communications. The strategy includes a prioritized national plan with actions for each watershed and a cost estimate. Investment would be €360 million, mostly in sewerage and treatment plants for municipal waste water and the protection of the aquifer supplying Skopje (Rasce Springs). The strategy has not yet been adopted by the Government.

In addition, various studies and plans have been carried out under the auspices of different ministries with external support (e.g. Integrated Management of the Quality of Water Resources, 1997, with support from France; Integrated Water Resources Development and Management Master Plan, 1999, with the support of the Japan International Cooperation Agency). It is extremely difficult to have a clear idea of what instruments have actually been adopted, which are binding and which are being implemented. The coordination among the different projects and ministries with relevant responsibility seems non-existent.

*Legislation*

The main pieces of legislation on water are summarized in Box 6.2. There is a Law on Waters. It defines the conditions and the methods for the use of waters, for protection from their harmful effects (floods), for their protection from contamination, for their management, and how to finance water management activities. The implementation of this Law is the task of the Ministry of Agriculture, Forestry and Water Economy.

The 1998 Law on Waters introduced new important features such as the creation of a water fund to cover expenses for water resources development and works of public interest; the establishment of a public water management enterprise (PWME) and of water users' associations, the introduction of waste-water standards and pollution charges; and the appointment of water management inspectors. Only a few of these instruments or institutions have been set up, and those that have been set up are finding it difficult to operate (e.g. Water Fund set up but under-financed, PWME in a critical financial situation, pollution charges not introduced).

Among the modern provisions of water legislation, permission is required for water abstraction and waste-water discharges. The Law also obliges the polluter to build waste-water treatment facilities. But all these obligations are badly enforced. For example, the user-pays principle exists but payments are increasingly neglected and there is no law obliging users to pay. There is a classification of water quality for rivers and lakes, but there are no quality standards or objectives to be met. The hydrographic basin management approach is not contained in the legislation, while a project for the transboundary water management of the Lake Ohrid catchment area was successfully developed a few years ago thanks to GEF financing (see more details in Box 6.1). According to a review of the legislation by EU PHARE in 2000, the approximation of the Law on Waters with the EU body of law still needs significant improvements and the Law on Waters is not fully efficient, due to the absence of a series of implementing ordinances.

A new law on water communities, requested by the World Bank for further cooperation in water

management, is before Parliament. The law proposes that water users should establish separate legal entities – water communities – responsible for irrigation and drainage. The water user communities would be granted the management and maintenance of the corresponding infrastructures. In this way it is expected that water users will become more interested in irrigation management, and that the collection of water charges will improve concomitantly.

*Institutions*

The current complex institutional arrangements for water management are the result of a long history and of frequent ministerial restructuring and reallocation of responsibilities over the past ten years. Five ministries share the management of water:

- The Ministry of Agriculture, Forestry and Water Economy manages water abstraction for all uses (including irrigation, public and industry supply) and is responsible for actions in the public interest such as flood control and drainage. The Ministry is responsible for the management of quantity and quality of surface and groundwater. It issues water abstraction and discharge permits;
- The Ministry of Environment and Physical Planning, with its inspectorate, is responsible for protecting water bodies against pollution;
- The Ministry of Health controls drinking and bathing water quality;
- The Ministry of Transport and Communications is in charge of public water supply and waste-water treatment infrastructures for municipalities. It also issues authorizations for building and operating industrial facilities and checks that these facilities have the necessary water-protection installations;
- The Ministry of the Economy is responsible for the construction of dams and hydroenergy production plants.

The Ministry of Agriculture, Forestry and Water Economy, through its Water Administration, is entrusted with the implementation of the Law on Waters. At present, it is the main actor in water management. The dispersion of responsibilities among five ministries is not compensated by close relationships and good cooperation among them all. This is reflected in the many fruitless attempts to set up water strategies.

---

**Box 6.2:        Legislation on water**

Law on Waters, Official Gazette, No. 4/98, amended 19/2000
Water Management Base, Skopje, 1977
By-law on the Quality and Safety of Drinking Water, Official Gazette, No. 5/84
By-law on the Sampling and Methods of Laboratory Analysis of Drinking Water, Official Gazette, No. 33/87
By-law on the Safety of Drinking Water, Official Gazette, Nos. 33/87 and 13/91
By-law on Determining and Maintaining Protection Zones Around Springs of Drinking Water, Official Gazette, No. 17/83
Decision on Maximum Permitted Concentrations of Radionuclides and Hazardous Substances in Inter-republic Water Currents, Inter-republic Waters and Waters of the Adriatic Coast of Yugoslavia, Official Gazette, No. 8/78
Decree on the Classification of Waters, Official Gazette, No. 18/99
Decree on the Classificiation of Water Currents, Lakes, Reservoirs and Underground Waters, Official Gazette, No.18/99
By-law on Natural Mineral Water Quality, Official Gazette of SFRY, No. 58/78.
Law on the Protection of Lakes Ohrid, Prespa and Dojran, Official Gazette, No. 45/77, and the Programme for the Protection of Lakes Ohrid, Prespa and Dojran, Official Gazette, No. 7/87.

---

Two types of public water enterprises see to the technical side of water management:

- Municipal Public Enterprises manage drinking water supply, sewage systems and waste-water treatment facilities in cities and villages. They abstract water (permits issued by the Water Administration of the Ministry of Agriculture, Forestry and Water Economy), disinfect it (chlorination), distribute it to the city users and maintain and operate the infrastructure network. They fix the water price in cooperation with the Association of Municipal Public Enterprises and their local governments. They also collect the water charges that are their only source of revenue, but over the past few years economic difficulties have led to the collection rate dropping dramatically, from 90 per cent in 1996 to 58 per cent in 2001 in Skopje. In such conditions, the enterprises can afford water disinfection, supply and maintenance but not big repairs such as renovating the distributing pipes or the sewage collectors. The draft law on water management enterprises before Parliament will open the way to a system of concessions.

- The Public Water Management Enterprise (PWME) was created in 1998 with 24 local branches. They supply irrigation water to farmers. They also supply water resources to municipalities and industries from their water storage reservoirs, and are responsible for flood protection infrastructure, measures against water erosion and drainage. They have two sources of finance: (1) a regular State budget line for the management of works of public interest (flood protection, erosion protection and drainage), which has been merely symbolic for years; and (2) water user charges that vary according to the local branch and the user. The

great economic difficulties of the past decade mean that most of the clients do not pay their bills. So the local infrastructures cannot be properly maintained, the staff of the local PWME are rarely paid and the enterprise itself has accumulated a considerable debt over time. Overall, this debt totals about $10 million today. At present, the PWME is being restructured, and its 24 local branches will become autonomous authorities. The PWME will stay as the regulatory body for these authorities. Those that cover the same river sub-catchment area may be merged. The restructuring will become effective in early 2003, when each autonomous authority will be headed by a council made up of representatives of the different stakeholders, including users. These water authorities will have the same responsibilities that they have now. They will be financed by the State budget for all tasks of public general interest (i.e. flood protection, erosion, drainage) and by the user for the water they supply. The secondary water supply infrastructure will be managed by water users' associations (WUAs), each responsible for collecting the money in its own territorial jurisdiction. If costumers fail to pay up, supply will simply be cut off, a measure that is not legal at present.

The draft law on water enterprises includes provisions for actions such as cutting off water when payments are not made. In recent years, the World Bank, through its Irrigation Rehabilitation and Restructuring Programme, has been working on the restructuring and rehabilitation of three of these irrigation schemes, and, through this programme, it has been pushing for a restructuring of the water enterprises and the creation of water users' associations.

*Standards*

Water standards are incorporated in the legal regulations listed in box 6.2. There are environmental quality standards (ambient standards) for different kinds of water bodies but no emission limits for the pollution discharged into water bodies. The standards on drinking-water quality comply with WHO guidelines, and in some cases are even stricter.

Rivers are classified according to the quality of their water (from class I to class V). Harmonization of the ambient standards for surface water quality with EU norms was completed in 1999. In theory, their implementation is controlled by the Water Management Inspection of the Ministry of Agriculture, Forestry and Water Economy, the Health Inspectorate of the Ministry of Health, the Inspectorate of the Ministry of Environment and local inspectorates.

*Monitoring*

According to the Law on Waters, the monitoring of all kinds of water is the responsibility of the Ministry of Agriculture, Forestry and Water Economy and is carried out by the Hydrometeorological Institute (table 6.4). The Institute monitors the quality of surface water in 60 measurement stations around the country. The Ministry of Environment and Physical Planning introduced more sophisticated monitoring equipment to measure the quality of the Vardar River (2 automatic stations giving online information – financed by PHARE) and other rivers in the country (18 automatic stations – financed by Switzerland). The Institute depends on the Ministry of Agriculture, Forestry and Water Economy. There is no biological monitoring of water ecosystems, except in Lakes Ohrid and Prespa by the Hydrobiological Institute. Because of financial constraints, the Hydrometeorological Institute stopped monitoring groundwaters in 1981, and now monitors only the water table. The Hydrometeorological Institute is also responsible for drawing up the water polluter cadaster. By law, the Institute is obliged to submit data to other relevant ministries, in particular the Ministry of Environment.

Monitoring the quality of drinking water and bathing water is the task of the Public Health Institute. It also investigates water contamination at the source or along the supply system, and checks the protection perimeters around the abstraction points. All municipal water enterprises have their laboratories, as they must control the quality of the water they supply to the users and adjust disinfection accordingly.

*Permits*

Water abstraction permits are issued by the Ministry of Agriculture, Forestry and Water Economy and are required for any kind of water use and discharge. Each local branch of PWME puts in a request for the amount of water it requires with its headquarters and the Ministry for approval. The priority ranking for water use and allocation is defined in the Law on Waters as follows: (1) municipal use, (2) agriculture, (3) industry, (4) hydropower generation and (5) other uses. This rule is not strictly followed: in 2001, the city of Prilep faced a severe water shortage while water was being used for the cooling system of the Oslomej thermal power plant, a facility that produces electricity for 200,000 people. Checking that facilities comply with the permit is the task of the inspectorate of the Ministry of Agriculture, Forestry and Water Economy.

Building permits are issued by the Ministry of Transport and Communications on the basis of an application that briefly describes the proposed activity. The Ministry requires documentation for facilities that are likely to have an impact on the environment and submits this documentation to the Environment Office. Operating permits require an opinion from the State Environment Inspectorate, which can lay down conditions for the proposed activities. There is no time limit for the permit. The State Communal Inspectorate verifies whether the facilities operate according to the law.

Regarding compliance, environmental inspections are based on standards. However, the regulations stipulating maximum allowable concentrations are outdated and inadequate. When regulatory levels are exceeded, environment inspectors may impose fines, lower production levels or require the installation of pollution control equipment (waste-water treatment systems). In extreme cases, facilities can be closed, a measure taken only exceptionally (for instance the zinc smelter factory in Veles in January 2001). Inspectors do not give technological advice, but rather push for end-of-pipe approaches.

**Table 6.4: Authorities that monitor water quality**

| Monitoring of: | Monitoring institution | Responsible agency |
|---|---|---|
| Rivers | Hydrometeorological Institute | Ministry of Agriculture, Forestry and Water Resource Management |
| Groundwater | Hydrometeorological Institute | Ministry of Agriculture, Forestry and Water Resource Management |
| Lakes | Hydrobiological Institute | |
| Pollution from industry | Inspection laboratory | Ministry of Environment |
| Domestic waste-water discharges | Municipal Water Enterprises | Municipalities |
| Monitoring of drinking water | Public Health Institute, Municipal Lab. | Ministry of Health, Municipalities (water enterprises) |
| Monitoring of bathing water | Public Health Institute | Ministry of Health |

*Source*: Ministry of Environment and Physical Planning, 2002.

### Water pricing

The Law on Waters regulates the price of water (i.e. sets a ceiling). Municipal water enterprises have two different prices for drinking water: one for households and another for enterprises. The water price is made up of a part for water supply and a part for sewage collection. Prices differ from one city to another, e.g. from $0.53/m$^3$ for households in Veles to 0.14 $/m$^3$ in Kavadardi. Enterprises pay about twice this price. In Skopje, it is $0.22/m$^3$ for households and $0.49/m$^3$ for enterprises. Today (2002), about 50 per cent of individual users and 60 per cent of other users (in particular institutions, such as hospitals and municipalities) cannot afford to pay.

The 1998 Law on Waters provides that public water enterprises should be paid for the raw water they supply to users (hydroelectricity, irrigation, municipalities and industry). However at present, few users pay.

### Financing water management

On the basis of the Law on Waters, the Water Fund was established in 1999 to participate in the financing of activities to ensure protection from the harmful effects of waters, water protection from pollution, construction, reconstruction and maintenance of irrigation and drainage systems and the preparation of water studies. The Water Fund proposes an annual activity programme to the Ministry of Agriculture, Forestry and Water Economy. The financial sources for carrying out this programme are set in the Law on Waters: a tax levied on the incomes of the public enterprises and governmental institutions, a tax on hydropower generation (0.5 per cent per kW), 1 per cent of the water user price from municipalities and industries, 3 per cent of the fish price from fish farms, 1 per cent on gravel extraction, a part of water pollution charges; and a regular State budget line for works of general public interest.

In fact, the Water Fund is far from being the powerful instrument it could be if it collected all the above-mentioned taxes. Water pollution charges have not been created and other incomes are not paid as they should be. The State contribution has never been paid. Actually, the Fund receives one eighth or one tenth of what it requires for its annual programme. In 2000, 2001 and 2002 (forecast), the Fund's total resources amounted to about 100 million denars per year (i.e. $1.5 million), far below what it would have been if it had collected all its dues. Of this sum, only 70 per cent was paid up, as part of the Fund is put to one side at the source for certain enterprises (Elektostopanstvo na Makedonija, public utility enterprises, users of industrial water, Public Water Management Enterprises). The Fund cannot grant credit since it cannot give guarantees to the banks, and the State does not guarantee the Fund's credit. For this reason the Fund cannot be an active player in infrastructure development. Currently, the Water Fund is drawing up the new water management plan developed under the auspices of the Ministry of Agriculture, Forestry and Water Economy.

The Environment Fund is also financing projects to protect water from pollution and prevent pollution. (see Chapter 3 on Economic instruments and privatization) Most of these projects concern waste water and some drinking water. In the portfolio, about 80 projects concern waste-water treatment plants for small and medium-size municipalities (under 15,000 population equivalent), 10 for industrial waste water, and 6 for waste water from pig farms. About $1 million has been spent on such projects as of early 2002, from funds received mostly from abroad.

*Projects*

At present, because of economic, social and political problems, the country cannot afford to invest in water management and related infrastructures. Over the past five years a variety of projects have been carried out, always with foreign partners. Most of them stopped shortly after the feasibility study either for political reasons and competition between different ministries, or because the country could not afford its share of the investments. Projects on monitoring (EU, Switzerland), policy and strategy development (France, Germany, Japan, EU, EBRD), protection of lakes, underground and surface waters quality (Denmark, Germany, Italy, Switzerland, Stability Pact, EU, GEF, World Bank), improvement of drinking-water supply and waste-water infrastructure (Japan, United States, World Bank, UNDP), improvement of irrigation infrastructures (Netherlands, World Bank), dams and reservoirs (France), have been or are being developed to the tune of a hundred thousand to a hundred million dollars.

## 6.6 Conclusions and Recommendations

Because of economic difficulties, the country has not been in a position to carry out most of the large projects that were started or envisaged in the development plan. These projects, in particular reservoirs, dams, irrigation schemes and flood protection works, may have an important impact on the environment, which should be prevented or mitigated. For this reason, it is urgent that a full-fledged environmental impact assessment (EIA) procedure should be set up with public participation, to alleviate this impact as far as possible.

The future water management plan is currently being prepared by the Ministry of Agriculture, Forestry and Water Economy, and does not involve any other key stakeholders. There is a strong need for better cooperation among the water managing institutions, in particular the five principal ones, i.e. the Ministry of Agriculture, Forestry and Water Economy, the Ministry of Environment and Physical Planning, the Ministry of Health, the Ministry of Transport and Communications and the Ministry of the Economy. Together, they should set up an inter-ministerial working group to participate in the current preparation of the integrated water management plan. The plan should cover water use and supply, water quality protection and conservation, and water flow management. This

inter-ministerial working group should be seen as a first step toward the creation of a water agency that would unite all the main responsibilities for the management and protection of water resources.

*Recommendation 6.1:*
*The Government should urgently set up an inter-ministerial working group consisting of the five key administrations in water management, i.e. the Ministry of Agriculture, Forestry and Water Economy, the Ministry of Environment and Physical Planning, the Ministry of Health, the Ministry of Transport and Communications and the Ministry of the Economy, together with their associated specialized institutions. This inter-ministerial group should be responsible for the further preparation of the upcoming integrated water management plan. The plan should cover water use and supply, water quality protection and conservation, and water flow management.*

The water situation in the former Yugoslav Republic of Macedonia is difficult, because water resources are scarce, unevenly distributed, used by a wide range of users and not managed in an integrated manner. Many cities face drinking-water shortages in the dry period, while simultaneously water resources are diverted to less vital uses. Till now, not enough attention has been paid and no real political will displayed to solve the problem.

At present, water management competencies are too dispersed among different ministries, thus preventing an integrated approach. Protecting water resources, guaranteeing that they are used in a sustainable way and alleviating their adverse impact (floods and droughts) is the task of the environmental protection authorities. Overall coordination of the management of water, including monitoring, licences and permits, should be the responsibility of the Ministry of Environment.

*Recommendation 6.2:*
*The Government should propose to Parliament that the Ministry of Environment and Physical Planning be the responsible authority for water resource management and protection. The Ministry of Environment should be entrusted with the implementation of the water management plan, including water monitoring, and it should be given the task of issuing licences and permits for water use and water discharges, and implementing the user-pays and polluter-pays principles.*

Experience in other countries as well as in the Lake Ohrid Conservation Project has largely proved that the management of water is most effective when the local population and users are closely involved in it and when it is seen in a territorially integrated manner. As joining the EU is one of its ambitions, the former Yugoslav Republic of Macedonia should move toward an integrated river basin management approach as required by EU Water Directive 2000/60/EC. A first step would be to identify river basins and sub-basins, and work out water management plans for each catchment and sub-catchment area. In line with the national water management plan, these plans would take into account water needs and the impact of human activities on water bodies, and would set objectives for water quality and quantity. The drawing-up of these plans should involve the participation of the main stakeholders. It should chiefly involve the local branch of the Public Water Management Enterprise and Municipal Public Water Enterprises and benefit from their long experience.

The Lake Ohrid Conservation Project has helped build capacity through a learning-by-doing approach. Not only has it helped inform the different national and local water entities and bring them together, but it has also shown how to manage when transboundary catchment areas are at stake and cooperation has to be established. This useful experience should not stop short simply because funds are lacking at the moment or political will is not strong enough. The project will be interrupted soon as its financing by international institutions and donors comes to an end. All efforts should be made to keep this "pilot experience" alive.

*Recommendation 6.3:*
*The Government, after designating the Ministry of Environment and Physical Planning as the responsible authority for water resource management and protection, should create an appropriate structure to assist the Ministry in implementing its enlarged tasks. These tasks should include the introduction of a river basin management planning approach working on the experience gained through the Lake Ohrid Conservation Project. Twinning arrangements with countries having experience in river basin management should be sought, together with their technical, financial and political support, to assist the country in its task.*

*Recommendation 6.4:*
*The Government should show its support for the Lake Ohrid watershed management by:*

- *Updating the legislation giving official status to the watershed management and related management objectives and institutions;*
- *Calling for the development of a management plan for the Lake;*
- *Giving official status to and reinforcing the present management board for the protection of Lakes Ohrid and Prespa;*
- *Mobilizing the international community and partner countries to help consolidate the integrated management approach of the transboundary Lake Ohrid catchment area.*

At the moment, neither the Municipal Public Enterprises nor the Public Water Management Enterprises have sufficient money to maintain and improve the infrastructure for which they are responsible. A major reason is that users are not paying their water bills and the water enterprises are not legally empowered to do anything about this. Legislation should give the water enterprises a real power to levy the water charges: they should be given the ability to suspend their services if they are not paid. The Government should work out special social measures or compensation for those citizens and public institutions that cannot afford to pay, so that the public water enterprises can be in a good position to compete with concessionaires, if the market were opened to concessions in the near future.

*Recommendation 6.5:*
*The Government should take measures to enforce the principle that all users should pay for the water they use. For those people who cannot afford to pay, the Government, together with the municipalities, should work out a system of social compensation.*

There can be no progress in the protection of water quality as long as polluters are not motivated to reduce their pollution load. While the Law on Waters makes it obligatory to treat waste water before it is released, command-and-control measures are not effective enough and are difficult to execute at the moment. They should be supplemented by economic instruments, starting with the step-by-step introduction of the polluter-pays principle. This should be combined with incentives to motivate polluters to decrease their pollution load and invest in cleaner production processes and abatement techniques. At the beginning, the pollution charges could target only a few major pollutants and toxic elements, and could be mostly applied to the key polluters on the State Environment Inspectorate's lists. Managing the user charges and the polluter charges, working out incentives to reduce pollution, and providing subsidies to help users and polluters improve water

management and protection should be among the tasks of the water agency.

*Recommendation 6.6:*
*The Government should prepare legislation to implement the polluter-pays principle according to the provisions of the Law on the Environment and Nature Protection and Promotion and the Law on Waters. Pollution charges should be introduced and in a first step implemented only according to few parameters, i.e. major pollutants and toxic elements. Collected pollution charges should be redistributed to stimulate the reduction of pollution discharges. (see also recommendation 3.1)*

# Chapter 7

# AIR MANAGEMENT

## 7.1    State and determinants

The National Environmental Action Plan (NEAP) adopted in 1996 identifies air pollution as a major environmental problem affecting the urban areas and a large part of the country's population. It originates in traffic, stationary sources – industry and energy production – and also in central and residential heating.

### Air Emissions

It is important to begin by noting the scarcity of reliable and harmonized information on air emissions. Data are fragmented, sometimes incoherent and their quality is questionable. Consequently, it is hard to get a comprehensive overview of the situation and at best only a broad qualitative assessment can be made.

Air emissions are said to have decreased significantly since the late 1980s. The main reason for this is the overall recession that followed the political changes resulting in reduced industrial production: the global index calculated by the State Agency for Statistics shows that industrial production decreased by around 50 per cent between 1990 and 1995 and has not shown any significant increase since then.

Unfortunately this cannot be illustrated with figures; nationwide air emission values are only available for 1997 and 1998 (see table 7.1). Furthermore, very large discrepancies can be observed between those two years, probably explained by the fact that different methodologies were followed for estimating emissions, the CORINAIR methodology (see http://www.eea.eu.int and http://air-climate. eionet.eu.int for more information) being applied for 1998 only. It can be seen that the estimated figures for $SO_2$ and $NO_2$ were much higher in 1998 than in 1997 although the inventory is incomplete for 1998 and includes only part of the mobile sources.

When expressed per capita (see figure 7.1), the 1998 levels for $NO_2$ and CO appear to be very low compared with other countries. But again in this case, it is not possible to draw any definitive conclusion as mobile sources are taken only partly into account for that year.

Air emission figures for the city of Skopje and some municipalities are available (table 7.2) but their validity is also questionable (emissions in these cities exceeding the national level). Bitola has the highest $NO_x$ and $SO_2$ emissions, representing 62 and 72 per cent of the national total. Dust emission in Jegunobce represents 85 per cent of the national total, while CO emissions are particularly high in Tetovo. In Skopje levels are high for all air pollutants.

### Table 7.1: Anthropogenic emissions

in thousand tons

|        | 1997 | 1998   |
|--------|------|--------|
| $SO_2$ | 17.0 | 105.6 a |
| $NO_2$ | 6.0  | 15.2 a |
| CO     | 23.0 | 25.8 a |

Sources: EMEP: http://www.emep.int. anthropogenic emissions - web site 01/2002. The Ministry of Environment and Physical Planning: EPR preparatory document - 01/2002.
Note: a) sectors 7 (transport) and 8 (other mobile sources) incomplete. No data for NMVOC, $NH_3$.

### Table 7.2: Air emissions from cities, 1998

in thousand tons

| Town | CO | $SO_2$ | $NO_x$ | dust |
|------|------|--------|--------|------|
| Total national | 25.8 | 105.6 | 15.2 | .. |
| Skopje | 4.2 | 6.3 | 3.3 | 0.3 |
| Bitola | 1.4 | 78.7 | 10.8 | 1.5 |
| Kicevo | 0.2 | 9.2 | 1.2 | 0.5 |
| Tetovo | 12.8 | 3.5 | 0.8 | 0.0 |
| Prilep | 0.0 | 0.0 | 0.0 | 0.0 |
| Gosrivar | 1.1 | 0.2 | 0.0 | 0.0 |
| Kocani | 2.1 | 1.7 | 0.1 | 0.0 |
| Veles | 0.9 | 4.8 | 0.1 | 0.1 |
| Kumanovo | 2.3 | 0.0 | 0.0 | 0.0 |
| Jegunobce | 1.4 | 3.8 | 1.0 | 23.2 |
| Total | 26.3 | 108.2 | 17.3 | 25.7 |

Source: The Ministry of Environment and Physical Planning: EPR preparatory document. 01/2002.

## Figure 7.1: Emission of $SO_2$, kg/capita, 1998

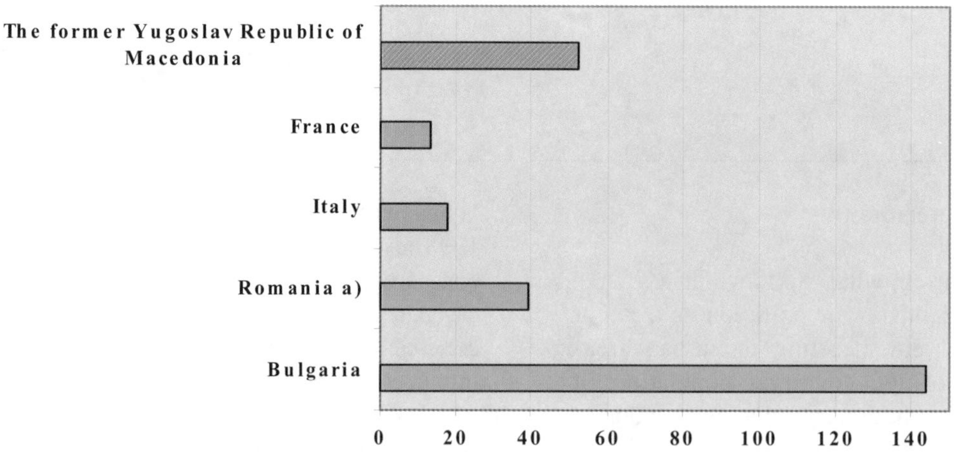

Source: computed by author from EMEP, 01/2002.
Note: a) for 1997.

### Sectoral pressures

Although incomplete, the 1998 inventory seems to show that the combustion and transformation of energy is the major contributor for $SO_2$, while production processes are the main sources of dust. CO is mainly produced by road traffic; both energy production and mobile sources are major emitters of $NO_2$.

### Industry

Because of obsolete or non-existent technology and equipment, industry is a major air polluter with sulphur, carbon and nitrogen oxide emissions. Moreover, significant environmental pressure originates in the metallurgy sector, metallurgical plants contaminating surrounding areas with heavy metals.

One of the most critical hot spots is the lead and zinc smelter "MHK Zletovo" in Veles. The factory, which was privatized, is located in a valley close to the city, and the prevailing winds tend to carry the air pollution to the urban area. The factory emits large amounts of $SO_2$ (4,000 tons per year), and also lead and zinc with cadmium (2.5 and 6.5 tons per year respectively). Although the factory's emissions are now reported to be lower than the permissible values, several studies have shown that sulphur dioxide, particles and heavy metal emissions have had a significant impact on public health. The factory is poorly equipped with de-polluting devices, and there is no coherent plan to improve the situation. The State Environment Inspectorate stopped the company's activities twice, in August 1998 and May 2001, for negligence.

Among the other major industrial air polluters in the country are the "OKTA2 refinery, the "OHIS" chemical complex, and the "USJE" cement factory in Skopje, and, in Jegunovce, the 'HEK Joguhrom' metal factory. (see also Chapter 11 on Industry, energy and the environment)

### Energy production

About 80 per cent of energy is generated in thermal power plants, with most of the remaining demand being met by hydro-electrical plants.

The most important power plant, generating 75 per cent of the country's annual demand in electricity, is located 12 km from Bitola. It burns the lignite produced in an adjacent mine; this lignite has a relatively low sulphur content.

However, the flue-gas desulphurization equipment and the filters are old and do not work properly. The $SO_2$ emissions are systematically well above the allowed limit value of 400 mg/m$^3$, with an average of between 1600 and 2000 mg/m$^3$. Dust and $NO_x$ emissions also breach the permissible values of respectively 50 and 150 mg/m$^3$, with observed mean values of 100 to 400 mg/m$^3$. For 1999 total emissions were estimated at around 46,000 tons of $SO_2$ and 2,400 tons of fly ash. The plant's stacks are more than 200 m high; this limits to some extent the air pollution impact on the immediate vicinity.

In Skopje $SO_2$ emissions from the three central heating power stations burning heavy fuel with a high sulphur content (2 to 4 per cent) are also above the limit values and significantly contribute to the city's air quality problems. However, with the completion of the gas pipeline, it is expected that there will be a 60 per cent drop in the use of heavy oil in Skopje with positive effects on air quality. In a later phase, gas should also be distributed to other cities such as Tetovo, Gostivar, Veles and Negotino (see Chapter 11 on Industry, energy and the environment).

Mobile sources

Emissions from mobile sources in the main cities with a high population density are also a factor in air pollution. The total number of registered vehicles, of which 83 per cent are private cars, was relatively stable over the past year increasing by only about 5 per cent between 1995 and 2000, that is, from approximately 327,000 to 342,000. The average age of the fleet is over 11 years, and it is estimated that 57 per cent of the cars are more than 15 years old. The Law amending and supplementing the Law on External Trade Operations- (Official Gazette, No. 2/2002) prohibits the import of cars older than 10 years.

By a 1998 regulation (Official Gazette No. 14/1998), technical inspection is mandatory once a year for all cars, trucks and lorries, and twice a year for buses. Performed under the responsibility of the Minister of Internal Affairs by technical centres authorized by the Ministry of Economy, inspection includes checking exhaust gases (CO content and opacity).

Most of the cars do not have catalytic converters. In any case, catalysers become inoperative due to the use of leaded petrol and are often removed. In 1995, only 9.3 per cent of motorists used unleaded petrol; by 1999, the figure had increased to only 15.5 per cent. The Government intends to phase out leaded petrol in several stages from the present standard of 0.6 g/l down to 0.0 g/l in 2008.

Poor technical maintenance and fuel quality, and, in particular, the high sulphur content of diesel (1 per cent), are also factors aggravating pollution.

*Air quality*

In this area, too, information is fragmented and its reliability questionable. The few statistical data collected during the EPR mission come from two of the three national networks operating monitoring stations in the country, i.e. the Environmental Information Centre and the State Public Health Institute. The Hydrometeorological Institute, operating the third network, refused to provide information directly since it reports regularly to the Ministry of Environment and Physical Planning.

These statistical data are of limited interest:

- They concern only Skopje and Veles;
- They cover only a few years and do not allow drawing any conclusion on trends;
- Only $SO_2$ and particulates are substantially covered.

Air pollutants monitored on a continuous basis include $SO_2$, smoke, $NO_2$, CO, total oxidants, ground-level ozone, inert dust and suspended particulate matter. Heavy metals in the air are measured only occasionally. It would be important to include PM10 and PM2.5 in future monitoring to allow exposure assessments.

Overall data quality is low and illustrates the lack of quality assurance and quality control procedures and harmonization between the different networks. They are also hardly comparable to EU standards and WHO guidelines; they use different averaging times, measurement techniques and other quality assurance and quality control criteria.

In practice the data just provide some clue as to pollution levels observed in Skopje and Veles (table 7.3). Apparently these levels are high, and the maximum permissible or allowable concentrations (MPC or MAC) are frequently exceeded. Finally, the most relevant information is found in the National Environmental Action Plan (NEAP). Although it was adopted in 1996, the findings can still be considered generally valid, although slightly mitigated both by the overall recession and by some technological improvements.

The air quality problems are limited to major areas. Specifically, Skopje, Veles Bitola and Tetovo, with approximately 60 per cent of the national population, have poor-quality air.

Ohrid is also classified in the NEAP as having poor air quality although this is supported neither by observed values nor by emission estimates. This statement has, however, been systematically repeated since the NEAP was adopted, including in the Japan International Cooperation Agency's study on air pollution monitoring in the country.

**Table 7.3: Indicative air pollution levels**

| Locality | Pollutant | Yearly average up to | Maximum daily value up to | |
|---|---|---|---|---|
| Skopje | SO$_2$ | 63 | 162 | tropical year 1998 |
| | SPM | 87 | 213 | tropical year 1998 |
| | NO$_2$ | 48 | 132 | tropical year 1998 |
| | CO | 2.4 | 6.8 | tropical year 1998 |
| | O$_3$ | 39 | 71 | tropical year 1998 |
| | Pb | 0.7 | 1.4 | calendar year 2000 |
| Veles | SO$_2$ | 111 | 380 | calendar year 2000 |
| | SPM | 128 | 495 | calendar year 2000 |

*Sources:* The Ministry of Environment and Physical Planning. Air qualilty in Skopje - Annual Report , 1999. Health Protection Institute. Report to EPR team. February 2002.

*Note :* CO expressed in mg/m$^3$, all other pollutants in µg/m$^3$.

### Skopje

The air quality problem in Skopje is due to both mobile and stationary pollution sources (central heating power plants, cement factory, chemical complex and refinery). The topography plays an important role in the pollution level as the city is surrounded by hills and has favourable conditions for temperature inversions, in particular during the winter.

Levels are reported to be high at least for SO$_2$ and black smoke, which frequently exceed the maximum daily concentration. Over the 1991–1994 period, the SO$_2$ maximum daily concentration of 150 µg/m$^3$ was exceeded up to 35 times a year, while for black smoke, concentrations above 50 µg/m$^3$ were recorded up to 123 times a year.

### Veles

Pollution levels in Veles are mainly due to the emissions from the "MHK Zletovo" zinc and lead smelter, which emits large amounts of SO$_2$ as well as zinc, cadmium and lead.

Between 1990 and 1993, the observed levels of SO$_2$ exceeded maximum allowable concentration (MAC) between 32 and 39 times per year depending on the location of the measurement site. More recent data indicate that the maximum allowable concentration for SO$_2$ was exceeded on 60 days in 2000, 43 days in 2001 and 9 days for the month of January alone in 2002.

### Bitola

Air quality in Bitola is mainly affected by emissions from the 'REK' power plant and the nearby mine. While SO$_2$ is mostly within acceptable limits, black smoke regularly breached the maximum allowable concentration between 1990 and 1994 (between 10 and 25 times per year).

### Tetovo

Pollution in Tetovo is related to the "HEK" metallurgical facilities and also to heating with high-sulphur fuel during winter.

Tetovo also had an excess of black smoke during the 1990-1994 period (16 to 78 times per year).

### *Impact on health*

Epidemiological studies, although limited, tend to indicate a correlation between pollution level and the morbidity and mortality from chronic respiratory diseases.

However, it must be noted that the morbidity trend has been decreasing since 1986. This could be explained by the fact that the health-care system has been modified but also by recession in the industrial sectors resulting in reduced emissions.

Most of the epidemiological studies were carried out in the periods 1973-1977, 1989-1993 and 1994-1997 by paediatricians and preventive medical institutions.

In Veles and Skopje a significant correlation has been established between respiratory illness and dust particles. A similar link also exists with the average monthly concentrations of $SO_2$. The air pollution problem is more acute in winter due to the effects of temperature inversion, combined with an increased combustion of fuel. For instance, in the winter of 1990, about 30 per cent of a sample of 36,000 children had serious respiratory symptoms.

In Veles, studies suggest that the population around the smelter has a higher concentration of lead in the blood and that there is a higher occurrence of cancer, respiratory diseases, miscarriages and birth defects.

### National Environmental Action Plan

The National Environmental Action Plan (NEAP) proposes goals for national environmental policy during the five years starting from 1997. Air quality-related priorities are:

- Decreasing the quantity of lead from mobile emissions and developing an action plan to phase out lead from petrol;
- Decreasing air pollution in Veles by introducing proper emission control methods;
- Developing an air quality monitoring programme for Skopje, which will identify the key emission sources and help enforce air pollution reduction;
- Phasing out the use of ozone-depleting substances (ODS) to allow the country to meet its commitments to the Montreal Protocol;
- Introducing self-monitoring for industries through regulations;
- Increasing enforcement to make the polluter comply with existing regulations; and
- Developing a comprehensive vehicle emission monitoring system.

More generally, the NEAP also recommends that the country should:
- Develop regulations in accordance with EU legislation;
- Create a system for issuing permits; and
- Increase penalties for non-compliance.

However, the NEAP includes neither a clear timetable nor the budget required for each of its projects.

## 7.2 Policy objectives and management practices

### Objectives and legislation

<u>Present situation</u>

The normative basis for all environmental action is contained primarily in the Law on the Environment and Nature Protection and Promotion adopted in 1996 and in a series of other laws that regulate issues related to the legal and institutional framework for the performance of the tasks in this area, for example, the Law on Health Protection (Official Gazette, Nos. 38/91 and 46/93) and several derived regulations.

The Law on Air Protection against Pollution adopted in 1990 and amended in 1993 is the central legal instrument for air quality management. It defines the framework for air protection against pollution. For details such as the maximum allowable concentrations set for 13 pollutants, specific regulations dating back to the 1970s are still in force.

This legal framework and the instruments governing air quality management are clearly outdated. This is illustrated in table 7.4, which compares the national MACs with the WHO guidelines and the EU limit values. The national standards are based on 24-hour values only, while WHO and EU values relate to a wider range of averaging times better or more appropriately related to health effects.

For stationary sources, there is no environmental permit system. However, according to the Law on the Environment and Nature Protection and Promotion, all polluting companies must prepare environmental plans and can be fined for failure to do so.

The country intends to approximate the EU Integrated Pollution Prevention and Control (IPPC) Directive, and the legal and institutional frameworks for an adequate permitting and enforcement system are being developed. The legal framework for mobile sources (fuel quality, lead and sulphur content, technical maintenance and control) is also weak. (see Chapter 13 on Transport and the environment)

<u>Draft law</u>

A draft law on air quality is now being prepared jointly by the Department for Legislation and Standardization and the Environmental Information Centre of the Ministry of Environment and Physical Planning, the Ministry of Health with the State Public Health Institute and the Hydrometeorological Institute, although the last one seems to have withdrawn from the process for reasons which are not clear.

The draft law, as it is formulated, would regulate "the conditions, the measures and the manner of organization and implementation of air quality protection and improvement". It would also regulate:

• Air quality limit values, including emission limit values and limit values for pollutants in fuel;

• Monitoring and the establishment of a monitoring information system, including an inventory of air polluters; and

• Management of air quality, measures for air pollution prevention and reduction, and plans for air protection against potential disasters.

It is intended to specify practical details such as limit values and monitoring conditions in subsequent legal acts at the proposal of the Ministry of Environment and Physical Planning with the consent of the Ministry of Health. The Ministry of Economy would be associated in this process for fuel quality standards, and the Ministry of Internal Affairs, for emissions standards for mobile sources.

The draft law on air does not clearly reassign air management competences to local administrations. In this respect, it must be stated that 21 of the 123 municipalities have developed or are developing local environmental action plans (LEAP).

**Table 7.4: Comparison of air quality standards and guidelines for the "classical" pollutants (in $\mu g/m^3$)**

| Pollutant | Average time | National limit value | WHO guideline value | New EU limit value |
|---|---|---|---|---|
| $SO_2$ | 10 minutes | | 500 | |
| | 1 hour | | | 350 a) |
| | 24 hours | 150 | 125 | 125 b) |
| | 1 year | | 50 | |
| PM | 24 hours | 50 c) | d) | 50 e) |
| | 1 year | | d) | 40 f) |
| CO | 15 min. | | 100,000 | |
| | 30 min. | | 60,000 | |
| | 1 hour | | 30,000 | |
| | 8 hours | | 10,000 | 10,000 |
| | 24 hours | 1,000 | | |
| Lead | 24 hours | 0.7 | | |
| | 1 year | | 0.5 | 0.5 |
| $NO_2$ | 1 hour | | 200 | 200 g) |
| | 24 hours | 85 | | |
| | 1 year | | 40 | 40 |
| $O_3$ | 1 hour | | | 180 - 240 h) |
| | 8 hours | | 120 | 120 i) |
| | 24 hours | 125 | | |

*Sources* :    WHO, Guidelines for Air Quality, Geneva, 2000.
EU directive 1999/30/EC ($SO_2$, PM, $NO_2$ and lead)
EU proposal COM (1999) 125 final - 99/0068 (COD) ($O_3$)
EU directive 2000/69/EC (CO)

*Notes* :
a) not to be exceeded more than 24 times per year.
b) not to be exceeded more than 3 times per year.
c) Black smoke.
d) not possible to determine a 'no-effect' level.
e) PM 10 not to be exceeded more than 35 times per year (stage 1 - 2005).

f) PM 10 (stage 1 - 2005).
g) not to be exceeded more than 18 times per year.
h) respectively information and warning threshold.
i) target value not to be exceeded on more than 20 days per year averaged over 3 years.

The draft, which is intended to approximate the legislation to the EU framework Directive on ambient air quality assessment and management (96/62/EC), in fact goes much further. In particular, it covers air emission and fuel quality, the organization of a monitoring system and an emissions inventory.

*Institutional framework*

The Ministry of Environment and Physical Planning is responsible for developing environmental policy, drafting legislation and regulations, implementing international agreements and conventions and also for monitoring the state of the environment. Within the Ministry, three bodies have specific responsibilities relating to air:

- The Environmental Information Centre, whose basic function is "to establish a base of relevant, properly processed (systematized and standardized), comprehensive, accurate, transparent and publicly accessible information on the state, quality and trends in all segments of the environment including air (pollution in urban and rural environments, global pollution, regional and transboundary emission)". The Centre is, in particular, responsible for air quality monitoring (see Chapter 2 on Institutional arrangements) and for developing and managing databases related to air pollution including emission registers. It is also in charge of maintaining permanent contact with the environmental information system of the European Environment Agency (EEA) and other international institutions and organizations. A Public Relations Office dedicated to communication with the public has also been established within the Centre.

- The State Environment Inspectorate, which checks the compliance of industry with current legislation, including legislation on air emissions. Measurements are performed by the Central Laboratory, which is the competent laboratory with special expertise in air emission monitoring.

- The Department for Legislation and Standardization responsible for developing new laws and setting standards.

There is no structure within the Ministry responsible for air management issues such as risk assessment, cost-benefit analysis, or the implementation of clean air plans.

Other ministries and State institutions involved are:

- The Ministry of Health and the State Public Health Institute for the monitoring of air pollution. The Ministry is in general responsible for monitoring the status of the protection of the population against harmful effects.

- The Ministry of Agriculture, Forestry and Water Economy through the State Hydrometeorological Institute, which operates the most important air-monitoring network of the country.

- The Ministry of Economy and the Standardization Institute for the setting of standards, including those related to fuel quality.

Although there is no regional level of public administration in the country, individual ministries and public services sometimes operate "regional" units responsible for several communes or municipalities. This is the case for the Public Health Institute but not for the Ministry of Environment and Physical Planning.

*Air quality monitoring*

The legal provision for monitoring is contained in the Law on Air Protection against Pollution. Although the Law fixes maximum allowable concentrations for 13 pollutants, only the most frequently present compounds are regularly monitored.

On the basis of the Law on the Environment and Nature Protection and Promotion (1996), air pollution monitoring is the responsibility of the Ministry of Environment and Physical Planning.

At present, the following institutions monitor air pollution in the country:

- The Ministry of Environment and Physical Planning. Within the Ministry, the Environmental Information Centre operates four automatic monitoring stations, all located in Skopje and measuring CO, $SO_2$, NO, $NO_2$, SPM, $O_3$ as well as several meteorological parameters. In addition to those stations, the network also includes one mobile system that can be used for both emission and immission measurement. The four stations were installed in 1998 in the context of a study financed by the Japan International Cooperation Agency to develop air pollution monitoring in the former Yugoslav Republic of Macedonia. Consistent with the guidelines fixed by this study, the country plans to install three additional stations in 2002, in Kicevo, Kumanovo and Kocani, and another five in 2003, in Veles, Bitola, Skopje and one or two other cities in the east of the country.

- The Hydrometeorological Institute under the Ministry of Agriculture, Forestry and Water Economy. The Hydrometeorological Institute has monitored air quality in urban centres for more than 20 years. It operates a network of 20 stations: 10 of them are located in Skopje while the rest are in other cities (Bitola, Veles, Tetovo, Kumanovo). One of these (Lazaropole) is registered as an EMEP station, but it has not reported since June 1992. The stations measure $SO_2$ and black smoke on a daily basis. At some locations $NO_2$ and total oxidants are also monitored. At present, the Institute has no concrete plans for strengthening or extending its network.

- The State Public Health Institute. Air monitoring and the measurement of $SO_2$, strong acidity, black smoke, TSP and CO are carried out through stations in the biggest towns (Skopje, Bitola, Veles, Tetovo, Kumanovo) managed by nine regional Public Health Institutes. Heavy metals (including lead) are measured but not routinely. The measurement techniques and the measuring times are not harmonized among the different stations in the network. At present, the Institute has no clear strategy for strengthening or extending its network.

Besides these three networks, the Law on the Environment and Nature Protection and Promotion also requires the major polluters to monitor air pollution in the vicinity of their facilities. Among those concerned are the "MHK – Zletovo" metallurgical and chemical company of Veles, the "REK Bitola" power plant, the three central heating power plants in Skopje and the "OKTA" refinery near Skopje.

Also in accordance with the Law, all of these air pollution data must be communicated to the Environmental Information Centre. The process for the exchange of data, however, is very poorly organized: there are no fixed and harmonized protocols for data transfer, no standard formats, most data being transmitted on paper and only a

few in computer files. In practice the data communicated from the external networks or stations are just piled up in the Centre and not even stored in databases. This explains why it is not possible to get a comprehensive overview of the present air quality situation.

Other major shortcomings observed in the existing system include:

- No clearly identified monitoring objectives for the different networks (compliance monitoring, policy development, trend qualification, population exposure) and, consequently, no definition of data quality objectives.

- No coordination and active cooperation among the different bodies involved in air quality monitoring, resulting in an inefficient use of resources. For example, $SO_2$ is measured at 18 monitoring sites and particulates at 44 in Skopje, while there is no systematic monitoring of metals in hot spots although this should deserve a high priority.

- Poor maintenance of the equipment, an aspect that seems to have been systematically underestimated in the past years although it is also clearly linked to the general lack of resources.

*Air emissions*

All polluting enterprises are subject to inspection by the State Environmental Inspectorate. The Inspectorate has seven inspectors. Inspections routinely cover different environmental "media" including air and noise. The Central Laboratory and its mobile measurement unit measure air emissions. The Inspectorate also relies on sampling data and monitoring supplied by the inspected companies and factories.

During 2001, the Inspectorate undertook approximately 1,800 inspections focusing on the most polluting industry, roughly 100 companies. Enterprises are generally inspected four to five times a year but more frequently in special cases.

When regulatory levels have been breached, inspectors may impose fines, lower production levels or require the installation of pollution control equipment. In extreme cases, facilities can be closed, a measure that has been taken on only a few occasions, for example "MHK Zletovo" in August 1998 and May 2001. Legal procedures to impose penalties are however very long and slow, resulting in either a relaxation of the pollution regulation or, as in most cases, imposing minimal fines (the highest penalty ever imposed was around €15,000).

An emission inventory is being developed in the Environmental Information Centre; at present it gathers information from about 200 emission sources.

*International conventions and activities*

On 30 December 1997, the former Yugoslav Republic of Macedonia became a Party to the Convention on Long-range Transboundary Air Pollution by succession with effect from 17 November 1991. But it has not yet ratified the Protocols to the Convention. The main reason for not ratifying these protocols is said to be the lack of information on the national situation and also of structural resources.

On 23 May 2001, the country signed the Stockholm Convention on Persistent Organic Pollutants, enabling preparatory activities to be carried out in 2002 under the GEF umbrella and strengthening the national capacity to manage these pollutants.

## 7.3   Noise

Noise measurements made by the Public Health Institute in Skopje show that 61 per cent of the results are above the WHO guide value of 65 dBA. This confirms the findings of a comprehensive survey carried out in 1997.

The Central Laboratory of the Ministry of Environment and Physical Planning and the Public Health Institute carry out noise measurement at respectively 5 and 14 sites in Skopje.

The noise issue is treated in the 1984 Law on the Prevention of Harmful Noise; the maximum allowed noise levels being prescribed by a specific decision adopted in 1993.

The intention is to draft a new law on noise in line with the EU strategy on noise management, which mainly includes a proposal for a directive on environmental noise, and also a new directive on

equipment used outdoors aiming at simplifying the legislation on noisy equipment.

## 7.4   Greenhouse Gases (GHG)

The former Yugoslav Republic of Macedonia acceded to the United Nations Framework Convention on Climate Change as a non-Annex 1 country in January 1998. A first step was undertaken in 2000 with the setting-up of a dedicated project unit within the Ministry of Environment and Physical Planning, with UNDP acting as implementing agency, and the establishment of working groups. The project aims at enabling the country to prepare its first national communication in response to its commitments to the Convention, including a nationwide inventory of GHG emissions by sources and removals by sinks. The communication is at present in its final phase and the inventory was produced in December 2001. The $CO_2$-equivalent emissions are shown in table 7.5 for the period 1990-1998: the energy sector represents around 75 per cent of the total emitted, followed by waste, agriculture and industrial process sectors, each of them contributing around 8 per cent.

## 7.5   Ozone-depleting Substances (ODS)

In 1994 the former Yugoslav Republic of Macedonia ratified the 1985 Vienna Convention for the Protection of the Ozone Layer and the 1987 Montreal Protocol on Substances that Deplete the Ozone Layer.

In 1997 the Ozone Unit was established within the Ministry of Environment and Physical Planning. The role of this Unit is to coordinate all the activities to protect the ozone layer. In the past four years with the financial support of the Multilateral Fund of the Montreal Protocol, several projects for phasing out or completely eliminating ODS have been or are being implemented.

The data on consumption from 1995 to 2000 show the effect of national action to phase out ODS (table 7.6). Over 80 per cent of the total consumption of these chemicals has already been eliminated, so fulfilling obligations under the Montreal Protocol, since the former Yugoslav Republic of Macedonia is classified as an Article 5 country.

## Table 7.5: CO₂-equivalent emissions for all sectors

kT

| | 1990 | 1991 | 1992 | 1993 | 1994 | 1995 | 1996 | 1997 | 1998 | Average |
|---|---|---|---|---|---|---|---|---|---|---|
| Total | 14,695 | 13,691 | 13,246 | 13,504 | 13,109 | 13,215 | 12,927 | 13,938 | 14,509 | 13,648 |

*Source*: United Nations Framework Convention on Climate Change, 2001.

## Table 7.6: ODS consumption

a) M T – quantity expressed in tons

| Substance | Consumption | | | | | |
|---|---|---|---|---|---|---|
| | 1995 | 1996 | 1997 | 1998 | 1999 | 2000 |
| CFC-11 | 464.8 | 420.0 | 420.8 | 7.0 | 8.8 | 7.1 |
| CFC-12 | 64.7 | 41.0 | 62.0 | 70.8 | 183.1 | 39.6 |
| Halon-1211 | .. | .. | 1.29 | .. | .. | .. |
| Halon-1301 | 3.0 | 3.0 | 3.24 | .. | .. | .. |
| HCFC-22 | 28.0 | 42.0 | 33.2 | 22.7 | 19.6 | 89.7 |
| HCFC-141b | .. | 1.0 | | 21.0 | 1.0 | 0.5 |
| M eBr | .. | 20.0 | 20.0 | 21.5 | 45.4 | 39.0 |
| Total | 560.5 | 527.0 | 540.5 | 143.0 | 257.9 | 175.9 |

b) ODP – quantity in tons multiplied with ODP value (ozone-depleting potential) = 1 for CFC-11

| Substance | Consumption | | | | | |
|---|---|---|---|---|---|---|
| | 1995 | 1996 | 1997 | 1998 | 1999 | 2000 |
| CFC-11 | 464.8 | 420.0 | 420.8 | 7.0 | 8.8 | 7.1 |
| CFC-12 | 64.7 | 41.0 | 62.0 | 70.8 | 183.1 | 39.6 |
| Halon-1211 | .. | .. | 3.87 | .. | .. | .. |
| Halon-1301 | 30.0 | 30.0 | 32.4 | .. | .. | .. |
| HCFC-22 | 1.5 | 2.31 | 1.8 | 1.2 | 1.1 | 4.9 |
| HCFC-141b | .. | 0.1 | .. | 2.31 | 0.1 | 0.1 |
| M eBr | .. | 12.0 | 12.0 | 12.9 | 27.3 | 23.4 |
| Total | 561.0 | 505.4 | 532.9 | 94.2 | 220.4 | 75.1 |

*Source*: GRID. Arendal web site. January 2002.

## 7.6 Conclusions and Recommendations

Although industrial emissions have likely decreased sharply in recent years following the overall recession, air quality has not significantly improved. Heavy industry together with the production of energy and the transport sector contribute to air pollution in the country's major cities. Obsolete technology at industrial facilities dating back to the 1980s, an ageing vehicle fleet and poor fuel quality are the main causes.

The National Environmental Action Plan (NEAP), adopted in 1996, has highlighted major air management issues that need to be tackled. It has also identified lines for action in that direction.

The Law on Air Protection against Pollution (1990, amended in 1993) and the instruments governing air quality management are outdated, some of them dating back to the 1970s. The development of a new law on air quality is an initiative in the right direction, in line with the NEAP recommendations.

*Recommendation 7.1:*
*The Ministry of Environment and Physical Planning, in cooperation with the Ministry of Health, should speed up the development of the new law on air quality including the development of the framework for air quality management and the setting of new air quality standards. In developing the new law, the Ministry should take into consideration not only European Union (EU) approximation but also a national air management strategy coherent with the Environmental Impact Assessment (EIA) and Integrated Pollution Prevention and Control (IPPC) strategy. Special attention should be paid to all issues relating to its enforcement, including the sharing of responsibilities between local self-government and national levels.*

Within the Ministry of Environment and Physical Planning, the Environmental Information Centre, the Environment Inspectorate and the Department for Legislation and Standardization all have specific responsibilities relating to air. However, there is no structure dealing specifically with air management issues.

*Recommendation 7.2:*
*The Ministry of Environment and Physical Planning should establish a unit dealing with air management issues which would be responsible for the preparation, implementation and evaluation of the national clean air strategy as well as for developing cooperation with all partners interested in air management. (ministries, industries, non-governmental organisations (NGOs))*

Although air quality monitoring is officially the responsibility of the Ministry of Environment and Physical Planning, three monitoring networks are currently in operation: the Ministry of Environment and Physical Planning's network (only in Skopje) managed by the Environmental Information Centre, the Hydrometeorological Institute's network and the State Public Health Institute's network. Their activities are not coordinated, resulting in wasted resources, and the relationship among the three bodies is sometimes conflictive. Monitoring objectives, data quality objectives, and quality

assurance and quality control procedures are not clearly defined.

*Recommendation 7.3:*

*(a) The Ministry of Environment and Physical Planning should coordinate and formalize the activities of the different networks involved in air quality monitoring through agreements and memoranda of understanding. (see also recommendation 4.2)*

*(b) The Ministry of Environment and Physical Planning in cooperation with the Ministry of Health should identify monitoring objectives, data quality objectives, quality assurance and quality control procedures. (see also recommendation 14.1)*

The former Yugoslav Republic of Macedonia has ratified the Convention on Long-range Transboundary Air Pollution but not the Protocols to it.

*Recommendation 7.4:*
*The Ministry of Environment and Physical Planning should develop appropriate strategies for implementation of the Protocols to the UNECE Convention on Long-range Transboundary Air Pollution. (see also recommendation 5.2)*

*Chapter 8*

# *WASTE MANAGEMENT*

## 8.1   Current situation

Waste is a major environmental challenge in the former Yugoslav Republic of Macedonia. Although the generation of waste has been influenced by the economic situation of the past ten years with its lower industrial output, the poor condition of existing landfills poses a continuous threat to the environment. With expected economic growth, the problem of waste may well worsen.

All hazardous and non-hazardous waste, except for some medical waste in Skopje, is stored at landfills. These landfills, which lack proper design and management, are the cause of a wide range of environmental problems, such as air pollution, and soil and groundwater contamination. Municipal waste and industrial waste are stored separately. Municipal waste is collected and deposited by public enterprises. Industrial waste is stored on, or close to, the industry's premises. There are officially 32 landfills operated by municipalities, but the total number of illegal landfills and dumps could be as high as 1000 according to the Ministry of Environment and Physical Planning. The Drisla landfill near Skopje is a landfill for municipal waste. It operates with a construction permit from the Ministry of Transport and Communications, making it the only legal landfill in the country.

Information on environmental pollution by landfills is limited. No comprehensive monitoring programme exists, nor are there sufficient facilities and monitoring equipment. Since 1981, there has been no monitoring of groundwater or of soil quality due to financial constraints. Some incidental samples have been taken, and these indicate that some places have high levels of pollution requiring urgent attention. In this regard, the comprehensive study on waste water, water quality and solid waste management funded by the European Union (EU) in 1999 and the post-conflict environmental assessment of the United Nations Environment Programme (UNEP) in 2000 gave a clearer idea of the problems associated with landfills (see box 8.1).

*Generation of waste*

Knowledge about waste generation, particularly of industrial waste, is scarce and incomplete. The most recent data – from 1999 – have been collected by consultants for the EU study for the solid waste management plan. Based on experiences in other countries in transition and a simple mathematical model, taking into consideration rising income levels, increasing urbanization and ever-smaller households, estimations have been made for waste generation trends from various sources, such as municipalities, industries, and kinds of waste, such as hazardous and radioactive waste.

---

**Box 8.1:        Waste problems at environmental hot spots**

In 2000-2001 UNEP undertook a rapid strategic assessment to identify the most urgent environmental needs of the former Yugoslav Republic of Macedonia. At a number of the hot spots that have been identified, waste causes severe negative environmental conditions:

- At the HEK Jugohrom ferro-alloy plant in Jegunovce, 466,000 tons of ferrochromium and 385,000 tons of chromate have been deposited in a landfill near the Vardar River. Soil and groundwater have been severely polluted. A groundwater sample taken by UNEP showed a chromium level of 12.2 mg/l. For comparison, the target and intervention values in the Netherlands are 0.001 mg/l and 0.03 mg/l.
- At the OHIS organic chemicals plant in Skopje, approximately 10,000 tons of hazardous chlorinated organic chemicals have been stored in inappropriate conditions for over 20 years. No samples of groundwater and soil have been taken, but the storage basins are suspected of leaching chemicals into the groundwater.
- The MHK Zletovo lead and zinc smelter in Veles has a landfill with 850,000 tons of solid waste containing heavy metals that may pollute the soil and groundwater.
- At the Rudnici Zletovo lead and zinc mine in Probistip, two hydro-tailing basins contain zinc, lead, cadmium and cyanide, posing a risk to soil and groundwater pollution.
- The REK Bitola lignite-fuelled thermal power plant in Bitola annually dumps 1.5 million tons of fly ash and slag that may pollute the soil and groundwater with heavy metals, including uranium compounds.

Source: *United Nations Environment Programme, 2001*

*Municipal waste*

It is estimated that 480,000 tons of municipal waste were generated in the former Yugoslav Republic of Macedonia in 1999, that is approximately 240 kg per person. On average, it is estimated that urban areas generate approximately 360 kg of waste per person per year, against approximately 120 kg for rural areas. These figures are just below the average for countries in transition (see figure 8.1).

The amount of municipal waste is expected to grow to 828,000 tons a year by 2025. According to the National Environmental Action Plan, average municipal waste composition in 1996 was 25 per cent ash and construction waste, 24 per cent paper, 20 per cent food scraps, 11 per cent plastics, 5 per cent glass and porcelain, 4 per cent textiles and leather, 3 per cent metals and 8 per cent other kinds of waste. There are no recent data on the composition of household waste.

*Industrial waste*

Large quantities of industrial waste are generated in the mining, metallurgical, fertilizer, and chemical industries, as well as in the coal-fired power plants. Most of the larger industries have their own industrial waste sites. Smaller enterprises whose

waste is more similar to the composition of household waste dispose of their waste at municipal landfills. Table 8.1 gives an overview of rough estimates of waste production requiring off-site treatment or landfilling.

*Medical waste*

The amount of medical waste generated by hospitals and laboratories ranges between 8,000 and 10,000 tons a year. Of this amount, 12 to 15 per cent is potentially infectious or toxic and the remaining is non-medical waste. It is expected that this amount will increase four- to eightfold in the long term. Medical waste is often radioactive and can lead to communicable diseases. All medical waste is currently mixed with municipal waste and dumped in the landfills. An exception to this is the medical waste from the main medical centre in Skopje, which is collected separately in special bags and burned in a small incinerator at the Drisla landfill site near Skopje. (see Box 8.2) The charge for collection and incineration is US$ 408 per ton. At the moment between 20 and 30 tons a year are burnt at a temperature of 1000 degrees Celsius. Their emissions are not monitored, nor are any pollution reduction measures in place. (see also Chapter 14 on Human health and the environment)

**Figure 8.1: Municipal waste production in selected countries in transition**

Annual municipal waste production in kg

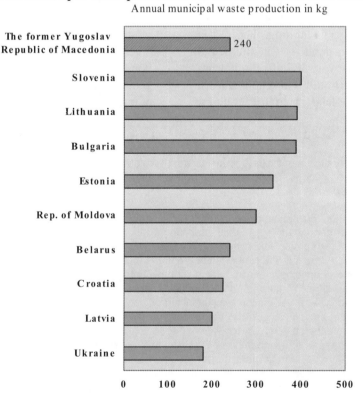

*Source*: UNECE. EPRs various issues.

**Table 8.1: Estimated quantities of industrial waste in 1996**

tons

| Sector of industry | Primary process waste | Other technological (industrial) waste |
|---|---|---|
| **T O T A L (rounded)** | **65,000** | **130,000** |
| Petroleum and chemical processing | 1,000 | 5,000 |
| Secondary processing of metal ores | 1,000 | 20,000 |
| Metal working and general manufacturing | 5,000 | 60,000 |
| Textile manufacturing | 1,750 | 12,500 |
| Food and drink processing | 50,970 | 12,500 |
| Other industrial sectors | 5,000 | 20,000 |

*Source*: Environment Office, 2001.

---

**Box 8.2:     The Drisla landfill**

The Drisla municipal landfill near Skopje has a capacity of 26 million $m^3$ and receives approximately 150,000 tons annually. Drisla is the only legal landfill in the former Republic of Macedonia, since it operates with a construction permit issued by the Ministry of Transport and Communications. This permit requires a letter of consent from all relevant ministries, including the Ministry of Environment and Physical Planning, the Ministry of Health, and the Ministry of Agriculture, Forestry and Water Economy. However, no formal guidelines exist on the construction and operating requirements for landfills. The landfill lacks lining and a drainage system to prevent potentially polluted leachate entering the groundwater. In addition, most of the pipes of the gas (methane) collection system are damaged, and the 'daily' covering of waste with inert material is very irregular. Although there are no legal requirements to do so, the Drisla public enterprise monitors on a monthly basis dissolved oxygen (DO), biological oxygen demand (BOD), acidity (pH) and chemical oxygen demand (COD). However, only two of the six boreholes are in operation. The price for the disposal of municipal waste is €11/ton.

*Source: Drisla Public Enterprise, 2002.*

---

*Agricultural waste*

In the State-of-the-Environment report of 2000, pesticide packaging was listed as being a major potential polluter of soil and groundwater. It is estimated that pesticide packaging, with minor quantities of residue attached, amounts to approximately 25 tons a year and ends up in one of the many illegal waste dumps. There are no official collection systems for manure, just the farmers' own systems. It is estimated in the NEAP that about 4 million tons of animal waste is disposed of annually (see Chapter 9 on Agriculture and forest management). Furthermore, no facilities exist for the disposal of carcasses and waste from slaughterhouses.

*Radioactive waste*

There are no official collection systems for radioactive waste and no facilities for its disposal. The amounts of radioactive waste are comparatively small and consist of low-level radioactive sources such as lightning conductors, industrial testing equipment, medical equipment and smoke detectors. Waste is usually stored at the location where it is produced. However, few of these locations are suitable for the long-term storage of radioactive wastes.

*Hazardous waste*

As no classification system exists for hazardous and non-hazardous waste, few data are available on the quantities and qualities of hazardous waste generated in the country. During the PHARE study on the solid waste management system industries proved reluctant to disclose the scale and nature of waste, and particularly hazardous waste. However, it has been estimated that approximately 46,000 tons of hazardous waste are generated a year, which might increase to about 75,000 tons or more by 2025. These amounts exclude the hazardous waste that industries retain on site.

*Waste management practices*

Currently the Ministry of Environment has no official programmes or instruments in place to reduce the amounts or the hazardousness of waste. Prevention, recovery, re-use and recycling practices are rare and mostly on the initiative of industry with the aim of improving process efficiency. For example, at the REK Bitola power station high-caloric slag is being mixed with lignite to see whether it can be used as a fuel source, instead of being dumped at the waste site. This method reduces the 150,000 tons of slag waste and increases the efficiency of the used fuel. Another example of waste reduction was developed at the Pivara brewery in Skopje. For the recycling of polyethylene bottles a first buy-back station will be opened at the plant's site using soft drinks as an incentive for returning empty bottles. However, of all methods for waste management, landfills are still the cheapest option but their full cost – including maintenance and rehabilitation after use – is not incorporated in the calculations.

*Cleaner production*

A national cleaner production centre was set up in the middle of 2000 with the help of the United Nations Industrial Development Organization (UNIDO) and the Czech centre for cleaner production. The national centre was initially placed within the Chamber of Commerce so as to give it direct access to the information on industries. The provision of information was, however, limited and currently the national cleaner production centre is based in the Environment Fund of the Ministry of Environment and Physical Planning.

In addition to the national centre, a regional centre exists in Veles, on the premises of the MHK Zletovo plant. This centre was set up as a non-governmental organization (NGO) and has 23 members, all of whom received training in cleaner production and environmental management systems from the Czech centre for cleaner production. As part of the training course, participants had to prepare proposals for cleaner production projects for their respective enterprises. This exercise resulted in seven feasibility studies in the fur, textile, fertilizer and ceramic industries.

## 8.2    Policies and instruments

*Policies*

There are two approved and two unapproved policy documents relevant to waste management: (i) the National Environmental Action Plan (NEAP), (ii) the National Environmental Health Action Plan (NEHAP), (iii) the draft spatial plan for solid waste management, and (iv) the draft national solid waste management plan. Only the NEAP and the NEHAP have been approved as official government policy.

Implementation of the NEAP has been lacking and by now it requires updating and harmonizing with the institutional changes since 1996. Due to the low political priority, the Kosovo crisis and internal unrest, few of the NEAP recommendations regarding waste management have been carried out. The NEAP recommendations included the development of regulations for the collection, transport, storage and disposal of solid, industrial and hazardous waste, including medical and radioactive waste and the development of a waste permitting system for industries based on their type and level of production.

The Ministry of Health, in cooperation with the Ministry of Environment and Physical Planning, developed the National Environmental Health Action Plan, which states that the cost of removal and final disposal of waste should be reflected in prices. It also lists five goals: (1) to minimize soil contamination and begin the phased clean-up of soil contamination, (2) to establish a modern legal basis (laws and regulations), (3) to ensure the safe collection, transport, neutralization and final disposal of household, medical and industrial waste, (4) to identify the status of existing landfills and assess their environmental health risks, and (5) to minimize waste and encourage recycling by introducing financial mechanisms and incentives. (see Chapter 14 on Human health and the environment)

The draft spatial plan for solid waste management was developed in 1998 but so far has not been approved by the Government (see Chapter 12 on Spatial planning). It is mainly based on the geographical characteristics of the country and identifies 14 regional landfills to be developed. The Ministry of Environment and Physical Planning was not approached for input to the report, which was published by the public enterprise for spatial planning.

The draft national solid waste management plan was prepared in 1999 with the financial support of the European Union's PHARE programme, but its status is unclear. Apparently only two hard copies – in English – of this plan were made available, one to the Ministry of Transport and Communications and the other to the Ministry of Environment and Physical Planning. By government decision of 18 October 2000 the latter has been made responsible for implementing the plan, which indicates its approval as an official government strategy. The same decision, however, states that translation and review of the plan are required before it is officially adopted. The plan is based on an extensive study of the characteristics of the current waste management system, including the amounts of waste generated and the means of disposal. The plan proposes short-medium- and long-term measures and aims to have an environmentally sound waste management system in full operation within 20 years. The measures would include extensive regulation and enforcement, economic incentives, reliable public waste collection and the development of environmentally acceptable waste management sites. The plan foresees eight regional landfills. These are not the same as the sites projected in the draft spatial plan for solid waste management.

The Ministry of Environment and Physical Planning was given authority at the beginning of 1999 to issue permits for 'temporary' landfills until the draft solid waste management plan has been approved. This permit allows for a speedy process, as the consent of the relevant ministries is not required, as is normally the case with the construction permit issued by the Ministry of Transport and Communications. In this way, the Ministry of Environment and Physical Planning can identify sites that are geologically most suitable as landfills and stop the current practice of random landfills at unsuitable sites, including wetlands. Four permits have been issued and the selected sites have been mainly abandoned mines with impermeable soil layers. Feasibility studies are part of the permit procedure.

### Institutional capacity

Responsibility for waste management is shared among the Ministry of Environment and Physical Planning, the Ministry of Transport and Communications, the Ministry of Health and the municipalities. The Environment Office within the Ministry of Environment and Physical Planning has only one staff member responsible for waste-related issues, and this person is also responsible for ecological-technological project preparation and monitoring. The Ministry of Transport issues construction permits for landfills and the Ministry of Health is responsible for medical waste. Municipalities are responsible for the collection and disposal of municipal waste.

### Regulatory instruments

Legislation on waste management is extensive. Over 18 separate laws have been passed as part of the legislative framework for waste management, of which the most important are:

- The Law on Waste, which sets out the manner and conditions of waste collection, transport and processing, waste disposal at organized landfills, and landfill maintenance;
- The Law on Communal Works (Official Gazette No. 45/1997), which regulates the organization of municipal services, including the treatment, collection and disposal of municipal solid waste; and
- The Law on Public Hygiene, and the Collection and Transport of Municipal Solid and Industrial Waste.

The aspirations of the Government are to harmonize with the legislation of the European Union. A comparative analysis of the formal legislative instruments in the former Yugoslav Republic of Macedonia and the EU, however, showed that none of the existing legislation respected EU legislation. In addition, there are no provisions for limiting the amounts of waste generated in industry. Permits and limits on waste generation are an important government instrument for reducing waste. Furthermore, there is no special legislation on the treatment, storage and disposal of hazardous waste as distinct from non-hazardous waste. Since 1997, on ratification of the Basel Convention, only the import and export of hazardous waste have been regulated by a permitting system. The comparative analysis prioritized a number of recommendations to harmonize the national legislation with the EU environmental legislation, but the Ministry of Environment and Physical Planning is not following them pending a more comprehensive programme for the harmonization of legislation. Only three directives (the Hazardous Waste Directive, the Waste Framework Directive and the Landfill Directive) are being translated into Macedonian. The IPPC legislation has already been translated.

According to the NEAP of 1996, potential investors would be required to submit an application for an environmental permit, which would be issued only if the proposed activity met EU standards. On the introduction of new standards, companies would be required to submit an environmental audit and a compliance plan within one year. However, these plans have not been implemented.

### Economic instruments and financing

Municipal waste collection is the task of the municipalities' public enterprises. The public enterprises are in principle financially independent and not allowed to make a profit. No public services exist for industrial waste, except for waste from small enterprises and offices which is similar to household waste. The Law on Communal Services states that the price of the waste service is to be established by the public enterprise with the approval of the city council. The waste collection and disposal fee is payable monthly and based on a household's floor space. On average in 1999 a household paid 2.15 denars/$m^2$ per month for municipal waste collection. Currently the price for household waste ranges from 0.44 to 3.07 denars/$m^2$ per month and for industrial waste from 0.44 to 6.00 denars/$m^2$. The collection rate ranges between 20 and 40 per cent. However, in 1995 the Government set a maximum price for public enterprise services in order to protect consumers. This price has not changed since then. The population's low purchasing power clearly stops the public enterprises from setting optimum prices that would cover maintenance and investments. Public enterprises are cross-subsidizing their activities, with fees collected from green markets and cemeteries being used to subsidize the loss-making waste collection and disposal sections.

The division of the former Yugoslav Republic of Macedonia into 123 municipalities created practical problems for many smaller and often rural municipalities. For example, the smallest municipality in area is Star Dojran with only 2 $km^2$, while the smallest municipality in population is Staravina with only 456 inhabitants. Certain municipalities therefore have public enterprises only on paper, as there is no sound financial basis for a public enterprise. The Ministry of Environment and Physical Planning estimates that approximately 80 per cent of the rural areas are not covered by public refuse collection.

In the draft national solid waste management plan rough cost estimates have been made and, based on

1999 figures, rates of €12.5/100 $m^2$ for domestic premises and €25/100 $m^2$ for commercial premises and €13.75/ton for non-hazardous industrial waste should be sufficient to cover the full cost of environmentally sound waste collection and disposal. This price, however, does not include the full cost of cleaning up all illegal sites.

Since 1997 the Law on Communal Works has provided for concessions and outsourcing as a means of operating public enterprises. However, since the municipalities did not own the assets, privatization was legally but not practically possible. While sewerage systems and waste collection trucks remained State property, no real privatization could take place. In January 2002 the ownership of assets was transferred from the State to the municipalities by amendment of the Law. Expectations among public enterprises that investors will come forward are high and possibly unrealistic as long as there is a price ceiling for municipal services. The German aid organization GTZ has started a project with the association of municipalities "ZELS" to help the 64 public enterprises in the country to become more commercially viable. Initial results of the project indicate three main problems: (i) the price setting by the national Government and the lack of understanding of real costs, (ii) 'social' employment, and (iii) the inefficient working practices of public enterprises.

The national Government has not placed solid waste management high on its agenda. The Public Investment Programme for 2001-2003 included only one hazardous waste management project, to be developed within two years at a total cost of US$ 710,000. This project would be funded by the sale of the State-owned telecommunications company, an indication that little structural funding would be made available.

---

**Box 8.3:      Clean and green**

One of the activities of the United Nations Development Programme (UNDP) is the "Clean and Green Macedonia" project. By employing unskilled workers to undertake the cleaning and disposal of waste two objectives are achieved. On the one hand, emergency employment is being provided to the most vulnerable municipalities, while on the other environmental degradation due to the lack of an effective solid waste management system is being reversed. The project was launched in April 1999 in Skopje and Tetovo. The project is currently in its last phase and has expanded to 71 municipalities.

Source: *http://www.undp.org.mk/nivogore/clean&grF.htm* , 2002

*Awareness and communication*

Environmental awareness–raising is an important element in any waste management strategy. It is a precondition for changing the behaviour of industries and consumers. Even though the draft national solid waste management plan has not been approved, it gives little place to awareness–raising. Providing best practice guidance to industry and demolition site managers are the only two actions included in the list of actions to be taken over the next five to seven years. After many years of non-payment, poor services and illegal dumping, awareness–raising is a much underestimated part of the draft national solid waste management plan and deserves a greater role in it.

The "Clean and Green Macedonia" project of UNDP contained a public awareness campaign at both the local and the national levels (see box 8.3). Several programmes on national television ensured a media coverage. Billboards were put up around the country. In addition an advertising campaign was launched involving radio and television clips, and daily and weekly newspaper advertisements. At the local level, the municipalities were helped to develop public awareness campaigns. Promotion materials were handed out and waste bins and information boards were placed at strategic locations. To prevent cleaned up waste sites from being fouled again, "clean and green" information boards were placed strategically.

## 8.3 Conclusions and recommendations

Waste in itself is not a problem though inappropriate treatment and disposal do cause health and environmental problems such as smell, soil pollution, visual pollution, air pollution through burning, emission of greenhouse gases and groundwater contamination. The magnitude of the environmental problems associated with waste is poorly monitored in the former Yugoslav Republic of Macedonia. The number of illegal dumpsites is unknown and there is no monitoring of soil and groundwater. The amounts of waste generated are estimated as no reliable measurements take place. Accurate data on environmental pollution are available for some 'hot spots' but these data are only incidental.

Five industrial sites have been identified as environmental hot spots, and another five have significant problems with hazardous waste. Both the groundwater and the soil are severely

contaminated, and untreated waste water is being allowed to flow into the Vardar River.

The Ministry of Environment and Physical Planning has no official programmes or instruments in place to reduce the amounts or the hazardousness of waste. Moreover, there is no classification system for waste and therefore few data on the amounts and kinds of hazardous waste generated in the country.

*Recommendation 8.1:*
*The Ministry of Environment and Physical Planning should establish a comprehensive strategy to stop the contamination of soil and groundwater by stored chemicals and other hazardous waste and to initiate soil remediation programmes in cooperation with the Ministry of Agriculture, Forestry and Water Economy. The strategy should include the establishment of a legal system for waste classification.*

With funding from the European Union, a draft plan has been developed to build a nationwide waste management system to put an end to many of the associated problems. This draft national solid waste management plan is, however, not in line with other strategies that have been developed such as the draft spatial plan for solid waste management and current practices such as the development of "temporary" landfills by the Ministry of Environment and Physical Planning. The draft national solid waste management plan has not officially been approved and no structural State funding is being provided for waste management issues. Staff dealing with waste management is insufficient as currently only one person is responsible for waste management, including the issuing of import and export permits for hazardous waste and the permits for temporary landfills.

*Recommendation 8.2:*
*The Ministry of Environment and Physical Planning should review the draft national solid waste management plan as soon as possible, taking into consideration the spatial plan for waste management and more awareness raising. Upon approval, the Government should allocate sufficient staff and financing to the Ministry of Environment and Physical Planning to guarantee successful implementation.*

Illegal waste sites crop up anywhere, regardless of planning or environmental requirements. As the draft national solid waste management plan has not yet been approved, the Ministry of Environment and Physical Planning has taken the initiative of countering the practice of illegal dumps by issuing permits for so-called temporary landfills. For a "temporary" landfill, the geologically most suitable place will be selected (i.e. abandoned opencast mines, sites with low permeability soils like clay) and subjected to an ecological-technological feasibility study. It is estimated that 80 per cent of the rural areas are not covered by public refuse collection services, which need to be expanded to put an end to illegal waste sites.

*Recommendation 8.3:*
*The Ministry of Environment and Physical Planning and the municipalities should act decisively to decrease the use of illegal dumps in rural areas.*

The incineration of medical waste from the Skopje medical centre at the Drisla landfill site is one of the few exceptions to the overall practice of waste disposal in landfills. It is an important example of waste separation and reduction of the risks associated with contagious and infectious waste.

*Recommendation 8.4:*
*The Ministry of Health and the Ministry of Environment and Physical Planning should extend the separate collection and incineration of medical waste to areas outside Skopje as a first step in a separate waste collection system.*

Implementing the draft national solid waste management plan requires major investments. Attracting private investments is therefore crucial. Privatization of public services has recently become possible. However, the national Government still caps the prices of public services. At municipal level there is little experience of the various forms of privatization, their benefits and shortcomings. In addition, the low collection rate of service fees,

'social' employment and high investments might limit the interest of the private sector.

*Recommendation 8.5:*
*The Ministry of Environment and Physical Planning together with the association of municipalities, "ZELS", should assist those municipalities interested in the privatization of public enterprises by developing a strategy to make public enterprises more economically attractive. A best practice guide based on experience in other countries, standard procedures for tendering, and studies into consumers' ability to pay should form part of this strategy.*

Cleaner production centres can fulfil an important role in countries in transition. Projects with low costs and even no-cost (good housekeeping projects), in particular, can often yield great environmental and financial benefits. Currently, the national cleaner production centre is strongly interlinked with the Environment Fund. One of the main projects of the regional centre concerns the fertilizer plant in Veles. According to the calculations of the regional centre for cleaner production, an investment of US$ 65,000 is required for quality and efficiency improvements in phosphoric acid production. The project would reduce oil consumption, local air pollution, electricity consumption and water pollution to the tune of US$ 1 million a year. These savings seem overestimated because of calculations using unrealistic electricity prices. Of the required investment, the company will pay US$ 27,000, while the remainder will be paid by the Environment Fund. As the fertilizer plant is privatized, the contribution from the Environment Fund could qualify as a subsidy. The Environment Fund is on the board of the cleaner production centre and most cleaner production projects listed require extensive external funding – some as much as €750,000. (see Chapter 11 on Industry, energy and the environment)

*Chapter 9*

# AGRICULTURE AND FOREST MANAGEMENT

## 9.1 Resources in agriculture

### Physical conditions

Due to its location and topography, the former Yugoslav Republic of Macedonia is exposed to three types of climate, the Mediterranean (suitable for vineyards, horticulture and early vegetables), the eastern European moderate continental (suitable for cereal and industrial crops) and one local mountain climate in the high mountains (suitable for livestock rearing). The country has limited rainfall that ranges from 400 to 1000 mm/year, with a significant difference between the regions. Rains are unequally distributed during the year: spring rains are followed by dry and hot summer months. Rainfalls occur mainly from October to December and from March to May; 75 per cent of the territory is characterized as semi-arid. Furthermore, in the past 10 years (1990-2000), the country has experienced droughts almost every year except 1995.

With but 36 per cent of the land in the valleys, the former Yugoslav Republic of Macedonia is a mountainous country. The climate and relatively good soils (two thirds of the arable lands are vertisol and terra rosa) offer comparative advantage for achieving high yields in agricultural production, if irrigation is provided. Half of the territory (50.8 per cent) is used for agriculture, split almost equally between arable land and pastures (see table 9.1). Very fertile land is scarce; only 7 per cent of arable land falls into classes I or II; 82 per cent into classes VI or VII. Because of the steady decline in rural population since 1948 (-30 per cent), it is reported that fallow land has increased in recent years (193,000 ha or 35.1 per cent of the arable land).

### Land distribution and farming structures

Arable land is shared between State enterprises and small private farmers (see table 9.2): 52 per cent of the households have less than half a hectare; 35 per cent have 0.5 to 3 ha; and 11 per cent have 3 to 5 ha. Large private professional farms are rare, and

agricultural activity is more an extension of household work where members are employed off-farm, and the farms are operated by the labour of the extended family, especially women. The considerable fragmentation into numerous small and irrational plots is an additional problem (average size of the plots: 0.4–0.7 ha). Individual households produce diversified crops for subsistence and sale and forage crops for supporting a mix of livestock. Grazing pastures in their turn are mostly socially (73 per cent) managed, and many farmers have access to the communal summer grazing pastures in the hills adjacent to their village.

Some 35 agro-kombinats, farming an average of 4,718 ha, were restructured and split into smaller units in the process of privatisation between 1997 and 1999. The 12 largest kombinats now have an average size of more than 2,500 ha, with about 1,000 employees, and several business units vertically connected, covering everything from primary production to retail.

In the absence of alternative market channels, agro-kombinats still play an important role as major employers in rural areas, sole distributors of farm inputs and purchasers of farm outputs. The agricultural combines are the main recipients of the Government's agricultural support policy (66 per cent of the subsidies for wheat, 56 per cent for cow's milk and 74 per cent for sheep's milk). However, unclear ownership of shares of agricultural land and organizational problems associated with oversized facilities have led to net losses, and the poor performance of the agro-kombinats jeopardizes their economic and social future.

Under the legal framework for denationalization, land reform was essentially linked to the return of State land that had been nationalized and farmed by the kombinats and to the privatization of State land through auction in order to encourage the development of a land market. Fifteen per cent of the land has been made available for rent by public auction, and preference is given to those who offer the best land-use programme (including soil protection).

### Rural employment and rural welfare

Agriculture employs 15 per cent of the labour force, but 41 per cent of the population lives in rural areas, and their existence is closely linked to agriculture. Individual agriculture is the symbol of the villagers' economic independence. According to the 1994 census, 226,000 persons (8.1 per cent of households) were engaged in agriculture, of whom only 53,000 were "engaged in agriculture as an occupation". Part-time farming with off-farm jobs is the lot of 50 to 60 per cent of the farmers. With the recent collapse of the manufacturing sector following transition and independence, an increasing number of people depend on agriculture for part or all of their income, and part-time farming plays an important role as a social buffer; rural families also provide foodstuffs to relatives in the cities. The poverty profile in the country is predominantly rural in large households with little education. Poverty leads to low environmental awareness, especially in rural areas.

### Economics and productions, markets

A full decade before independence, agriculture in the country was marked by a modest but constant increase and an unvarying 14-16 per cent share in GDP; after independence, deep economic difficulties arose with high unemployment. In October 2000, 57 per cent of the population had incomes just at or below the value of the consumer's basket, and there was a drop in the quality of nutrition (less dairy products and meat). (see also Chapter 14 on Human health and the environment) However, agricultural output has been relatively more buoyant than the rest of the economy: 15-20 per cent of GDP is produced by the agricultural sector, and it is the only sector that

has shown an increase: 8 per cent in 1994, 3 per cent in 1995 and 10.7 per cent in 1997. In contrast with other sectors, agriculture has always been predominantly a private sector activity. Public farm production accounted for only 23 per cent of GDP but its share of the value of the total agricultural market surplus is 67 per cent, twice that of the private sector. There is a permanent shortage of wheat, and of oil, sugar, milk and meat, which must be imported. Lamb meat, fruits, tomatoes, peppers, grapes, tobacco, wine and brandy are exported.

In 1994 the Government started liberalizing agricultural prices (phasing out direct budget support for market interventions and lowering custom tariffs in accordance with the world trade agreements), and agricultural subsidies declined from 23 per cent to 6 per cent between 1993 and 1995. These subsidies included subsidized loans, rebates on the purchase of inputs, price support and export subsidies together with support for the socially owned agro-kombinats.

### Crops

Sixty-two per cent of the arable land is used for cereal production, with more than half for maize. The yield (23 metric quintals/ha) is considered low. The country also produces rice with a fairly good yield (54 metric quintals/ha). Industrial crops (10 per cent of the arable land) are mainly sunflowers and tobacco, and vegetables cover 17 per cent of the arable land (peppers, tomatoes, gourds). After the loss of the Yugoslav market, a shift took place from vegetables to barley and alfalfa for livestock. Vineyards (28,000 ha) are an important tradition in the country and are cultivated intensively, mainly in Povadarie and Pelagonija Polog. The average yield is 0.75 $kg/m^2$. Tobacco (25,000 ha in 1998) is largely oriented towards export (28 million tons of the 33 million tons produced in 1998).

### Table 9.1: Agricultural land use, 1999

|  | in 1000 ha | in % |
|---|---|---|
| Total | 1,282 | 99.3 |
| Arable land: field crops and vegetables | 534 | 41.4 |
| Perennial crops: orchards and vineyards | 45 | 3.5 |
| Meadows | 54 | 4.2 |
| Pastures | 649 | 50.3 |

Source: Efremov, G. et al. Academy of Sciences and Arts.
Agricultural Development Strategy in the Republic of Macedonia to 2005. Skopje, July 2001.

**Table 9.2: Farming structures, 1998-1999**

|  | Number of farms | Average size ha | Use of arable land % | Share of GDP 1960 % | Share of GDP 1996 % |
|---|---|---|---|---|---|
| Social sector: State entreprises | 168 | 983 | 27.0 | 15.0 | 23.0 |
| Social sector: Cooperatives | 24 | 163 | 0.5 | .. | .. |
| Private sector | 178,087 | 1.3 | 72.5 | 85.0 | 77.0 |

*Source*: Efremov, G. et al. Academy of Sciences and Arts. Agricultural Development Strategy in the Republic of Macedonia to 2005. Skopje, July 2001.

---

**Box 9.1:     Tobacco**

The former Yugoslav Republic of Macedonia is a traditional producer of the well-known aromatic oriental tobacco types Prilep (15,000 tons in 1998), Yaka and Dzebel, which it exports. However, there is a tendency to introduce more and more Virginia tobaccos for domestic consumption because domestic production satisfies only 20 to 25 per cent of the market.

The Tobacco Institute in Prilep, founded in 1924 as a trial station, is solely responsible for the selection of varieties, and it is the main internationally renowned research centre in the Balkans. It carries out research in all tobacco-related fields, mainly in the selection of tobacco quality and resistance to disease. It also ensures the technical organization and extension of tobacco production in the country. The tobacco companies play a leading role in the cultivation of tobacco, not only because they buy all the production by contract, but also because they are the only distributors of the treated seeds (against *Peronospora tabacina*) exclusively produced in the Tobacco Institute, and they ensure the technical follow-up of the cultivation by transmitting the warnings and the instructions for compulsory plant protection measures issued by the Tobacco Institute, according to the Law on the Protection of Plants .

In Pelagonija especially, the main economic activity is the production of tobacco. A large number of families in the Prilep region working on small farms and on leased land depend on tobacco growing as their cash crop. Some individual non-farmer producers have grown tobacco for more than 20 years on the same plot with no crop rotation, and pests and diseases have become a huge problem. Chemicals must be bought in private shops and many producers do not know which products they should use. Those producers who run a farm can practise crop rotation, use animal dung and small amounts of synthetic fertilizers, and avoid the use of pesticides and still obtain normal yields despite the fact that they do not irrigate, for instance in northern Pelagonija, where there is no irrigation system.

Present applied research in the Tobacco Institute addresses mainly the adaptation of irrigation and fertilization levels for Virginia types in the country's conditions, in order to increase both the quantities and the quality produced for the manufacturers. Tobacco research is carried out only in irrigated cultures, despite the current lack of irrigation water (Pelagonija has a total irrigable area of 29,000 ha, and the World Bank project speaks of increasing this capacity).

However, research has shown that diseases such as black shank (*Phytophotora Parasitica var. nicotianae*) appear more frequently in irrigated fields and that their spread depends also on growing techniques. Only the use of chemicals can provide effective protection against this very serious pathogen. In the framework of the Montreal Protocol, the use of methyl bromide for tobacco seedlings should be phased out. This project is viewed as an acceptance of alternative technologies in the agriculture of the former Yugoslav Republic of Macedonia.

---

### Livestock

Livestock numbers in the country are relatively small with 166,000 head of cattle and 947,000 sheep in 1998 and, except for goats (85,000), numbers have been declining for many years because the industry overall has not developed as foreseen (45 per cent of the feed requirements must be imported) and because processing facilities were not adapted to production (non-existent or oversized). Eighty-four per cent of the total livestock is owned by private farmers. Except for lamb meat, there are no market surpluses for export; milk productivity is low in the private sector (1700 kg/cow in 1998); and local requirements are met with imported products.

### Agro-processing

The participation of the food-processing industry (drinks and tobacco) in GDP is 5.5 per cent and it represents 62 per cent of exports. It helps to reduce the balance-of-payments deficit. The sector employs 17,000 workers. Capacities were built for the large Yugoslav market and are now underused and obsolete.

In the former Yugoslavia, the (then) Republic of Macedonia played an important role as an agricultural producer serving an internal market of 23 million people. The dissolution of the Federation, followed by the Greek blockade and then the embargo on Yugoslavia by the international community (1992) disrupted many production chains and market links. Today, the internal market of about 2 million people is too small to absorb the production of export-oriented sectors. So far, these sectors have failed to capture new markets due to supply unreliability, inadequate product quality, relatively high costs, lack of diversification and poor marketing. The large vegetable sector experienced a 20 to 70 per cent decline between 1990 and 1998. It comprises thousands of mainly private producers, who will have to adjust to the demands of new export markets to make up for the loss of the traditional outlets in the region. The fruit sector, dominated by apples (35 per cent of the 17 thousand ha orchards), suffered a decline of 30 per cent in the same years. Production may expand if value can be added through better post-harvest handling and storage. The wine, tobacco, sheep and goat sectors are evaluated separately in this chapter.

## 9.2    Environmental concerns in agriculture

*Water and Land Use*

Irrigation and drainage

Except in the west, the former Yugoslav Republic of Macedonia has few water resources, resulting in a water deficiency during the summer (springs dry out). Drought is usual (more than 100 days in the centre of the country). During the growing period evapo-transpiration (about 640 mm) is much higher than rainfall (190 mm). High-crop yields and optimization of production are possible only with irrigation. Irrigation is the country's largest consumer of water (34 per cent).

The irrigation (land reclamation) system includes the main dams that provide irrigation water by gravitation, 61 pumping stations and 1364 km of open concrete canals. The total area under irrigation amounts theoretically to about 163,000 ha, 100,000 with sprinklers and the rest with other types of surface irrigation systems, using 900 million $m^3$ or 25 per cent of the river water available during an average dry year. In fact, schemes have not been completed or properly maintained so that only 126 thousand ha can be irrigated (23 per cent of the arable land, see table 9.3). Of the 6746 km of the

detailed ditch network, 40 per cent are open (in the oldest systems, or where rice is grown) and 60 per cent are underground pipes. The main irrigated crops are vegetables (18 per cent) and cereals (35 per cent), orchards (8 per cent) and vineyards (14 per cent). Rice accounts for 3 per cent. (see also Chapter 6 on Water management, including protection of lakes)

The irrigation system was developed over three periods: up to 1958; between 1958 and 1975; and from 1975 to the present. During the first period, 27 irrigation schemes were built covering an area of 19,026 hectares. During the second period the biggest schemes were constructed, such as Tikvesh, Bregalnitsa, and Strumitsa, with three independent schemes, Turija, Vodocha and Mantovo, covering a total of 68,448 hectares of fertile arable land, as well as a few smaller schemes covering 39,514 hectares. During the third period, 28 irrigation schemes were built, with an area of 36,704 hectares, including the irrigation of the biggest grain production field, Pelagonija with 20,200 hectares.

The irrigation systems are complex engineering systems made of numerous, widely dispersed facilities. They consist of basic constructions (dams, intakes, pumping stations, main and secondary canals), local irrigation networks and irrigation equipment. Almost all big systems are supplied with water from reservoirs usually built in the upper course of the rivers and providing gravity irrigation.

The systems constructed in the 1980s and later are in good condition, but those built in the 1970s have deteriorated considerably due to the poor quality of the initial design and poor maintenance, which result in high seepage, sometimes more than 50 per cent (Tikvesh, Bregalnica). The level of finance (payment of water user charges) and the budgeting system are not sufficient to pay for the maintenance of the now 30-year-old systems.

Very few environmental issues arise from the proposed irrigation rehabilitation, since the water quality is adequate (no salinity) and the reduction of water losses and hence the run-off of fertilizers and pesticides will have only positive effects. However, the use of agrochemicals is expected to rise. Furthermore, the Tikvesh and Bregalnica systems suffer from the formation of algae. The origin of the algae remains unknown, but it is building up to such an extent that it is preventing irrigation (clogging of the hydrants) and requires regular manual cleaning. The recommended measures (use of chemicals) should not affect the

quality of the water and the health of the irrigation workers.

---

**Box 9.2:    Wine**

With more than 28,000 ha of vineyards, the former Yugoslav Republic of Macedonia is a wine-growing country. Sixty-four per cent of the surface belongs to small private producers. Table grapes account for 35 per cent of the plantations (Afusali variety); the Smeredevka and Vranec varieties account for 80 per cent of the plantations for wine production. In recent years, foreign varieties have been more intensively planted in order to satisfy the needs of quality exports. Yields have not been satisfactory (0.6 to 0.9 kg/m$^2$). The plantations suffered from a lack of water and cold winters, as well as from the ageing of the plantations. The processed part of the private sector (26 – 45 per cent) is well below the corresponding surfaces, and the quantities produced did not fully use the capacities of the processing units.

In the Vardar lower basin including Kavadarci in the Crna River basin, agriculture specializes in fruit, vegetable and grape production, and wine is the main product, with a tradition that seems to go back even before Roman times. Most private farmers are into grape production as a high-value, profitable crop.

Tikves AK is one of the country's major agro-kombinats; established in 1946 with 66 ha of vineyards, it developed to 1,750 ha in 1996. It buys and processes grapes from individual producers throughout the entire region covering a surface of 6,500 ha. Tikves AK is a very successful wine producer with a major share of the domestic market as well as being the country's leading wine exporter (62 per cent of market share, with 40 per cent of its exports just to Germany). Tikves AK wines (the famous Smeredevka) have often won medals at international exhibitions (Bordeaux (France), Ljubljana). It is also the country's largest table grape exporter to Western Europe (Austria, Germany, Netherlands), with a market share ranging from 50 to 70 per cent.

Tikves AK was the first to begin to grow grapes applying artificial irrigation: yields were increased from 0.4 kg/m$^2$ to 1 – 1.2 kg/m$^2$, or 1.5 – 2.0 kg/m$^2$ for table grapes (peak yields of 4 kg/m$^2$ are mentioned). The vineyards of the kombinat receive chemical fertilizers and cow manure (the best farm dung promoting soil activity) every three years (no manure in private vineyards). Fungicides (Cu preparations against *botrytis cinerea* and *plasmopara viticola*) and insecticides (against grape moth, *polychrosis botrana*) are applied according to a treatment plan (four or five times a year). Generally, fertilizer applications correspond to normal levels in Western Europe. The director of the kombinat, as well as the small private producers, have recently become interested in organic methods, because they could help save on expensive agrochemicals, but they fear a severe drop in yields and are still not sure whether lower yields could be compensated by lower expenses.

In the vineyards more than 50 years ago, traditional production was naturally "organic", but this is rarely the case now because of the efficient expansion of the use of agrochemicals, including among small part-time farmers who benefited from the irrigation systems. Treatments lead to the appearance of chemical-resistant pests (grape moth). New cheap organic methods (installation of predators such as the ladybirds *coccinella septempunctata*) have to be introduced, but also old ones revived (such as bottle traps filled with sugar and vinegar). Without irrigation, yields are cut by half, but old Macedonian varieties (such as Stanushina) are more resistant to drought and pests and can be cultivated without irrigation.

---

**Table 9.3: Status of irrigated land**

|  | in 1000 ha | in % of arable land |
|---|---|---|
| "Suitable for irrigation" *) | 421 | 76 |
| "Total irrigation" (system extension) *) | 370 | 67 |
| "Optimistic" prediction 2020 *) | 266 | 48 |
| "Optimal" prediction 2020 *) | 136 | 25 |
| Theoretical potential (if current systems completed) ** | 173 | 31 |
| Actual potential of irrigation **) | 126 | 23 |
| Irrigated 1987 **) | 82 | 15 |
| Irrigated 2000 **) | 42 | 8 |

*Sources* :
*) Efremov, G. et al. Academy of Sciences and Arts. Agricultural Development Strategy in the Republic of Macedonia to 2005. Skopje, July 2001.
**) see chapter 6 on Water management.

### Land management and erosion

Most of the territory of the former Yugoslav Republic of Macedonia is vulnerable to erosion, and 38 per cent (9,423.6 km$^2$) is subject to strong erosion processes (see table 9.4). Deforestation (the wood floated down the Vardar River to the port of Thessaloniki) was large-scale under the Ottoman Empire, turning the central part of the country (25,000 ha in Krivolak) from a dry area to a semi-desert. The western part (from Struga to Tetovo) is characterized by pasture run-off from torrential rains due to overgrazing and scarce soil cover, and the north-eastern part around Delcevo has steep barren mountains, where poor farmers use forage cut from trees for feeding their cattle. Short and intensive rainfalls are typical, producing intensive erosion, local floods and landslides.

An erosion map was prepared (1980-1997) in a database version (scale 1:50,000) based on the Gavrilovic-Poljakov empiric methodology (1992), but no printout was made. The intensity of erosion was classified into three categories: deep erosion (gully erosion), mixed erosion and minor surface erosion.

The total annual production of erosive deposits is 17 million m$^3$ or 685 m$^3$/km$^2$. Almost half of it ends up in the rivers and is carried downstream – the Vardar, for instance, collects 3.9 million m$^3$ annually from its tributaries – and the other half becomes sediment in natural lakes and artificial reservoirs. The annual amount of debris in watersheds and the volume of deposition in the reservoirs of the major dams were analysed in the National Erosion Survey. The Crni Drim watersheds have little debris (less than 0.1 mm/year) compared to that in the Vardar and Strumica basins (about 0.5 mm a year). Debris in the Kalimanci is as high as 1.0 mm/year. Torrential floods cover agricultural land with sterile sediments such as stones and gravel, which damage the irrigation infrastructures and build up about 3 million m$^3$ of erosive detritus a year. The erosion of riverbanks (for instance, along the Vardar River approximately 20 km upstream from Gevgelija) is also a problem. The heavy siltation (Sateska estuary) and thus pollution of Lake Ohrid have been studied. Some 193,000 ha of total ploughing land is left uncultivated, because of its low fertility and a lack of labour (old age) or mechanization. The fallow areas represent a latent focal point of erosion resulting in the degradation and impoverishment of the soil layers.

The annual erosion of the cultivated soil layer to a depth of 20 cm affects 8,500 ha, or 0.33 per cent of the total surface of the country. About 40 thousand ha (annual soil loss of 308,000 m$^3$) of irrigated land is subject to erosion, due to furrow irrigation on sloping land.

The intensive rotation of crops, the use of agrochemicals and heavy machinery damage the soil in some parts of the country. There are serious compaction problems in some irrigated systems particularly with fluvisols and colluvial soils. Stubble burning is widespread and leads to a reduction of organic substances in the soil. Eleven thousand hectares are reported to be saline, but this is not yet considered a problem. Saline soils might be created by improper irrigation practices.

---

**Box 9.3:     The Lisice dam on the Topolka River**

The Lisice dam, started in 1991, is being constructed on the Topolka River near Veles, although construction has been halted because of financial constraints. Veles has a drinking water shortage throughout the year. The dam is only one of the components of the Lisice hydro-system (supply pipeline of 20 km, pipeline for the irrigation network, filter station, temporary intake), a multipurpose structure of the highest priority in the water management of the former Yugoslav Republic of Macedonia. The first objective is a supply of clean drinking water for the town of Veles and its surroundings (50,000 inhabitants, 75,000 in the conurbation) and water for the local economy and industry. The irrigation of approximately 4,000 ha is also planned.

The diversion canal for supplying drinking water is already operating, and the farmers who used to grow rice in Risice (the village takes its name from "rice"), Topolka Valley, using water taken directly from the river have to turn to other crops less water-intensive, but also less profitable (wheat and barley), especially if irrigation has to be reduced. Rice is concentrated now on the best lands (classes I and II) and crop rotation is non-existent.

According to the Law on Waters (art. 11), the supply of drinking water has priority over the supply of irrigation water. So, farmers doubt that they will recover their entire irrigation capacity after completion of the hydro-system. At the same time, rice growing suffers from the competition of now freely imported and much cheaper rice (about half of the price), and the rice area and production declined by 47 per cent following the termination of price support. Private farmers in Topolka, however, do seem to be able to sell directly to customers at good prices. Finally, not only is rice threatened by the shortage of water, but it might also be the cause of water shortage itself, as it is the most water-consuming crop in the country.

## Table 9.4: Soil erosion

| Erosion process category | area (km$^2$) | % |
|---|---|---|
| Extremely high | 698 | 3 |
| High | 1,832 | 7 |
| Medium | 6,893 | 27 |
| Low | 7,936 | 32 |
| Very low | 7,463 | 31 |

*Source*: Gorgevik, M. et al. University "Cyrill and Method" Skopje. Kartana Erozija Republika Makedonija, Kniga 1.

Measures to protect rivers and reservoirs from erosion were initiated in the early 1900s, and since 1945 measures have been taken to control erosion on deforested barren land such as the banning of nomadic goat and sheep breeding by the Law on Erosion (1951, abrogated in 1989). This very unpopular measure proved effective for the recovery of degraded shrub land. The Law on Soil Conservation and Torrent Control was applied between 1950 and 1980, and 285 basins were regulated. In 1970, the Rural Afforestation Fund was established and, by 1990, 164,360 ha had been reforested. Since 1990 this activity has been strongly reduced (10 per cent of the previous decade) due to budget constraints. Currently, the usual measures are debris flow control structures such as low dams together with afforestation in the watersheds.

Erosion is still a problem in steep bare lands or where forests have been clear-cut. Migration from the countryside led to abandoned land and its regeneration, which, allied to the erosion control programmes after 1945, eased erosion. Although erosion of agricultural land is considered "less serious", the long-term effect of erosion on arable land, reducing the fertility of the best soils, is indeed a priority. Land susceptible to erosion must be classified and measures evaluated according to the return on investment, integrated with a watershed approach. Simple and imaginative measures (planting of raspberry bushes and cherry trees) can be taken against erosion. These measures do not always have to be costly reforestation with pine trees from nurseries, which may lead to soil acidification. Improved grazing management practices have to be introduced and imposed on local farmers. Finally, it must be noted that the World Bank's rehabilitation and restructuring irrigation project does not contain any provisions for the control of erosion, the mastering of the sediment deposits in the reservoirs or the reforestation of the catchment areas.

---

**Box 9.4: Sheep and goats**

Given its climatic and geographic characteristics, it is not surprising that the country has a strong tradition in sheep and goat husbandry, both for milk and for meat products. Some of the sheep are raised nomadically: 300,000 head graze from mid-May until the beginning of November in the hills in the west and east of the country; in winter the herds are kept mainly in the Vardar River plains. Winter pasture forage is poor and does not meet the needs of the ewes at the end of gestation, so that imported expensive complement feeds are necessary. Sheep production is largely in private hands, on farms with flock sizes of between 50 and 150 ewes. But 49 larger companies, which emerged from the collectivized State enterprises, have flocks ranging from 1,000 to 12,500 ewes (60 per cent of the nomadic herd).

In 2001 official statistics showed 1,315,000 head: some 600,000 lambs were fattened, corresponding to 4,700 tons of lamb meat, half of it was exported. Lambs are sold to the main EU-registered slaughterhouses (agro-kombinats at Stip, Gostivar and Kumanovo) that produce mainly whole carcasses for export. Since the outbreak of foot-and-mouth disease in 1996, followed by an EU ban on lamb meat from the former Yugoslav Republic of Macedonia, the sheep herd decreased by one third. The sector also suffered from the drought years (1998-2001) in the winter pastures and the real number could be well below 1 million head.

Roughly 40,000 tons of sheep's milk are produced for cheese to meet the strong domestic demand. After weaning the lambs (slaughtered at Easter time), ewes continue to be milked until mid-July, often under poor hygienic conditions (brucellosis infections). After the collapse of the export market for lambs, sheep farmers turned to milk products. Therefore, many small sheep farmers are reluctant to switch from the native Pramenka breeds (Ovcepolian and Sarplaninian) and their crossbreeds with Merinos – with relatively low yields in milk and in meat – to new, subsidized one-purpose breeds (for meat only, such as Awassi and Chios).

In order to control erosion, in 1951, goat breeding was banned by law and the goat population dropped from 517,000 head in 1947 to 1,000 in 1956. Goat breeding was permitted again in 1989, and since then the number of goats has increased rapidly (200,000 head in 2001) in small (< 100 head) private flocks, but some larger specialized farms are emerging. In contrast to sheep, goat herds are sedentary. This sector's conditions (production more focused on cheese with uncontrolled hygienic conditions) and prospects are similar to those of sheep production.

*Water and soil pollution*

Water pollution by agricultural activities

Discharges and serious contamination from livestock farms (especially pig farms, with slaughterhouses) is a serious source of pollution in certain parts of the country, for instance in the Pchinja (near Kumanovo), the Bregalnica (Sveti Nikole) and the Strumica rivers. Two thirds of the cattle herd is concentrated in the north (Skopje, see table 9.5).

There is limited information on non-point pollution from agricultural sources, and its effects on the water basins are not clearly known. The consumption of agrochemicals continues to decrease (see table 9.6): pesticide consumption dropped from 2,706 tons in 1983 to 659 tons in 1993. The use of agrochemicals in the private sector does not seem to be controlled. No contamination of products exceeding the permitted limits could be shown in the analysis. Organochlorine and organophosphorus pesticides are not a problem, whilst herbicides have not been examined so far. However, problems with waste water from agriculture are noted in the River Bregalnica (Delchevo and Kochani), in the Vardar near Gostivar and near Negotino from newly developed areas and in Pelagonija. Lake Ohrid is reported to suffer from pollution by agricultural run-off (phosphorus).

Most drinking water sources are unpolluted mountain springs and, in general, the analysed water samples range within accepted limits. But the percentage of examined water samples that do not match the class specified in the 1999 Decree on the Classification of Waters is still high in rural settlements. There are no sanitary protection zones round the water-abstraction points limiting agricultural use in compliance with the 1983 Regulations on Sanitary Protection Zones. In the past 20 years this has contributed to several water-borne epidemics. The nitrates in the examined waterways are within the limits, and seem restricted to a small number of individual water-supply facilities in some plains villages where the land is used intensively for agriculture (Prilep and Radovici). Irrigation water from surface and groundwater is of satisfactory quality; groundwater quality is not monitored; and migration patterns of pollution are not known.

Although waste water from animal farms might not be a priority now, the production and discharge of cattle manure from large farms will have to be studied in the near future, especially units whose size is well above the limit set by the EU Directive on EIAs (97/11/EC, annex I, para. 17). Waste-water management is the task of the Ministry of Environment and Physical Planning. (see Chapter 6 on Water management, including protection of lakes)

Soil pollution

The contaminated areas that must be given priority are the hot spots and the industrial sites investigated by UNEP in its post-conflict environmental assessment of the former Yugoslav Republic of Macedonia: their air, water and soils are severely contaminated. The NEAP reported that cadmium, lead and zinc levels were 10-15 times higher in vegetables grown in Veles than in those from control regions. As much as 4 to 10 times the acceptable levels for lead and cadmium were found in spinach and lettuce (which are plants with a very high uptake) due to soil contamination, but no soil investigations are available. Epidemiological data suggest that the population in Veles has a higher blood lead level than a control population. The effects of heavy metals intoxication (Sn, Cd, Zn) on the health of domestic animals were already studied in the country in the 1970s. A UNEP soil sample taken at the OHIS A.D. Chemical Factory in Skopje showed 51 mg of Cr/kg, 55 mg of Cu, 189 mg of Zn, 36 mg of Ni, 224 mg of Mn, 503 mg of Pb, and 500 mg of Hg. Mercury and lead are the main contaminants of concern. Mercury is extremely dangerous to human health and bioaccumulates in the food chain. Contamination has been studied mainly in alluvial soils (see table 9.7).

Pesticide and herbicide residues in soils, also not seriously investigated, showed low levels (propanil and molinate in rice fields). DDT as well as other slowly degrading pesticides and herbicides (atrazine, prometryn, aldrin and dieldrin) are still present in rice fields in some regions (Kochani), and will be for a long time.

**Table 9.5: Large animal farms, 2002**

heads

| Name of farms | Dairy cows | Beef cattle | Pigs |
|---|---|---|---|
| Trubarevo - Skokpje region | 300 | .. | .. |
| Trubarevo - Skokpje region | 300 | .. | .. |
| Rzanicino - Skopje region | 300 | .. | .. |
| Cento - Skopje region | 300 | .. | .. |
| Skopje - Konjare | .. | 100 | .. |
| Skopje - Petrovec (military farm) | .. | .. | 3,000 |
| Kumanovo | .. | 300 | 10,000 |
| Tetovo - Celopek | .. | .. | 3,000 |
| Sveti Nicole | 300 | 500 | 10,000 |
| Krivolak | .. | 800 | .. |
| Kavadarci - Sopot | .. | 100 | .. |
| Stip | .. | .. | 10,000 |
| Gradsko - (Veles) D.Cicevo | .. | .. | 20,000 |

*Source*: Author's estimation.

**Table 9.6: Use of agrochemicals**

in tons

| | Fertilizers | Pesticides |
|---|---|---|
| 1996 | 10,339 | 556 |
| 1997 | 17,021 | 506 |
| 1998 | 21,617 | 529 |
| 1999 | 18,270 | 462 |
| 2000 | 16,416 | 308 |

*Source*: Republic of Macedonia. State Statistical Office. Statistical Yearbook 2001.

As an exporter of agricultural products, the former Yugoslav Republic of Macedonia must be particularly strict about the heavy metal and pesticide residue content of the soil, and exert strong control over their use. Research in the rice fields in Kochani showed that cadmium contents of 0.0 to 0.1 are below the maximum tolerated limit (1 ppm). However, as a rice and tobacco exporter, the country must give special attention to the cadmium levels in the soils, because of the high uptake by those plants in particular. Besides industrial pollution (in the Veles region), sludge from cleaning irrigation canals, urban sludge used in agriculture and certain phosphate fertilizers are also sources of cadmium contamination.

There is no monitoring system yet and the spread of pollution on a wider scale over agricultural land, limiting the cultivation of crops, has not yet been investigated. For many heavy metals plant uptake from polluted soils might be quite low, but grazing, with its direct uptake from the soil to animals in the form of dust, must absolutely be avoided. The irregular dissemination pattern of pollutants is difficult to assess, and for food exports at least, soil analysis must ensure that the agricultural produce does not come from contaminated soils.

*Biodiversity and agriculture*

In the former Yugoslav Republic of Macedonia, 18.5 per cent of the ecosystems are grassy (meadows and pastures) and 45 per cent agrarian.

Since there is no monitoring system, changes in agricultural practices induced by changes in the natural world have been noted but not quantified. For example, long periods of drought and the lack of irrigation water in the reservoirs have changed the use of rice paddies, and this has led to the disappearance of migratory birds from the region. Due to the drastic decrease in the number of cattle in the mountains, there has also been a marked reduction in predator birds which feed on carcasses. The ploughing of new fields has led to the destruction of natural habitats, such as that of the almond tree (*Amygdalus nana* in Lubas, Kavadarsci and Vaksinci and Kumanovo).

A semi-natural habitat: pastures and meadows

The pastures and similar grazing grounds support the important livestock subsector. The 634,000 ha of pastures (of which only 550,000 are actually used because of reforestation programmes) are divided into winter pastures (40 per cent of the surface) and summer pastures (60 per cent of the surface, of which 85 per cent are in the western mountains). They produce yields well below their potential (estimated at 800 kg dry matter/ha), with an average about 270 kg dry matter/ha. (see table 9.8) (see Chapter 10 on Nature and biodiversity management)

Low yields can be explained also by the use of pastures in marginal land that should be covered by forests, as was previously the case in the Balkans. The burning of pastures for clearing bushes (*Juniperus* sp.) is a problem. Overgrazing and erosion are a matter of concern in the winter Mediterranean pastures (Vardar plains) and in the eastern summer pastures (Delcevo), not in the western part (alpine pastures: Sar Planina, Korab, Bistra and Karaoman Stegovo). Because of the decrease in herds, enormous surfaces are not used to their full potential. Furthermore, because of the political upheavals of the past years, the western summer pastures are much less accessible to the

herds from the central part of the country. It is one of the objectives of the World Bank's private farmers support project, 1997, to improve pasture and range management, so as to protect less productive, more fragile surfaces, as farmers seek to increase profitable small ruminant production in upland areas.

The pastures belong to the State, which in 1998 created a "public enterprise for pasture" whose income relies on contract grazing fees. Sheep companies consider the grazing fees to be very high and rarely pay them. As a result there is no investment, pastures are generally not well kept (e.g. there is no resowing of damaged surfaces), there is no management plan, and infrastructure (drinking points, bathing pools, access roads, or even cheese-making units) is lacking.

### Table 9.7: Content of heavy metals in examined soils in the country and CEE limit values, 2001

| Site | Heavy metal | Contents (mg / kg soil) | Limit value CEE (total form in mg/kg soil) |
|------|-------------|-------------------------|--------------------------------------------|
| River Kumanovo | Arsenic | 30 - 83 | no |
| Dracevo - Skopje region | Cadmium | 4.1 - 16.6 | 1.0 - 1.5 |
| River Kumanovo | Cadmium | 5.6 - 7.6 | 1.0 - 1.5 |
| Trubarevo (Skopje region) | Chromium | 14 - 208 | no |
| Chernozems | Chromium | 40 - 193 | no |
| River Zletovica | Copper | 395 | 50 - 140 |
| Trubarevo (Skopje region) | Nickel | 11 - 458 | 100 |
| Chernozems | Nickel | 24 - 260 | 100 |
| River Zletovica | Zinc | 4083 | 150 - 200 |
| Veles | Zinc | 92 - 2105 | 150 - 200 |
| Avtocomanda (Skopje region) | Zinc | 652 | 150 - 200 |

*Source*: Mitrikeski, J. and Mitkova, T. Faculty of Agriculture. Assesssment of the quality of the contaminated soils in Republic of Macedonia, 2001.

### Table 9.8: Main pasture ecosystems

| Associations | type | site | yield kg DM/ha* | feed quality |
|--------------|------|------|-----------------|--------------|
| Trifolium resupinati balansae | mediterran. | valleys+ hills | 2,000 | +++ |
| Hordeta-Caricetum distantis | mediterran. | hills | 1,800 | ++ |
| Cyperetum longi | mediterran. | hills | 2,500 | --- |
| Tunoco -Trisetetum myrianthi | wet sites | hills + uphills | 1,000 | + |
| Cynosureto - Caricetum hirtae | alpine | 800-1200 m alt. | 1,200 | ++ |
| Brachypodio - Onobrycetum pindicolae | mediterran. | hills | 1,300 | ++(+) |
| Erysimo - Trifolietum | mediterran. | > 1000 m alt. | 800 | + |
| Geranieto - Poetum violaceae | alpine | Galicica | 500 | + |
| Festucetum duriusculata | alpine | Western part | 2,000 | --(-) |
| Festucetum paniculatae (syn.Festucetum spadiaceae) | alpine | Western part | 2,500 | --- |
| Nardetum stricta | alpine | Western part | 600 | -- |

*Source*: Ivanovcki, P. Furagno Proizvodstvo. Skopje, 2000.
*Note*: * DM stands for dry matter.

<u>Exploiting natural resources: medicinal and aromatic herbs</u>

Thanks to the geographical location and the climatic and relief conditions of the country, there is an abundance of various sorts of medicinal and aromatic herbs and forest fruits, which are widely used in the pharmaceutical, food and cosmetic industries. Wild herb harvesting has a long tradition in the country. The wild-growing herbs are collected even in the barely accessible mountainous areas, and processed and packed in manufacturing plants, such as Alkaloid's "Botanicals" Profit Centre, founded in 1936. Alkaloid exports chemicals all over Europe. The pharmaceutical effects of the medicinal products are certified by the State Analytical and Control Institute, and the products are given a green ECO mark after an audit conducted in accordance with European Union Directive 2092/91 on organic origin of agricultural production. Finally, the quality of the production process meets ISO 9001 and ISO 14001 standards.

Picking is well organized with Alkaloid, but the uncontrolled picking of medicinal and aromatic herbs in the mountains for export in large quantities by very poor retired or unemployed people is more and more a problem. *Gentiana lutea,* for instance, is already extinct in the Jablanica, Baba, Korab and Sar mountains.

Experiments in cultivating *Thymus* and *Origanum vulgare* have started. Well-selected and cultivated species would be preferred by manufacturers because of their higher content of the desired substances (essential oils, flavonoids). Even if the results are satisfactory, investments would be considerable, and processing factories are only likely to be interested if the red list becomes applicable (see table 9.9). A transition period allowing the development of cultivation methods would be welcome.

The introduction of good agricultural practice guidelines for the cultivation of medicinal and aromatic plants in the Balkans has been proposed by the Faculty of Engineering of Novi Sad (Yugoslavia), in order to ensure product quality. Organic cultivation is not demanded, but the use of agrochemicals has to be reduced to a minimum (integrated production) and documented. Cultivation on polluted soils and irrigation with polluted waters are prohibited. Products made out of organically cultivated raw materials – and not collected wild – could be awarded a special label.

This activity could provide an income to mountain people living on marginal lands. The problem has been tackled only marginally at the Faculty of Agriculture of Skopje.

**Table 9.9: List of collected herbs and plants to be put on the red list, 2002**

| |
|---|
| Arctostaphylos uva-ursi |
| Digitalis grandiflora |
| Gentiana lutea |
| Hypericum perforatum |
| Hyssopus officinalis |
| Juniperus communis |
| Origanum vulgare |
| Primula veris |
| Pulmonaria officinalis |
| Salvia officinalis |
| Sambucus nigra |
| Sideritis scardica |

*Source:* Brajanoska, R. The Ministry of Environment and Physical Planning, 2002.

## 9.3 Policy objectives and management

*Institutional Responsibilities*

The Ministry of Agriculture, Forestry and Water Economy is responsible for agricultural and rural development. The Ministry of Environment and Physical Planning is responsible for soil protection.

The Agricultural Inspectorate of the Ministry of Agriculture, Forestry and Water Economy controls the use of fertilizers and pesticides according to the product instructions. Inspectors of the Ministry of Environment and Physical Planning are responsible for supervising the implementation of measures for protecting the soil against pollution and erosion, and its rehabilitation.

The country's extension service was first established in 1975, to promote private agriculture, often in close association with agro-kombinat out-grower programmes. Support for the establishment of a national extension agency came from the Ministry of Agriculture, Forests and Water Economy and from the private farmers support project financed by the World Bank. The Agency is headquartered in Bitola, but its operations are dispersed countrywide and grouped in six regional centres. The Agency employs 140 well-qualified professionals in 30 working units, each of which covers more than 30,000 farmers in all types of activities.

The main constraints of the extension service are a lack of applied research, inadequate attention to production economics and farm management, and insufficient knowledge of both the resources at the disposal of the farmers and their difficulties.

The National Extension Agency is currently working with the World Bank's private farmers support project. Through this project, 300 farms (50 from each of 6 regions) are being monitored for a period of one calendar year, ending in 2002. The project also includes technical assistance and aims to strengthen the supply of technology and information services to private farmers, to improve access to extension services and relevant research, and to raise production and farm income.

The project also supports the creation of farmers' associations with membership fees. It is foreseen that, by 2010, half of the activities of the official extension service will be privatized.

*Policy Framework*

The Agricultural Development Strategy to 2005 (Skopje, July 2001) is a comprehensive document that addresses all sectors of agricultural production. The general objectives – besides integration into the European Union – include better use of the natural advantages of the country, with the completion and development of irrigation schemes; improving the quality, processing and packaging especially of agricultural products, especially those with greater market potential; and better management and use of natural grassland.

Agricultural production should be stimulated in order both to meet domestic demand, especially for basic products such as wheat, oil, sugar, milk and meat, and to develop further traditional agricultural exports (see key sectors below). However, the Yugoslav markets need to be restored and the agricultural policy of the European Union may well be an impediment.

Restoration of the deteriorated irrigation systems has been given a high priority. The use of irrigation together with modern production methods is viewed as essential if farmers are to produce a surplus for sale. The rehabilitation of the three irrigation systems supported by the World Bank will help to ensure the livelihoods of 25,000 farmers, increasing their income by about 50 per cent on average. The impact on mid-scale farms would be greatest since they would benefit from the intensification of agriculture. The aim is to ensure

high yields and good product quality for commercial agriculture and especially exports, and to provide adequate incomes and higher living standards in the rural areas.

The environmental chapter of the Agricultural Development Strategy deals exclusively with the implementation of organic farming and presents no other concrete environmental objectives. The Agricultural Development Strategy also addresses rural development, but is directed primarily at general measures, such as credit, the development of cooperatives, basic infrastructures and rural centres, the training of the young in agriculture, support for farmers-workers, and the creation of small enterprises.

*Legislation*

The Law on the Protection of Plants passed in 1998 is now being revised to comply with EU Directive 91/414/EEC. Revision concerns the establishment of a committee to choose the chemicals to be put on the official list and the registration of the chemicals (see art. 39). The Law itself deals with the protection of plants from diseases and pests (warning system), protection from imported diseases and pests (custom controls), the production of and trade in plant products and measures to prevent effects on animal and human health, and on the environment and nature. Priority must be given to integrated pest management (art. 6). Plant owners who use plant protection products must keep records of the treatments (art. 15) and businesses producing, importing or marketing products must be officially registered (art. 35) because they must fulfil the prescribed conditions for the storage and destruction of the products and have a permit to do so (art. 39).

Soil protection is addressed in different laws. The Law on the Environment and Nature Protection and Promotion (1996) specifies in article 17 that degraded soils must be rehabilitated by the legal entity or person responsible for their degradation. The Law on Agricultural Land (implemented by the Ministry of Agriculture, Forestry and Water Economy) enforces "the rational use of agricultural land," including anti-erosive measures (art. 11) with the support of the extension service (art. 13). Articles 75 and 76 of the same Law provide detailed provisions on soil protection against erosion (such as a ban on cutting trees, the rational use of pastures, the protection of slope lands, the obligation to plant perennial crops or build protective works, carry out measures against fires, see art. 79). The Law also specifies that the maximum allowed concentration of harmful substances will be set in a regulation.

According to the Law on Waters, water enterprises have to take measures to protect reservoirs from sediments and take anti-erosion measures for that purpose. Large enterprises have departments dealing especially with erosion and torrent control.

The legal framework for denationalization comprises the Law for Agricultural Land (Official Gazette No. 40/76), the Law on the Transformation of Enterprises with State Capital and the Law on the Transformation of Enterprises and Cooperatives with State Capital Managing Agricultural Land (Official Gazette No. 19/96).

A law on organic farming is still in preparation; in the meantime, national certification of organic products for export is not possible. There are companies such as Tajmishte in Kicevo, which is developing "healthy food production", or "Eko-Gradinar" in Dobreijci/Strumitsa, which is striving to comply with "environmental standards for the quality of vegetables for European markets", but there is no reference to certification. To help the Environmental Movement (DEM), an environmental NGO, the Swiss Government supports activities promoting organic farming with projects in five regions (Veles, Maleshavia, Strumitsa, Ovce Pole, Tikvesh). The Ministry of Agriculture, Forestry and Water Economy does not consider the prospects of organic farming to be bright, even in the relatively extensive agriculture systems of the former Yugoslav Republic of Macedonia, not only because of the farmers' inexperience and the lack of interest shown by competent bodies, but also because of the higher price of the products and the limited purchasing power of domestic consumers. However, export of such products once properly certified is by no means excluded.

## 9.4    Conclusions and recommendations

More water needs to be made available for agriculture in the former Yugoslav Republic of Macedonia, especially to grow produce which would be competitive on world markets. This requires rehabilitating the irrigation infrastructure and reducing current water losses through, inter alia, improved irrigation systems (dripping), the measuring of water use, transparent pricing of consumed water (and sanctions against users who do not pay), the promotion of water restrictions for

end-users at the hydrant, and the introduction of conservation tillage for keeping moisture in the soil. The country needs to have a better knowledge of available groundwater resources, and it should promote the integrated management of water resources.

*Recommendation 9. 1:*
*The Ministry of Agriculture, Forestry and Water Economy should urgently promote rational water use and strategies to lower the demand for water in the agriculture sector rather than support increased supply. The impacts of agricultural practices on water quantities and quality should be studied and reduced with the implementation of guidelines for operating irrigation facilities and the pumping of groundwater. The construction of additional surface water reservoirs should be re-examined under the principle of sustainable and efficient use of limited resources.*

The current Law on Waters does not contain any specific regulations on pollutant loads from agriculture, nor is there a "code of good agriculture practices". Only article 9 of the Law on the Protection of the Lakes (45/77) specifies that the development of horticulture must be in accordance with regional planning. The increased use of agrochemicals following the rehabilitation of irrigation systems should be controlled through the extension services. The private farmers support project is intended to monitor and control pollution loads at various important points in the systems, including downstream. It will be the responsibility of the Public Water Management Enterprise to ensure that concentrations of substances do not exceed the levels prescribed in the Law on the Quality and Safety of Drinking Water.

*Recommendation 9.2:*
*The Ministry of Agriculture, Forestry and Water Economy and other relevant bodies should ensure that irrigation systems, particularly following their rehabilitation, are protected from the leaching of chemicals and from erosion.*

Protection of the soil is addressed through several laws, including those dealing with the environment and nature protection, with forests, with water and with waste. Consequently, enforcement of the laws also lies with different entities, including, for example, the State Environment Inspectorate and the Agricultural Inspectorate. The lack of a clear definition of institutional responsibility and the absence of controls and penalties make these regulations ineffective.

*Recommendation 9.3:*
*The Ministry of Environment and Physical Planning, in cooperation with the Ministry of Agriculture, Forestry and Water Economy, should prepare comprehensive legislation on soil protection in order to substitute existing laws and to define respective responsibilities clearly. The law should contain provisions on protecting the soil and remediation measures for contaminated soils, compulsory measures against erosion and compaction, and provisions for the use of the best agricultural practices.*

In the industrial hot spots, the soil is seriously contaminated with cadmium, mercury and lead, and these are now being found in plants with a high uptake, such as spinach and lettuce. Mercury is extremely dangerous to human health and bioaccumulates in the food chain. Pesticide residues, including DDT, are also found in the soil. As an exporter of agricultural products, the former Yugoslav Republic of Macedonia must be particularly strict about the heavy metal and pesticide residue content of the soil, and exert a strong control over their use.

For many heavy metals, plant uptake from polluted soils might be low, but grazing, with its direct uptake from the soil to animals in the form of dust, must absolutely be avoided. There is, however, no system to monitor soil contamination.

*Recommendation 9.4:*
*(a) The Ministry of Environment and Physical Planning should initiate a programme analysing and monitoring soils for heavy metal and pesticide contamination and develop a comprehensive programme for prevention and clean-up.*

*(b) Agricultural activities, including plant production and animal grazing, should be prohibited in areas where the soil is contaminated.*

Extension services have traditionally focused on the most effective ways to get good economic returns through better yields with less input. These services need to be broadened to encompass sustainable development practices through better pasture and meadow management, integrated pest management, conservation tillage, improved cropping patterns, and organic farming (combined into "technical packages"). The 1998 Report on the Survey of Small-scale Farmers showed that 80 per cent of farmers use information from sources other than extension services.

*Recommendation 9.5:*
*The Ministry of Agriculture, Forestry and Water Economy should further develop and strengthen agricultural extension services with comprehensive information programmes based on the principles of integrated and organic farming. Where farmers cannot pay, these extension services should be provided free of charge.*

The former Yugoslav Republic of Macedonia has the potential to increase exports of some of its major crops. With the rehabilitation of the irrigation system, it is expected that the production of irrigated grapes (wine and table grapes) would return to its 1990 level, since it has already captured a strong market, and more marginal pasture land could be turned to intensive vineyards. Tobacco remains an important export, and the demand for lamb meat in particular is strong outside the country and exports of it could be increased.

"Environmentally friendly" product labelling, as proposed, for example, in EU Regulation 2081/92, is an important tool to promote both the sustainable management of agriculture and exports.

*Recommendation 9.6:*
*The Ministry of Agriculture, Forestry and Water Economy, in collaboration with the Ministry of Environment and Physical Planning, should establish the pre-requisites for marketing major agricultural products under an eco-label, and particularly those products intended for export (such as wine, tobacco and lamb).*

# Chapter 10

# NATURE AND BIODIVERSITY MANAGEMENT

## 10.1 Nature Management and Forestry

### Introduction

The former Yugoslav Republic of Macedonia is a landlocked country, where high mountains and hills alternate with deep valleys (Mount Korab, on the Albanian border, is the highest peak, 2764 m). Its climate differs according to the relief and the type of terrain: hot summers and short, cold winters in the steppes, with heavy snowfalls in the mountains. The climate in the valleys is moderate.

Three glacial lakes, Ohrid, Prespa and Dojran, are very important, particularly for their rich biodiversity, their water resources, the tourism they generate and their transboundary significance. The country shares the lakes' resources with two neighbouring countries – Greece (Lakes Prespa and Dojran) and Albania (Lakes Ohrid and Prespa). So, unified monitoring and the integrated management systems of these lakes are necessary for all these countries in order to conserve and enhance the lakes' biodiversity and ecological values.

### Biological-geographic provinces

*Mediterranean forests and maquis* are typical forest biotopes with evergreen shrubs and mesophyllous trees and herb vegetation, close to water bodies. *Mediterranean semi-deserts* occupy the stony sites of hilly zones and the lowland sites on deep soils, where semi-shrubs and sclerophyllous grasses can be found.

In the *sub-Mediterranean-Balkan forests,* oak, hornbeam, pine, and chestnut species prevail. *Middle-European Balkan forests* include mountain beech, mixed beech and fir, maple and birch, and spruce forests, as well as alder and other lowland forests. *European forests of the taiga type* can be found in fragments of spruce, Scots pine, fir and beech forests, in mixed or pure stands, comprising peat bogs, creeks, swamps and lakes.

*European high-mountain rocky ecosystems, tundra and alpine pastures* can be found at altitudes higher than 1500 m. *Macedonian molika pine (Pinus peuce) and Pinus pallasiana forests,* in the zone of alpine rocky pastures, represent Mediterranean mountain forests on rocky terrain. *South-Balkan rocky mountain terrain and dry pastures* are typical alpine biotopes, covered with berry shrubs.

### Current state of flora and fauna

Various climatic influences and relief forms on a relatively small territory result in the occurrence of 3200-3500 species of vascular plants, 485 species of vertebrates and 6,844 species of invertebrates.

The flora contains 260 associations, joined in 90 unions, about 50 orders and about 30 classes. Some types of vegetation are thoroughly studied (the aquatic, muddy, halophytic and the vegetation on the plain meadows), while the vegetation of hilly, mountain and sub-alpine zones is in the phase of intensive study. (table 10.1)

A number of these species are endemic, relict and rare. (table 10.2)

From a mycological point of view, the territory of the former Yugoslav Republic of Macedonia is not very well researched. There are 1500 known fungi species in the country (table 10.3), but further research is necessary to complete the inventory. There are about 66 endangered fungus species; they are either collected for food and horticultural uses, or disappear from their natural sites due to habitat changes.

The total number of known fauna species in the country is 4,014. Some of the fauna species (the invertebrate and mono-cellular animal species) have not been studied thoroughly, while the vertebrate species are well studied. (table 10.4)

So far, 6,844 invertebrate species are known, including 4,665 insects, of which 2,295 are butterflies. The number of butterfly species in the country significantly exceeds their numbers in neighbouring countries.

## Table 10.1: Diversity of flora

| Vegetation | Number of known taxa |
|---|---|
| **Total** | **3,701** |
| Algae *(Algae)* | |
| Bluegreen algae (Cyanophyta) | 220 |
| Silicate algae *(Bacillarophyta)* | 450 |
| Total | 670 |
| Higher plants *(Cormophyta)* | |
| Lycopodium plants *(Lycopsida)* | 6 |
| *(Sphenopsida)* | 13 |
| *(Filicinae)* | 60 |
| *(Coniferophyta)* | 22 |
| *(Dicotyledonae)* | 1,630 |
| other | 1,300 |
| Total | 3,031 |

*Source*: The Ministry of Environment and Physical Planning, 2002.

## Table 10.2: Endemic and relict types of plants

| Vegetation | Number of known types | Note |
|---|---|---|
| Total | 89 | |
| Endemic | 61 | Illyrian, Scardopinian and Mezian endemites included |
| Relicts | 28 | Boreal relicts included |

*Source*: The Ministry of Environment and Physical Planning, 2002.

## Table 10.3: Number of fungi

| Fungi | Number of known types | Note |
|---|---|---|
| Total | 1,500 | |
| Fungi *(Mycophyta)* | 1,400 | Basidiomycetes |
| | 100 | Ascomycetes |

*Source*: The Ministry of Environment and Physical Planning, 2002.

Economically, the most important endemic fish species are the Ohrid trout (*Salmo letnica*), the Ohrid bleak (*Alburnus alburnus alborella*), and the Dojran roach *(Rutilus rutilus dojranensis)*. Of the amphibian and reptile species, 24 per cent are endemic. There are three endemic mammal species. These are the Balkan mole (*Talpa stankovici*), the Balkan pine vole (*Microtus felteni*), and the Balkan short-tailed mouse (*Mus macedonica*).

There are 425 protected vertebrate taxa, of which 133 (26 per cent) have "endangered" status, i.e. strictly protected species.

## 10.2   Protected Areas

The country's protected areas are classified into six categories according to the criteria of the World Conservation Union (IUCN) and the Law on the Protection of Rare Species (adopted in 1973). The protected area network covers 184,137 ha (7.16 per cent) of the territory (table 10.5).

The National Parks are Mavrovo (73,088 ha) (see box 10.1), Galicica (22,750 ha) and Pelister (12,500 ha). The strict natural reserves are Ezerani (2,080 ha) and Tikves (10,650 ha). The natural monuments are Lake Ohrid (23,000 ha), Demir Kapija (200 ha), Arboretum Gazi Baba (3.3 ha), Lake Dojran (2,730 ha), Ostrovo Gazi Baba (13 ha), Gol Covek (5 ha), Lake Prespa (17,680 ha), Matka Canyon (5 443 ha), Katlanovo area (5,442 ha), Markovi Kuli (23,400 ha), Monospitovo Blato (250 ha), Drenak Canyon (5 ha), Karsi Bavci (10 ha), Murite (10 ha), Konce (0.7ha) and Morodvis (0.5 ha).

The other protected areas with special natural characteristics are Leskoec (300 ha), Vodno (1,953 ha) and Kozle (85 ha). There are 14 natural habitat localities (2,465 ha) with protected species of dendroflora (pine, fir, spruce, yew, juniper, oak, beech, birch, wild chestnut tree, plane tree).

There are two aquatic ecosystems in the former Yugoslav Republic of Macedonia on the international lists of the protected world natural heritage. These are Lake Prespa (18,920 ha), which is a Ramsar site, and Lake Ohrid (38 000 ha), which is a UNESCO World Heritage site.

## Table 10.4: Diversity of fauna

| Fauna | Number of taxa |
|---|---|
| **Total** | 4,014 |
| Invertebrates *(Invertebrate)* | |
| Worms *(Annelids)* | 130 |
| Molluscs *(Mollusca)* | 208 |
| Crabs *(Crustacea)* | 277 |
| Insects *(Insecta)* | 2,888 |
| Total | 3,503 |
| Vertebrates *(Vertebrata)* | |
| Fish *(Pisces)* | 58 |
| Amphibians *(Amphibia)* | 21 |
| Reptiles *(Reptilia)* | 37 |
| Birds *(Aves)* | 311 |
| Mammals *(Mammalia)* | 84 |
| Total | 511 |

*Source*: The Ministry of Environment and Physical Planning, 2002.

## 10.3 Pressures on Nature

### Agriculture

Agricultural impact on nature does not differ from that in other European countries. Agricultural land occupies about 50 per cent of the territory; it has spread due to natural conditions. Irrigation, drainage, the reclamation of swamps, terracing, and grazing by livestock took place in the past century, but no exceptional events have been reported in recent years. The use of pesticides and fertilizers has decreased in the past decade due to economic problems, so industry and traffic are the main sources of soil and water pollution. (see Chapter 9 on Agriculture and forest management)

### Forestry

Data on the forest area vary. According to the Spatial Plan of the former Yugoslav Republic of Macedonia (1996), forests and forest plantations cover 934,128 ha or 36.7 per cent of the total area. According to the Ministry of Agriculture, Forestry and Water Economy, the forest area included in the management plan accounts for 998,054 ha. Most of the forests are State-owned (82.9 per cent), and used for timber production. (table 10.6)

The first forest inventory was carried out after the Second World War. The first forest management studies date back to 1961. Since then, forests have been managed on the basis of ten-year management plans. Although the forest area has increased in recent decades (table 10.8), the timber stock per hectare has decreased (from a reported 350-550 $m^3$/ha to 43-179 $m^3$/ha). This is indicative of a deterioration in forest quality, due to either poor management practice or habitat degradation, or both.

The maximum annual cut is 1,118,000 $m^3$, or 56.8 per cent of the annual increment. The share of timber cut in State-owned forests was 90.52 per cent (against 9.48 per cent in private forests). Deciduous tree species make up 93.5 per cent of the annual cut (conifer species 6.5 per cent). Economic problems have led to illegal forest cutting, amounting, in 1996, to 7,868 $m^3$ or less than 1 per cent of the average annual cut.

During the recent dry periods (1984-1994 and 1995-2000), there were about 500 fires with an average burnt area of 800 ha. The annual cost of direct and indirect damage was about €75,000.

---

**Box 10.1:    The Mavrovo National Park**

The total park area is 73,088 ha (about 40,000 ha of pastureland and about 33,000 of the forestland). There are three zones within the park: (1) tourist/recreational (36,088 ha), (2) melioration (32,000 ha), and (3) strictly protected (5,000 ha). Economic activities are allowed in the melioration zone (forestry, hunting, livestock grazing, and fishing), according to their respective 10-year management plans. Fishing is managed by the public water management company, under a long-term contract, and according to the Law on Fishery. A public pastureland company manages the grassland, also according to a long-term contract.

There are 32 inhabited settlements within the park area. The population is mainly occupied in livestock-breeding and seasonal work.

The only income of the Mavrovo National Park comes from the sale of timber. The park's total stock amounts to about 5 million $m^3$. The annual increment is about 120,000 $m^3$, of which 15 per cent is cut each year. Therefore, the job structure in the park management follows the typical organization of a forest company.

There are no biologists or other nature protection experts, or tourist guides (interpreters) employed in the park.

The construction of an information centre inside the park has begun, but it is not yet completed due to a lack of financing.

**Table 10.5: Biodiversity in the protected areas**

| Protected area category | Area (ha) | Number of protected species | Note |
|---|---|---|---|
| Strict natural Reserves | 12,730 | 61 | Water birds |
| (IUCN cat. I) | | 22 | Predator birds |
| | | 14 | Other aquatic animals |
| | | 32 | Hairy wild animals |
| | | 24 | Bats |
| | | 13 | Reptiles |
| | | 42 | Plant species |
| National Parks | 108,338 | 134 | Ornitofauna |
| (IUCN cat. II) | | 37 | Hairy animals |
| | | | Fish and amphibians |
| | | 45 | Reptiles |
| | | 16 | Bats |
| | | 27 | Plant species |
| | | 83 | |
| Natural monuments | 58,084 | | Representatives of the above mentioned categories |
| (IUCN cat. III) | | | |
| Other protected regions | 2,338 | | |
| (IUCN cat. IV - VI) | | | |
| Total | 181,490 | | |
| Ramsar region | 18,920 | 62 | Water birds |
| | | 17 | Predator birds |
| | | 34 | Other aquatic animals |
| | | 24 | Bats |
| | | 7 | Reptiles |
| | | 42 | Plant species |
| Regions of world importance | 38,000 | 142 | Aquatic fauna |
| | | 19 | Aquatic flora |
| | | 36 | Coastal vegetation |
| Total | 238,410* | | |

*Source*: The Ministry of Environment and Physical Planning, 2002.
* The data on the areas of the SNR Ezerani, the Ramsar site-Lake Prespa and the region of world importance Lake Ohrid and its coast are included in the category of natural monuments.

**Table 10.6: Types of forests according to ownership and use**

| Forest types | Area | |
|---|---|---|
| | ha | % |
| Economic forests - State-owned | 859,427 | 82.9 |
| Economic forests - privately owned | 106,427 | 10.2 |
| Forests in national parks | 43,589 | 4.2 |
| Protected forests | 17,617 | 1.7 |
| Picking places | 1,101 | 0.1 |
| Other forests for special use | 8,897 | 0.9 |

*Source*: PHARE Multi Country Programme for the Republic of Macedonia, "St. Cyril and Methodius" University, Faculty of Forestry. Skopje, 1996.

*Hunting*

Hunting is an important source of income (no data on revenue were available). There are 249 hunting grounds; four of them are State-owned (Lesnica, Polaki, Trubarevo and Jasen). All the others are leased by bidding, based on the four application criteria for bidders, who must:

- Be registered for hunting activities;
- Have 10-year developmental programmes;
- Prove their material status and viability (maintenance of feeding and salt-lick places, cottages for hunters, weapons, equipment, vehicles, communication equipment); and
- Employ a forest engineer or a forest technician.

The Government appoints a committee for proposals and evaluation. It consists of five members; three are from the Ministry of Agriculture, Forestry and Water Economy and one each from the Ministry of Finance and the Ministry of Justice.

There are 48 big and small game species (15 mammal and 33 bird species). The game of special economic interest includes: deer, chamois, wild boar, wild rabbit, partridge and pheasant. Introduced species are fallow deer and mouflon. Poaching is not a serious problem.

*Urbanization*

The increasing trend toward greater urbanization is also impacting negatively on biodiversity and nature management. There is no zoning of endangered habitats outside protected areas. (see Chapter 12 on Spatial Planning)

## 10.4 Responsible institutions, policy objectives, and legal framework

*Responsible institutions*

The responsibility for nature and biodiversity management is shared between the Ministry of Environment and Physical Planning and the Ministry of Agriculture, Forestry and Water Economy.

Ministry of Environment and Physical Planning

Nature and biodiversity management is under the responsibility of the Environment Office. Among other tasks, the Office is responsible for:

- The provision of guidelines for the purpose of developing spatial and urban plans for the sustainable exploitation of natural resources and the protection of the natural heritage;

- Strategies for the application of environmental parameters aimed at sustainable use and the protection of biological and geological diversity;

- The identification of ecological areas for ecological production;

- Geological issues; and

- Monitoring, implementing and specifying the instruments for the acceptable use of biological diversity, participating in the implementation of the strategy for biological diversity, and the enforcement of the relevant national and international legislation.

The Office is divided into four divisions, for biodiversity, protection of rare species, monitoring and environmental impact assessment and laboratory study.

There are no nature conservation units at regional and local authority levels.

There are two inspectorates responsible for nature protection: the Forestry Police of the Ministry of Agriculture, Forestry and Water Economy (for protected areas), and the State Environment Inspectorate of the Ministry of Environment and Physical Planning (in cases of ecological accidents and illegal building). It is not clear which inspectorate is responsible for protected species outside protected areas. However, the Environment Inspectorate lacks staff and equipment, at both national and local levels.

The Minister of Environment and Physical Planning is a member of the Government Commission for Sustainable Development.

Ministry of Agriculture, Forestry and Water Economy

The Ministry of Agriculture, Forestry and Water Economy is responsible for forest management. The State Secretary of Forestry and the Assistant Minister of Forestry hold the highest forestry positions in the Ministry. The Forestry Division has five departments, dealing with:

- Forest inventory and use

- Silviculture and afforestation

- Hunting

- Forest protection and

- Public relations

There are 17 regional forest offices responsible for regional forest administration.

Other government institutions involved

Nature conservation policy is also the task of two Parliamentary Commissions: Commission of Foreign Affairs, and Commission for Environment, Youth and Sport. In addition, in the sphere of nature management, the Ministry of Transport and Communications deals with environmental impact assessment procedures.

## Table 10.7: Forest fund by tree species

| Tree species | Forest fund (on 31. 12. 1994) (ha) | Forests according to ownership (on 31. 12. 1995) | | |
|---|---|---|---|---|
| | | Total | State-owned | Private |
| **Total** | **965,941** | **965,650** | **859,427** | **106,223** |
| Plantations of deciduous trees | 545,047 | 541,730 | 466,475 | 75,255 |
| Beech | 226,016 | 225,766 | 210,832 | 14,537 |
| Oaks (all) | 283,050 | 280,039 | 226,552 | 55,840 |
| Other deciduous hard leaf trees | 31,363 | 31,796 | 25,575 | 6,094 |
| Poplar | 775 | 775 | 486 | 279 |
| Other deciduous soft leaf trees | 3,843 | 3,354 | 3,039 | 315 |
| Unmixed plantations of coniferous trees | 81,905 | 81,673 | 72,242 | 9,431 |
| Spruce | 1,253 | 1,298 | 1,297 | 1 |
| Fir | 3,124 | 3,098 | 2,698 | 400 |
| Black pine | 64,465 | 63,958 | 56,301 | 7,657 |
| White pine | 7,687 | 7,864 | 7,112 | 752 |
| Other with coniferous trees | .. | .. | .. | .. |
| Mixed plantations of deciduous trees | 277,341 | 277,146 | 258,666 | 18,480 |
| Beech, oaks and others | 28,594 | 28,601 | 24,735 | 3,866 |
| Beech and other deciduous trees | 25,412 | 25,826 | 23,033 | 2,793 |
| Oaks and other deciduous trees | 193,522 | 193,594 | 182,240 | 10,354 |
| Oaks and other deciduous trees | 29,813 | 29,125 | 27,658 | 1,467 |
| Other deciduous trees | .. | .. | .. | .. |
| Mixed plantations of coniferous trees | 9,610 | 7,656 | 6,356 | 1,300 |
| Spruce - Fir | 598 | 598 | 598 | .. |
| Black - white pine | 3,410 | 3,260 | 1,960 | .. |
| Other coniferous trees | 5,602 | 3,798 | 3,798 | .. |
| Mixed plantations of deciduous coniferous trees | 52,038 | 57,445 | 55,688 | 1,757 |
| Beech-spruce-fir | 8,169 | 10,055 | 10,055 | .. |
| Black and white pine and other coniferous | 2,932 | 3,832 | 3,815 | 17 |
| Other deciduous and other coniferous | 40,937 | 43,558 | 41,818 | 1,740 |

*Source*: The Ministry of Environment and Physical Planning, 2002.

## Table 10.8: Forest according to ownership

| Census Year | Forest fund ha | State-owned ha | State-owned % | Private ha | Private % |
|---|---|---|---|---|---|
| 1939 | 551,000 | 469,000 | 85.27 | 81,000 | 14.73 |
| 1961 | 888,000 | 817,000 | 92.00 | 71,000 | 8.00 |
| 1993 | 964,000 | 858,000 | 89.00 | 106,000 | 11.00 |
| 1994 | 964,941 | 859,427 | 89.00 | 106,223 | 11.00 |

*Source*: The Ministry of Environment and Physical Planning, 2002.

The National Committee for Biodiversity Conservation was established in 2000 to enforce the development and implementation of the National Biodiversity Strategy. The Committee consists of 20 representatives of scientific institutes and faculties, the Ministry of Agriculture, Forestry and Water Economy, and the Ministry of Foreign Affairs. The Committee has a secretariat, with an executive secretary who comes from the Ministry of Environment and Physical Planning.

The institution responsible for national park management is the "Work Organization National Parks and Hunting Areas," under the responsibility of the Ministry of Agriculture, Forestry and Water Economy. Parliament appoints the park directors, as well as the director of the Organization. The Organization has legal and accounting departments (each of the three National Parks has its own account).

The State Enterprise 'Macedonian Forests' manages the State-owned forests. It has 2600-2800 employees, working in 30 regional forest offices. Reforestation of harvested forest areas is financed from the income of the Enterprise, while afforestation of new areas is financed from the State budget. Private contractors harvest the timber.

There are two inspection bodies in the forestry sector. Forestry activities are supervised by the Forestry Inspectorate, which is responsible for tree selection and marking for harvesting, and approval of cutting. There are 4 inspectors in the Ministry and 14 regional inspectors. The number of inspectors is not sufficient for the whole forest area, which delays the cut approval process. The Forestry Police is responsible for the prevention and control of illegal activities (e.g., illegal felling). Currently, there are 70 Forestry Police.

The Forest Management Institute draws up hunting management plans, in cooperation with the Forestry Faculty. The Ministry of Agriculture, Forestry and Water Economy approves the plans. The Institute is no longer an independent organization, but a unit under the responsibility of the State Enterprise 'Macedonian Forests'.

The Faculty of Natural Sciences, the Faculty of Forestry and the Museum of Nature are the main scientific institutions for biodiversity management and protection. Experts from these institutions are involved in most of the nature conservation projects (the development of the National Biodiversity Strategy and Action Plan, the Red Data Book, biodiversity monitoring, protected area network, etc.).

*Biodiversity Strategy*

The National Biodiversity Strategy was initiated during the drafting of the NEAP in 1996. It should have been completed in 2000, but, due to long bureaucratic procedures for the grant approval, the project was launched only in 2001. A project coordinator has been appointed, and a steering committee established. The steering committee has 13 members, including representatives of the Ministry of Environment and Physical Planning, the Ministry of Finance, the Ministry of Foreign Affairs, the Ministry of Agriculture, Forestry and

Water Economy, the Ministry of Economy, the National Committee on Biological Diversity, the Chamber of Commerce, an NGO, and the Pelister National Park.

*Legislation*

The following laws regulate biodiversity protection and management:

- The 1997 Law on Forests regulates forest and forest land management, protection and inventory. Under this law, national parks and forest reserves are excluded from the commercial forests and are treated as special purpose forests.

- The 1996 Law on the Environment and Nature Protection and Promotion includes nature protection in general environmental issues (i.e. monitoring, reporting), but there are no provisions that regulate species or protected area conservation and management.

- The 1996 Law Proclaiming the Ezerani Ornithological Site a strict nature reserve at the Lake Prespa.

- The 1996 Law Proclaiming the Tikves Ornithological Site a strict nature reserve at the Crna Reka Gorge.

- The 1996 Law on Hunting defines the breeding, protection and hunting of game species, and hunting grounds (these provisions are not harmonized with protected area management regimes).

- The 1980 Law on the Conservation of National Parks.

- The 1977 Law on the Protection of Lakes Ohrid, Prespa and Dojran defines these lakes as nature monuments with special social importance.

- The 1973 Law on the Protection of Rare Species defines rare species, the purpose of their protection, protection organization, and staffing. It lacks provisions on owners' rights and obligations, management and protection regimes.

- The 1965 Law Proclaiming Forest Areas on Pelister Mountain a National Park.

- The 1965 Law Proclaiming Forest Areas around Mavrovo Valley a National Park.

- The 1958 Law Proclaiming Forest Areas on Galicica Mountain a National Park.

Proposals for two new laws on nature protection were completed in 2000 (the first one is on general biodiversity protection, and the other on protected areas). Since they were assessed as not compatible with EU legislation, they were withdrawn.

### International agreements

The former Yugoslav Republic of Macedonia has ratified the following conventions related to biodiversity:

- *The Convention on Biological Diversity* (Rio de Janeiro, 1992), ratified in 1997. The development of the National Biodiversity Strategy and Action Plan is an ongoing project.

- *The Convention on the Conservation of European Wildlife and Natural Habitats* (Bern, 1979), ratified in 1997. The enlargement of the protected area network, from 7.2 to 11.1 per cent of the total territory, is envisaged in the National Biodiversity Strategy and Action Plan.

- *The Convention on Wetlands of International Importance Especially as Waterfowl Habitat* (Ramsar, 1971), ratified in 1997. The conservation programmes for Lake Prespa and other water bodies include the preservation of ornithological sites in wetlands.

- *The Convention on International Trade in Endangered Species of Wild Fauna and Flora* (CITES) *(Washington, 1979),* ratified in 2000. The procedure for issuing licences has been established. Moreover, there is a government decision imposing export licences for endangered species on the national list.

There are several agreements on the conservation or protection of wild species that it has not yet ratified. The exception is the Agreement on the Conservation of African-Eurasian Migratory Waterbirds, which it ratified in 1999.

### Registers, monitoring, databases

The former Yugoslav Republic of Macedonia does not have an information system or a monitoring system for biodiversity. The main sources of biodiversity data are scientific case studies and projects. Since April 2000, the Ornithological Information Centre has been working in the Lake Prespa area (strict nature reserve "Ezerani"). The Centre gathers data from supervisors, local environmental NGOs, and ornithological associations in the Prespa region. It processes and publishes the data in cooperation with the Birds Study and Protection Association.

### Public participation

Local communities are not involved in protected area management. A stronger engagement of environmental NGOs and the establishment of mechanisms for dialogue between municipalities and the central government could improve this. The role of NGOs in public awareness raising and nature protection education (particularly in support of protected areas) needs to be encouraged. (see Chapter 4 on Environmental information and public participation)

## 10.5 Conclusions and Recommendations

Since all national parks are under the responsibility of the Ministry of Agriculture, Forestry and Water Economy, the Ministry of Environment and Physical Planning does not have the most important nature conservation tools. There are three main limiting factors to possible solutions: (1) monetary policy does not allow the recruitment of new employees in the State administration, (2) current forestry staff in national parks management are the only ones with experience, and (3) the only income of national parks is obtained from selling timber from sanitary forest felling. Therefore, as a first step, the only solution is to use the existing capacities and financing scheme.

*Recommendation 10.1:*
*(a) The Government should put the "Work Organization National Parks and Hunting Areas," as well as the Galicica, Mavrovo, and Pelister National Parks, under the responsibility of the Ministry of Environment and Physical Planning, with the existing personnel, equipment and financing.*

*(b) The competent authority should, as soon as possible, develop integrated management plans for the national parks, in cooperation with the Ministry of Agriculture, Forestry and Water Economy, and the Ministry of Finance, with the broad involvement of environmental NGOs and*

*local communities. Adequate financing schemes for the implementation of the management plans should be developed and introduced.*

The Bern Convention (1979) regulates in detail the protection of endangered species, with special emphasis on their habitats. This Convention serves as the basis of European Council and European Union nature conservation policy. EU Directive 92/43/EEC on habitat protection aims at the conservation of wild flora and fauna habitats, by establishing a coherent ecological network of protected areas (Natura 2000). This network is particularly important for the conservation of endangered habitat types or sites of endangered species, and consists of Special Areas of Conservation (SACs). Each country is also obliged to establish the protected areas of regional (European) importance – the Sites of Community Interest (SCIs), on which disturbing animals and habitat degradation are forbidden. The EU member countries are obliged to establish the SCI network by 2004; their total area should be at least 10 per cent of the total territory.

All these obligations also apply to new EU member countries and they are supposed to submit their proposals for protected area systems (Natura 2000) by the date of accession. Other pre-accession countries should join the Emerald protected area network, the programme adjusted to countries in transition, within the framework of the Bern Convention.

By establishing the Ministry of Environment and Physical Planning, by signing up to international conventions on nature conservation, and by developing the Pan-European Biodiversity Strategy (including the Emerald network), the former Yugoslav Republic of Macedonia has taken the most important steps towards meeting the above-mentioned requirements. The main obstacles that currently stand in the way of further progress in nature conservation are non-harmonized legislation, unclear institutional responsibilities, a lack of trained staff and a lack of financing, particularly for protected areas.

*Recommendation 10.2:*
*In the process of harmonizing its legislation with European Union requirements, the Ministry of Environment and Physical Planning should, as soon as possible, prepare a unified law on nature protection*

The current Law on Forests contains provisions on special purpose forests (forests intended for recreation, tourism, science, military activities), and these include the forests in the national parks. Each public institution that carries out silvicultural and forest protection, pays 5 per cent of the income from the timber sold to the State Enterprise "Macedonian Forests". Therefore, the national parks are treated as business companies, although the forest cut in the national parks is sanitary. Additionally, there is no park control over fish populations in lakes, since the Ministry of Agriculture, Forestry and Water Economy is responsible for long-term leasing contracts on fishing in lakes.

*Recommendation 10.3:*
*The Ministry of Agriculture, Forestry and Water Economy and other ministries responsible for the use of natural resources, should harmonize their existing or new legislation with the new unified law on nature protection as well as with nature conservation requirements set by the European Union, and should incorporate the nature conservation measures into the management plans of the natural resources for which they are responsible.*

Sustainable forest management is essential, particularly for the former Yugoslav Republic of Macedonia, where most forests (over 70 per cent) have a protective role. Additionally, decreasing stand quality (standing volume per hectare) over the past 50 years indicates constant forest degradation. A shift from timber-oriented forest management to a multifunctional one is particularly difficult for a country in transition. It is therefore important that both a national forestry strategy and economic instruments should be developed for forest management. In the medium term, forest management plans should be adjusted to forest certification requirements.

*Recommendation 10.4:*
*The Ministry of Agriculture, Forestry and Water Economy should, as soon as possible, develop a national forestry strategy that will ensure sustainable forest management based on internationally recognized principles. The strategy should be developed with the participation of the Ministry of Environment and Physical Planning, scientific institutions, non-governmental organisations (NGOs) and other stakeholders. The strategy should also include economic instruments that would facilitate introduction of sustainable forest management practices.*

# PART III: ECONOMIC AND SECTORAL INTEGRATION

*Chapter 11*

# INDUSTRY, ENERGY AND THE ENVIRONMENT

The situation in the former Yugoslav Republic of Macedonia reflects the legacy shared by many countries of industrial and energy-related activity implemented without due regard for the environment. However, the former Yugoslav Republic of Macedonia has now embarked on the path of environmental protection and clean-up, with significant implications for the industrial and energy sectors – two of the largest contributors to the current state of the environment.

## 11.1 Current Situation in Industry and Energy

The security crisis in February 2001 had a highly detrimental impact on the country both economically and socially. Following a generally favourable 2000, economic activity slowed down markedly during the first three quarters of 2001 due to the disruption of production and export markets and a sharp deterioration in consumer and business confidence. During this period real GDP declined by nearly 6 per cent compared to the same period in 2000. The contraction of output was broad-based and affected most sectors of the economy. Industrial output fell by 8.8 per cent in the first half of 2001 compared to the same period in 2000. Industrial production trends are shown in table 11.1.

**Table 11.1: Industrial production**

annual % change

| 1995 | 1996 | 1997 | 1998 | 1999 | 2000 |
|------|------|------|------|------|------|
| -11.0 | 3.2 | 1.5 | 4.5 | -2.6 | 3.5 |

*Source*: State Statistical Office of Macedonia, 2001.

Industry, including mining, is the main sector of the national economy, contributing 35.8 per cent to GDP in 1990 and 26.4 per cent in 2000. Table I.3 highlights the major economic activities by sector as a percentage of GDP.

*Structure of Industry*

According to the Labour Force Survey, the average number of employees in industry, including mining, in 2000 was approximately 114,400, equivalent to 37 per cent of the total workforce. This compares with 206,200 in 1990, which was equivalent to 41 per cent of the total workforce.

Most industrial plants were built in the 1960s and 1970s, and more than 80 per cent of the sector's equipment is economically and physically obsolete. The energy sector has similar features, notably a lack of modern power-generation technologies resulting in increased environmental pollution. When the former Yugoslav Republic of Macedonia entered its transition period, the industrial sector was characterized by stagnant production, a high level of technological depreciation, high import dependency, inadequate and uncompetitive export capacity, a long-term lack of investments, operational losses, high over-employment and a low level of profitability. Industrial production declined drastically, with a fall of more than 50 per cent in the period from 1989 to 1997. The Chamber of Commerce estimates that the industrial sector is currently operating on average at 50 per cent of capacity. The revival of the industrial sector is a key factor in the country's economic prospects.

In 2000, industry was responsible for 33 per cent of total final energy consumption and transport accounted for 23 per cent, with households, commerce, public authorities and agriculture responsible for the remaining 44 per cent. Of the consumption by industry, the iron and steel sector was responsible for 32 per cent, glass, pottery and building materials for 21 per cent, non-ferrous metallurgy for 16.5 per cent, and food, drink and tobacco for 15 per cent. It is estimated that in 2000, six large industrial companies (Toplifikacija AD, Fenimak, HEK Jugohrom, ESM, OKTA and Makstil) consumed around 33 per cent of total energy, 40 per cent of total oil and 80 per cent of total electricity (these figures also include transport and other services and commerce).

During the period from 1989 to 1993, industry was the major consumer of electricity, with 60 per cent of total consumption. However, in 2000 this had fallen to 30 per cent, half of which was consumed by the iron and steel sector. Owing to its affordability, the consumption of electricity by households has increased and in 2000 they consumed just over 50 per cent of the total electricity generated.

### *Structure of the Energy Sector*

The energy sector is highly polluting and is in critical need of modernization. The ongoing transition process towards a free-market economy has created the need for more effective, energy-efficient technologies.

The basic energy infrastructure comprises: coal mines, a crude oil refinery, a gas pipeline network, thermal and hydropower plants (their characteristics are provided in tables 11.2 and 11.3 respectively), electricity transmission and distribution networks, district heating systems, geothermal systems and firewood. Much of this energy infrastructure will have reached (or be nearing) the end of its economic life by 2020, which predicates decisions on major reconstruction and revitalization in the short term.

The primary energy balance (see table 11.4) highlights the limited indigenous energy resources: low-quality coal (lignite), hydropower, biomass and wood, and geothermal energy. Lignite plays a key role being used for 80 per cent of primary indigenous energy production; however, there are significant environmental problems associated with its production and combustion.

The coal mines can be divided into two separate categories: those that are vertically integrated with power plants and those with smaller capacities supplying industry and households directly. The key mines are Suvodol, Oslomej, Brik Berovo and Piskupstina, which at current exploitation rates will be depleted by around 2014, 2012, 2021 and 2021, respectively. Options for extending the future supply of lignite are currently being explored.

Total available electricity in 2000 was 6619.6 GWh, of which 78 per cent was generated by thermal power plants, 18 per cent by hydropower and 4 per cent was imported. The country is extremely reliant on one State-owned lignite-fired power plant, REK Bitola, which generates over 65 per cent of total electricity. The generation, transmission and distribution of electricity are the responsibility of the vertically integrated public enterprise for electricity, JP Elektrostopanstvo na Makedonija (ESM). All the lignite mines supplying lignite for electricity generation are also part of ESM and are State-owned.

Taking into consideration the current adverse economic circumstances, ESM is achieving considerable results. However, it also faces severe problems including the non-payment of invoiced electricity, a lack of financial resources for the rehabilitation and modernization of existing technologies and infrastructure, high system losses, high operating costs and its unattractiveness to foreign investors. To address these problems, the process of transformation and privatization has begun with financial assistance from Germany.

Until 1991 the power system was an integral part of the European power transmission system. ESM is a member of the Union for the Co-ordination of Transmission of Electricity (UCTE), which facilitates bulk power exchange between its members. However, today the power system is isolated from the main part of the UCTE network and is connected only with neighbouring systems in the Balkans.

### Table 11.2: Characteristics of thermal power plants

| Plant | Capacity (MW) | Net annual production (GWh) | Year of installation | Hours of operation in 2000 | Main fuel | Energy value of fuel (kj/kg) |
|---|---|---|---|---|---|---|
| Bitola I | 225 | 376.8 | 1982 | 7,480 | Lignite | 7,908 |
| Bitola II | 225 | 43.2 | 1984 | 7,867 | Lignite | 7,908 |
| Bitola III | 225 | 31.4 | 1988 | 8,100 | Lignite | 7,908 |
| Oslomej | 125 | 178.2 | 1980 | 4,580 | Lignite | 7,667 |
| Negotino | 210 | 128.3 | 1978 | 45 | Oil | 40,190 |
| **TOTAL** | **1,010.0** | **5,159.0** | | | | |

*Source*: ESM. The Electric Power Company of Macedonia. 2000 Annual Report. Skopje, 2001.

## Table 11.3: Characteristics of hydropower plants

| Plant | Net annual production (GWh) | Year of installation/ rehab | Plant type |
|---|---|---|---|
| Vrutok | 376.8 | 1957/1973 | Reservoir |
| Raven | 43.2 | 1959/1973 | Run of river |
| Vrben | 31.4 | 1959 | Run of river |
| Globocica | 178.2 | 1965 | Reservoir |
| Tikves | 128.3 | 1968/1981 | Reservoir |
| Spilje | 289.9 | 1970 | Reservoir |
| Small HPPs | 122.2 | 1938-1993 | River/Reservoir |
| Kozjak* | | Under construction | Reservoir |
| **TOTAL** | **1,170.0** | | |

*Source*: ESM. The Electric Power Company of Macedonia. 2000 Annual Report. Skopje, 2001.

There are currently no nuclear energy facilities. Studies undertaken for the Government by the Academy of Sciences and Arts on electricity system expansion planning to 2030 indicate that the introduction of a 600 MW nuclear power plant may be necessary post-2020.

As at July 2001, out of the total US$ 596 million lent to the former Yugoslav Republic of Macedonia by the World Bank since 1993, US$ 35 million had been allocated to the electric power and energy sector.

### Electricity Demand Projections

Electricity consumption is expected to double from 6,200 GWh in 1995 to 12,400 GWh in 2020, with an average annual increase of 3.1 per cent.

ESM forecasts that an additional 809 MW of installed capacity will be needed by 2015 to meet projected energy demand, which is equivalent to an increased annual production of 3,300 GWh. ESM has developed a priority list of new projects based on hydro and gas. Its development plan outlines the environmentally beneficial rehabilitation and modernization of the existing production capacity for the period to 2015, including: the rehabilitation of large and small hydropower plants, the rehabilitation of basic equipment and installations at all thermal power plants, together with adaptation to natural gas at all thermal power plants.

### Energy Prices

The Law on Energy stipulates that the prices of electricity, natural gas, heat energy, geothermal energy and oil derivatives are set in accordance with the methodology for the pricing of certain forms of energy adopted in 1998 (Official Gazette No. 43/98). The price structure consists of normalized costs, taxes, contributions and profits.

## Table 11.4: Primary energy balance, 2000

| Energy resources | TJ | % | Total |
|---|---|---|---|
| Production: | | | |
| Lignite | 53,295 | 80 | |
| Biomass (including firewood) | 8,635 | 13 | |
| Hydropower | 4,212 | 6 | |
| Geothermal | 653 | 1 | |
| Sub-total | 66,795 | 100 | 54% |
| Imports: | | | |
| Crude Oil, NGL and feedstock | 33,979 | 60 | |
| Natural gas | 2,227 | 4 | |
| Petroleum products | 15,748 | 28 | |
| Electricity (net import) | 404 | 1 | |
| Biomass | 315 | 1 | |
| Coal and lignite | 1,701 | 3 | |
| Fuels from coal and lignite | 2,213 | 4 | |
| Sub-total: | 56,587 | 100 | 46% |
| **TOTAL** | **123,382** | | **100%** |

*Source*: Statistical Yearbook of Macedonia, 2001.
*Notes*: Import data is provisional. Exports and stock changes excluded.
TJ = tera joules

A third amendment to the Law on Energy has now been drafted to establish an independent energy-pricing regulatory body. The amendment is intended to create local conditions for a more efficient transformation and privatization of the energy sector and the development of the natural gas network in line with European Directives 96/92/EC (internal market in electricity) and 98/30/EC (internal market in natural gas).

Electricity prices charged in 2001, according to category were:

- Industry (total average): 3.08 US cents/kWh
- Large metallurgical industry: 2.1-2.2 cents/kWh
- Households: 3.49 cents/kWh
- Commercial (services and others): 6.25 cents/kWh
- Total average price: 3.67 cents/kWh.

By comparison, in 2000, the average EU price of electricity for industry and households was 5.4 cents/kWh and 12.4 cents/kWh, respectively, and in the United States 4.4 cents/kWh and 8.5 cents/kWh, respectively.

According to officials from the Ministry of Economy, energy prices are not subsidized. However, lower-than-average electricity prices are charged to large energy-intensive industrial customers through special contracts.

There are problems with the payment of electricity and district heating by both industry and households. All households have electricity meters. ESM estimates that 90 per cent of households are able to pay for electricity compared to 20-25 per cent of industry, which reflects the very serious financial state of many major industrial enterprises at this time. HEK Jugohrom, a ferro-alloy producer representing around 60 per cent of ESM industrial customers, is unable to pay for its electricity. In countries that have faced similar situations, such as the Russian Federation and Kazakhstan, highly targeted (in terms of objectives and time lines) temporary subsidies were provided by the Government to a number of very energy-intensive industrial enterprises (in particular metallurgical). The temporary subsidies, which were supplemented by government-approved technical measures for

reducing energy consumption, were granted so as to allow the enterprises to continue to operate during the crucial transition period. These measures were applied only to enterprises that were perceived to be economically viable in the long term.

Following privatization, ESM expects the price of electricity to increase to an average of around 5.4 c/kWh. This price rise would be gradual, i.e. not more than 10 per cent a year. However, such an increase has social implications and the percentage of households unable to pay their electricity bills will rise.

## 11.2 Environmental Considerations in Industry and Energy

*Selected Environmental Concerns in Industry*

The NEAP highlighted the pollution due to industrial sources, with most of the country's key polluting industries clearly located in Skopje. The country's industry-related environmental hot spots are highlighted in Figure 11.1.

In autumn 2000, in collaboration with the national authorities, UNEP undertook an environmental assessment of the former Yugoslav Republic of Macedonia, which found that five industrial sites required urgent attention in order to halt serious risks to public health and the environment. These sites are the HEK Jugohrom ferro-alloy factory, the OHIS AD Chemical Complex, the MHK Zletovo Lead and Zinc Smelter, Zletovo Lead and Zinc Mine and the REK Bitola Thermal Power Plant.

### Environmental Concerns Associated with Radioactivity from Coal and Fly Ash

There is significant concerns over the potential radiation hazard posed by the fly ash dumpsite at REK Bitola, but no scientific data were made available to corroborate this concern. All coals contain trace elements that are naturally radioactive including uranium, thorium and their numerous decay products. Although these elements are less chemically toxic than other coal constituents, such as arsenic, selenium or mercury, they can present a potential risk of radiation. Assessment of this level of radiation is critically dependent on the concentration of radioactive elements in the coal and the fly ash that remains post combustion.

---

**Box 11.1: Selected Environmental Issues at REK Bitola Thermal Power Plant, Bitola**

REK Bitola is a 27-year-old vertically integrated lignite-fired power plant, comprising three units of 225 MW each. The plant generates most of the country's electricity and is of strategic national importance. Lignite is supplied from the adjacent Suvodol lignite mine (some 7.2 Mt in 2001). Approximately 700 workers are employed at the power plant and 1,400 at the mine. The plant and mine, which operate 365 days a year, are located around 12 km from Bitola, the country's second largest city with a population of over 75,000.

Each unit has an electrostatic precipitator (ESP), but there is no flue gas desulphurization system. The low-grade indigenous lignite has a low sulphur content of 0.6 per cent and an ash content of around 13 per cent, a combination which results in a high fly ash resistivity. This impacts the ESPs, which are not able to perform at design efficiency and also appear to be beyond their effective life. Around 1-1.5 million tons of fly ash and 70,000 to 150,000 tons of slag are produced annually. In 2000, the German company Pentol GmbH put forward a proposal to install a flue gas conditioning system that would have resulted in a 95 per cent reduction in solid emissions. The estimated cost was €700,000, for which international funding would be required. None, however, has been obtained to date.

The fly ash and slag, containing silicate and heavy metals, including uranium compounds, are dumped in an open field 4-5 km from the plant. Once a week 50 cm of soil is placed over the top of the spoil pile in order to mitigate wind erosion. However, significant areas of fly ash are always left uncovered, allowing air pollution from dust containing heavy metals and uranium compounds to occur. Similar contamination of the soil and groundwater can be assumed to occur, with concern for the quality of water draining into the nearby river, which supplies local villages with drinking and irrigation water. No specific data were available regarding this pollution, as the plant does not monitor it.

The recycling of bottom ash or slag was carried out for a number of years. A separation plant was installed and the recycled bottom ash was transported to Skopje for use in the USJE cement factory. However, when in 1998 USJE was purchased by the Greek Titan Cement Company, the use of Bitola recycled bottom ash ceased due to Titan's sourcing its raw material from alternative suppliers. The separation plant has not operated since then and the bottom ash is dumped together with the fly ash. An internal proposal has been put to senior ESM management to restart the separation plant for the production of briquettes for use in the power plant.

The power plant management is aware of the pollution problems associated with the fly ash dumpsite and is undertaking an industrial trial to reduce air pollution, which involves spraying a chemical on the fly ash before it reaches the conveyor belt prior to transport to the dumpsite. A proposal is also being considered to dispose of all the fly ash generated during the future expected life of the power plant, to 2015, which would be funded by ESM. In cooperation with the Ministry of Environment and Physical Planning over 100,000 acacia trees have been planted in the vicinity of the dumpsite to mitigate dust emissions.

There is no waste-water treatment plant, so untreated process waste water containing dissolved oil compounds and heavy metals is being discharged directly into the river via an open canal – a further source of possible soil, groundwater and drinking water contamination. Again, this situation is not being monitored.

Air quality is monitored at the stack and at three sites located a few kilometres away. The emission levels of $SO_2$, NOx and dust in 2001, together with the national and EU emission limits are shown in Figure 11.2. Average $SO_2$ emissions are more than four times the permissible limit set by the Government. The potential problem of acid rain is not being monitored. Additionally, the plant has not started to implement environmental management systems and has no concrete plans to do so in the near future.

---

Radioactive elements from coal and fly ash impact the population only when they are dispersed into the air or water or are included in products that contain fly ash, such as building materials. At REK Bitola there is clear evidence of airborne emissions of fly ash and groundwater contamination, hence of a potential radiation hazard, which merits urgent further formal investigation.

### Chemicals and Persistent Organic Pollutants (POPs)

Environmental pollution from chemical waste, including POPs, is acknowledged to be a problem, but to what degree is not yet clear. The industrial and energy sectors are key contributors to this pollution. It is estimated that at least 6 Mt of 'cinder' waste, containing manganese, chromium and heavy metal ions, have been produced by the metallurgical sector. Waste from the mining sector is estimated to be at least 150 Mt containing lead, cadmium, zinc and copper ions and organic substances from flotation reagents. OHIS AD is the largest producer of chemically contaminated waste producing 4 Mt a day.

There is also a significant environmental problem with POPs in the electricity distribution network. ESM currently uses over 6,000 capacitors or condenser batteries in its distribution network, of which 300 are large. Half of these capacitors are not operating because they are defective – although their recommended operating life is only 7-10 years, their average age is 20 years. The capacitors pose a significant environmental hazard as their cooling fluids contain polychlorinated biphenyls (PCBs). PCBs are one of the key 12 POPs under the Stockholm Convention. The use and production of PCBs was prohibited in Japan in 1992, in the United States in 1977, in Germany in 1983 and in France in 1987. A report by ESM in 2001

concluded that all the capacitors need replacing at an estimated cost of €168,700. However, this amount does not include the costs associated with the transport and permanent disposal or storage of the present capacitors. Replacement of the capacitors was one of three projects proposed by ESM for potential Swiss funding.

---

**Box 11.2:    Selected Environmental Issues at HEK Jugohrom Ferro-Alloy Plant, Jegunovce**

HEK Jugohrom was established by the Government in 1952 as the country's sole producer of chromium minerals and ferro-alloys. Employing almost 2,000 workers and with an annual production capacity of around 69,000 tons, it is currently reported to be operating at or below 80 per cent of capacity and at a financial loss (net loss in 1999 of Euro 14,916,941 .After privatization Jugohrom became an independent legal entity – 11 per cent is owned by individual shareholders and the remaining 89 per cent is up for sale.

The uncontrolled disposal of waste material from the plant and the improper handling of material containing chromium salts have led to severe chromium contamination of groundwater and soil, including in the vicinity of the River Vardar. In 1982 the plant began monitoring soil and groundwater and the data confirmed contamination of the water by chromium. To address this problem the plant designed, installed and financed a groundwater abstraction system, which resulted in the concentrations of $Cr^{6+}$ decreasing by 200-800 mg/l to total contamination levels of 5-15 mg/l. The plant's target is 1 mg/l (for comparison the target and intervention levels in the Netherlands are 0.001 mg/l and 0.03 mg/l) – if this is to be achieved remediation measures will need to be stepped up. Chromium production ceased in 1993 and the shed where chromium was produced and used has neither been cleared of chromium nor secured.

Significant air pollution from the stacks, notably an estimated 9,000 to 17,000 tons of dust and fly ash a year, is due to the plant's electric furnaces operating without any form of gas cleaning. A project to reduce these emissions and recycle energy from a number of the furnaces has been proposed by the plant management, but requires funding. According to the NEAP, total dust, black smoke and particle-borne chromium standards have been breached in the past years in the vicinity of the plant. Lack of data makes it impossible to assess any health impacts on workers.

HEK Jugohrom plans to undertake three remedial activities under the direction of the Ministry of Environment and Physical Planning with EU funding. The measures include keeping the bottom of the dumpsite drier, installing a drainage system to catch leachate and divert it to the waste treatment plant and further recultivating the dumpsite to abate rainwater infiltration.

---

**Box 11.3:    Selected Environmental Issues at OHIS AD Chemical Complex, Skopje**

OHIS AD has been in operation since 1964 and was one of the country's largest industrial producers manufacturing a range of chemical products and employing around 3,900 workers. It is a currently classified as a joint-stock company – around 48 per cent of the company is privately owned by individual shareholders.

According to the UNEP August 2001 'Feasibility Study for Urgent Risk Reduction Measures at Hot Spots in the former Yugoslav Republic of Macedonia' at least four locations at the chemical complex pose unacceptable risks to human health and require urgent environmental clean-up. In the now-closed lindane plant, dermal and inhalation contact with lindane (and other HCH isomers) contaminated soil, air, water and floors are possible. The use of lindane has been banned in a number of European countries since 1974-1978. For over 20 years, approximately 10,000 tons of a technical mixture of HCH isomers (hazardous chlorinated organic chemicals) have been stored on-site in several uncovered concrete basins leading to air, soil and groundwater pollution. There is a perceptible risk of inhaling HCH contamination at this waste dump. The former electrolysis plant used mercury and both dermal and inhalation contact with mercury contamination are possible from the soil, walls, air, floors and equipment. The large quantities of other improperly stored hazardous materials, including eight tons of mercury, pose the risk of contaminant inhalation and soil and groundwater contamination. OHIS AD has resorted to this on-site waste dump in the absence of a proper national industrial and hazardous waste treatment facility (see Chapter 8 on Waste management). At all of these sites contamination has already leached into the groundwater or may do so. UNEP outlined a number of remedial options for each of the sites.

A further environmental problem at the complex is caused by the fact that the waste-water treatment plant, which was built in the 1980s, is not currently operating so that untreated water from the plant is being discharged directly into the River Vardar. The plant reportedly used two tons of mercury a year and mercury-laden waste water was allowed to drain directly into the river. In 2000, the Enviro Group undertook a feasibility study for the rehabilitation of the waste-water treatment system. USAID has been approached to fund the US$ 4 million rehabilitation, but according to OHIS no progress has been made.

# Figure 11.1: Industrial Environmental Polluters and Hot Spots

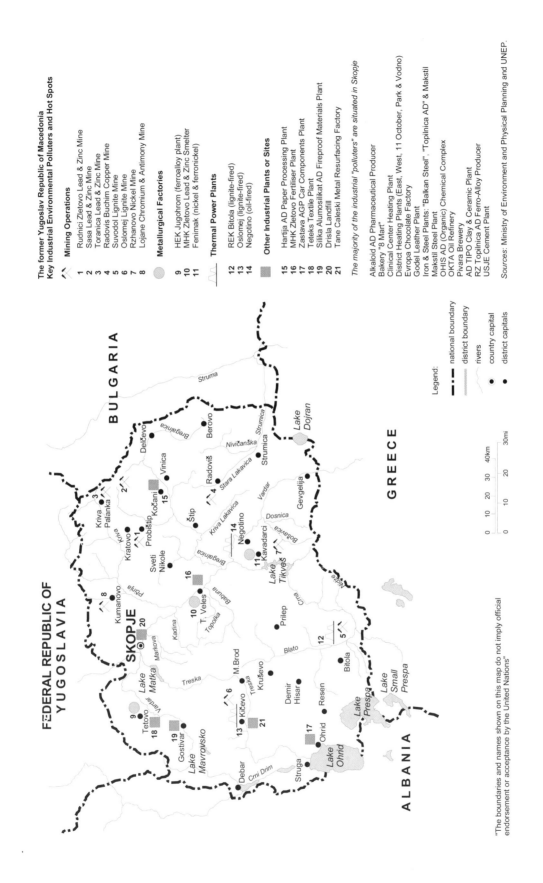

**The former Yugoslav Republic of Macedonia**
**Key Industrial Environmental Polluters and Hot Spots**

**Mining Operations**

1  Rudnici Zletovo Lead & Zinc Mine
2  Sasa Lead & Zinc Mine
3  Toranica Lead & Zinc Mine
4  Radovis Buchim Copper Mine
5  Suvodol Lignite Mine
6  Oslomej Lignite Mine
7  Rzhanovo Nickel Mine
8  Lojane Chromium & Antimony Mine

**Metallurgical Factories**

9  HEK Jugohrom (ferroalloy plant)
10  MHK Zletovo Lead & Zinc Smelter
11  Fenimak (nickel & ferronickel)

**Thermal Power Plants**

12  REK Bitola (lignite-fired)
13  Oslomej (lignite-fired)
14  Negotino (oil-fired)

**Other Industrial Plants or Sites**

15  Hartija AD Paper Processing Plant
16  MHK Zletovo Fertiliser Plant
17  Zastava AGP Car Components Plant
18  Teteks Textile Plant
19  Silika Alumosilikat AD Fireproof Materials Plant
20  Drisla Landfill
21  Tane Caleski Metal Resurfacing Factory

*The majority of the industrial "polluters" are situated in Skopje*

Alkaloid AD Pharmaceutical Producer
Bakery "8 Mart"
Clinical Center Heating Plant
District Heating Plants (East, West, 11 October, Park & Vodno)
Evropa Chocolate Factory
Godel Leather Plant
Iron & Steel Plants: "Balkan Steel", "Toplinica AD" & Makstil
Makstil Steel Plant
OHIS AD (Organic) Chemical Complex
OKTA Oil Refinery
Pivara Brewery
AD TIPO Clay & Ceramic Plant
RZ Toplinica AD Ferro-Alloy Producer
USJE Cement Plant

*Sources: Ministry of Environment and Physical Planning and UNEP.*

Legend:
— · — · national boundary
——— district boundary
rivers
● country capital
● district capitals

"The boundaries and names shown on this map do not imply official
endorsement or acceptance by the United Nations"

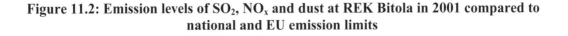

**Figure 11.2: Emission levels of SO₂, NOₓ and dust at REK Bitola in 2001 compared to national and EU emission limits**

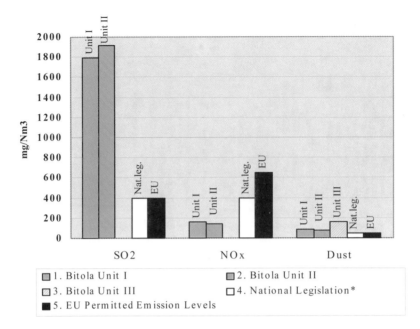

*Source*: REK Bitola as reported to the Ministry of Environment and Physical Planning.

NB Emissions of SO₂ and NOₓ are not measured (nm) for Unit III.

*Book of regulations for maxium permitted concentrations and quantities of harmful substances "Official Gazette No 3/1990".

Air pollution emissions, notably SO₂, have been reduced as a result of a joint project with the Ministry of Environment and Physical Planning to switch the on-site power plant from oil to gas. Plans for additional cleaner production projects, for which details were not available, are reported to be progressing.

*Selected Environmental Considerations in the Energy Sector*

The energy sector is responsible for 80 per cent of current greenhouse gas emissions, the remainder being shared equally by industrial processes, waste and agriculture. Within the energy sector, power generation represents some 73 per cent of these emissions due to the dominance of lignite as an energy resource.

*Lignite.* The use of lignite for electricity production in the former Yugoslav Republic of Macedonia has serious environmental impacts, particularly in terms of emissions of SO₂ and particulates. However, lignite is the most dominant domestic energy resource and its continued use is critical to present economic activity and social well-being. Close attention needs to be given to the future environmental management of emissions from the

lignite-fired power plants, particularly with regard to SO₂, NOₓ and particulate matter. Soil and groundwater pollution also occurs during the lignite extraction process.

*Oil.* With no indigenous reserves, the country is dependent on imported oil. Crude oil is imported by rail from Thessaloniki to the OKTA refinery in Skopje, with transport a larger cost component of the final product than refining. EBRD has lent US$ 50 million towards the construction of a new 221 km oil pipeline, linking Thessaloniki to Skopje, which commenced in 1999. The pipeline, which will carry up to 2.5 million tons (Mt) of crude oil per year, will provide a cheaper and more environmentally sound alternative to the current road and rail transport. The course of the new pipeline also dramatically reduces the risk of an oil spill into the River Vardar. Furthermore, the equipment at the OKTA refinery will require modernizing if it is to manufacture products that meet the new environmental legislation on the production of unleaded petrol and for lowering the sulphur content in diesel fuel. (see Chapter 13 on Transport and the environment)

The Albanian-Macedonian-Bulgarian Oil Pipeline Corporation (AMBO) also plans to develop a 910 km long pipeline, with an annual capacity of 40 Mt of crude oil, from the port of Burgas (Bulgaria) through Bulgaria, the former Yugoslav Republic of Macedonia and Albania to the port of Vlore. Such an extensive and high-capacity development raises the risk of environmental damage from any oil spillage, especially because the current pipeline routing will follow the roads and railways and run relatively close to the northwestern perimeter of Lake Ohrid.

*Gas.* As with oil, there are no domestic gas reserves. An 800 million m$^3$/year natural gas pipeline from Ukraine through Bulgaria to Skopje was completed in 1995. The State-owned GAMA controls the supply, transport and distribution of gas. The pipeline does not operate at full capacity due to the current economic situation. The market for natural gas is only 250 to 300 million m$^3$/year.

The increasing use of natural gas (fuel switching and to meet increasing energy demand) entails significant environmental benefits and long-term plans to achieve this include:

- A gas-fired cogeneration power plant in Skopje (2005);
- Two combined cycle gas-fired plants in Skopje (2010/2013);
- The construction of a pipeline to the currently oil-fired Negotino power plant;
- A supply to industrial cities between Skopje and Negotino;
- The interconnection of existing pipelines to enable the formation of a regional network; and
- The reopening of the existing Kosovo pipeline and the construction of a second pipeline after 2020.

One industrial plant (Zelezara) transferred ownership of its oil-fired cogeneration plant to ESM to settle non-paid invoices. ESM intends to convert this plant into a combined cycle gas combined heat and power plant (180-200 MW$_e$/150 MW$_t$) as an independent power producer project. An environmental assessment carried out in 1999 by the Japan Consulting Institute indicated significant environmental improvements would be achieved through annual emission reductions of: 752,847 tons $CO_2$ (55 per cent reduction), 6,674 tons $SO_2$ (99 per cent reduction) and 2,459 tons $NO_2$ (80 per cent reduction).

## Promotion of Renewable Energy Sources

The Government recognizes the importance of renewable energy in the reduction of negative energy-related environmental impacts.

*Hydro Power.* Only 20 per cent of the country's hydroelectric potential is currently exploited and emphasis has been placed on addressing this situation, particularly in the rehabilitation of existing plants and the construction of new small hydropower plants (HPPs). The bulk of the existing hydro capacity is classified as large hydro, with 22 small HPPs representing 10 per cent of total capacity.

The 1976 Water Resources Master Plan (based on pre-1970 data) estimated the "technically usable" annual electric power potential of the rivers as 6,520 GWh; however, there has been no review of this estimation to reflect more recent river flow data. The draft energy sector strategy plan estimates that this power potential is only around 5,020 GWh annually and if the additional potential of mini hydro is included this rises to about 5,460 GWh annually, still 16 per cent less than the 1976 Master Plan.

The existing plants are all in need of rehabilitation, some urgently. Rehabilitation of the six large HPPs is planned by ESM with the help of World Bank and Swiss Government aid and there is currently a tender for the rehabilitation-operation-transfer (ROT) of seven small HPPs.

The development of small HPPs is being actively pursued on a concession basis. Compared to large HPPs they have a small environmental impact and are cheaper to build (larger plants would require foreign investment). From an original list of some 80 small HPP projects, 40 licences have recently been issued and are now under review with the final decision resting with the Ministry of Environment and Physical Planning. An environmental assessment may be undertaken on each project on a voluntary basis, as there is currently no legal requirement for it. Previously there was no consultation with the public even on the potential environmental impact associated with the development of hydropower plants, but there are now plans to include a public consultation process commencing with this current list.

In the water supply, government policy gives use for drinking a legal priority over irrigation and industrial use. However, in mid-2001 during an unusually dry spell there was a water shortage in Prilep and the Government decreed that the supply of water to the strategic REK Bitola power plant for use in the cooling towers should take priority over drinking water for the town. Wells are now being drilled in the locality to ensure a similar situation does not arise again.

*Alternative Energy Sources*

The current use of geothermal, biomass, solar and wind energy resources is not significant. The Ministry of Economy as part of its policy to promote renewable energy sources on a concession basis is investigating the potential for future exploitation.

Geothermal energy comprises around 0.5 per cent of the total energy balance. The quantities and temperature of the geothermal energy, however, limit the production of electricity. There are some 15 projects in operation or under development including heating greenhouses, drying agricultural products, space heating and industrial uses. Over 80 per cent of the installed capacity is for heating greenhouses. The sector can be extended by modernizing the technology and re-establishing markets for heat energy.

Wind power is not currently exploited and the scarcity of data makes it difficult to estimate its development potential.

Solar installations offer a promising source of power. The average solar irradiation is 4.2 $KWh/m^2$/day, which is some 30 per cent higher than in a number of European countries. There are only a few photovoltaic systems in the country. ESM has reported that the summer electricity consumption profile has changed with the increased use of air conditioning systems. These daily loads can potentially be closely matched by photovoltaic generation.

Firewood represented almost 11 per cent of indigenous energy production in 1997. The average production of 800,000 $m^3$ a year generates around 8.57 PJ of energy, which is used for residential heating. No increase in this level of consumption is forecast. For financial reasons a number of households continue to use firewood for residential heating despite being connected to the district heating system. It is generally admitted that the unregulated use of firewood is prevalent throughout the country.

District Heating

There are five district heating systems, three in Skopje, one in Bitola and one in Makedonska Kamenica, with the last reportedly not operating for financial reasons. The largest system in Skopje is a modern system privately-owned by Toplifikacija AD and operated on 80 per cent heavy fuel oil (with an annual consumption of 70,000 tons) and 20 per cent natural gas. Some 40,000 households are connected to the State-owned network. During the heating season approximately 725,000 GWh of heat energy is produced. The use of heavy fuel oil leads to significantly increased air pollution in Skopje, particularly in winter. The other two district heating systems are much smaller – one operates on gas and is connected to some 6,000 households and the other operates on heavy fuel oil and is connected to some 2,000 households. It is estimated that some 35 per cent of households in Skopje are connected to district heating systems, of whom around 90-94 per cent are able to pay. There are plans to build new systems, based on heavy fuel oil, in Ohrid, Kavadarci, Kicevo and Stumica.

It is widely acknowledged that in cities and urban areas, district heating is one of the best economically competitive and environmentally friendly alternatives to individual heating from oil or gas, particularly when coupled with the generation of electricity in combined heat and power plants using natural gas.

## 11.3  Selected Areas of Policy Engagement to Mitigate Environmental Impacts

*Cleaner Production*

The increasing role of and plans for the implementation of cleaner production techniques is covered in section 11.4 below.

*Energy Intensity*

The former Yugoslav Republic of Macedonia has a high energy intensity, which can be attributed to a number of factors – industry represents a relatively high share of GDP, a number of industrial sectors are relatively energy-intensive (such as chemicals, metallurgy and cement); the technology used by large and small-scale industry is less energy-efficient than in Western countries; and buildings and houses are poorly insulated. The high energy intensity of existing industry is highlighted by a recent study on future energy, which found that, if HEK Jugohrom and Fenimak were to be closed, no new thermal power plant would be needed until 2006, but if they remained operational the immediate construction of a 270 MW plant would be required.

The high energy intensity offers significant opportunities for energy savings bringing both environmental and economic benefits. Using energy-saving practices results in reduced energy consumption and wastage, thus requiring the production of less energy with a subsequent reduction in potentially polluting emissions. A reduced requirement for natural resources also leads to a decreased environmental impact.

### Energy Efficiency

The former Yugoslav Republic of Macedonia ratified the Energy Charter Treaty and the Protocol on Energy Efficiency and Related Environmental Aspects in September 1998.

There is currently no specific legislation in force on energy efficiency, it is only provided for in the Law on Energy. The NEAP proposed the development of an energy conservation plan, but this has not been introduced. 1988 saw the adoption of the Programme for Savings, Substitution and the Rational Use of all Energy Types up to the Year 2000, which set the framework for the country's energy efficiency policy. Under this Programme more than 100 projects were carried out, which according to the Ministry of Economy resulted in an annual reduction of 8 per cent in total energy consumption. These projects included the development of geothermal energy, solar applications, heat recovery from condensers, the production of briquettes from waste wood and the use of natural gas.

At the end of 1999 the Government passed a new Programme for the Efficient Use of Energy up to the Year 2020, the development of which is mandated by the Law on Energy and therefore falls under the responsibility of the Ministry of Economy. Whilst this programme is a continuation of the previous one, it also includes new elements, of which a key one is the preparation of a strategy for energy efficiency to 2020 and the establishment of an energy efficiency fund. The Ministry of Environment and Physical Planning is actively collaborating in the development of the strategy. Other features of the Programme are legislative and

other incentives (for example import duties and tax deductions for energy efficiency projects); the adoption of a combination of appropriate financial and legislative measures for the promotion of energy efficiency and renewable energy projects; the development of regulations and standards for the efficient use of energy; training and information dissemination; the implementation of projects; international cooperation and the fulfilment of international obligations. Table 11.5 gives the key energy efficiency indicators.

One of the projects proposed under the Southeast European Cooperative Initiative (SECI) was the Skopje Energy Efficiency Demonstration Zone (1998-2000). Costing US$ 7.7 million, the project proposal focused on energy savings and environmental protection through the increased use of photovoltaics and improved district heating systems, in particular in the Skopje Clinical Centre. Due to obsolete equipment and techniques, the Centre's heating system is one of the main polluters in the locality. ESM provided funding for the preparation of the project proposal; however, the project has not been carried out due to the lack of financial support from the Government and foreign donors.

Makstil AD, the country's largest steel producer, received a seven-year US$15 million loan in 1998 from EBRD for modernization, in particular the installation of continuous casting, which will result in reduced dust emissions and improved energy efficiency.

## 11.4 Policy, legislative and institutional framework

### Policy Objectives

One of the main objectives of the Government, in the light of its desire to accede to the European Union, is to harmonize existing and new legislation with that of the EU in accordance with the Stabilization and Association Agreement. This is evident in the studies being undertaken and the policies and strategies planned or being developed in the industrial and energy sector.

An intense industrial privatization programme has been widely implemented. By mid-1999 around 90 per cent of all former "socially owned" enterprises identified for privatization had already changed ownership, mostly through a management employee-buy-out. (see Chapter 3 on Economic instruments and privatization)

**Table 11.5: Main energy efficiency indicators**

| Year | Population (in millions) | GDP (billion US $) | Electricity (TWh) | Energy per capita (kWh/PC) | Energy intensity (kWh/US $) |
|------|------|------|------|------|------|
| 1990 | 2.033 | 4.32 | 5.25 | 2.58 | 1.22 |
| 1995 | 1.966 | 4.17 | 5.80 | 2.95 | 1.39 |
| 1997 | 1.990 | 3.49 | 6.33 | 3.17 | 1.81 |
| 2000 | 1.993 | 4.68 | 6.35 | 3.18 | 1.28 |
| 2010 | 2.024 | 7.16 | 8.33 | 4.11 | 1.16 |
| 2020 | 2.022 | 13.52 | 12.58 | 6.22 | 0.93 |

*Sources* : Black Sea Regional Energy Centre and Economic Chamber of Macedonia, 2002.

The importance of cleaner production in industry to reduce environmental pollution and energy consumption is recognized and policies are being worked out for the adoption of such techniques. There are plans to increase the use of natural gas in industrial processes and for the production of electricity.

The introduction of energy efficiency measures and the development of renewable energy sources are being pursued – both are recognized as tools for reducing negative environmental impacts in the industrial and energy sectors. Activities currently being processed by the Ministry of Economy in this area include: the preparation of a strategy for the complex development of energy for the period to 2020; the preparation of an energy efficiency strategy for the period to 2020; the establishment of a special body to take responsibility for energy efficiency issues; the establishment of a fund for energy efficiency initiatives; the preparation of promotional material to highlight the benefits of rational energy use; and the increased use of renewable energy, in particular biomass and geothermal energy. The underlying policy in the development of the energy sector strategy is reliance on market mechanisms and an acknowledgement that: (i) energy prices should cover operating costs with a margin to fund future investments; (ii) energy companies should not rely on government financing; (iii) energy companies should operate as commercial entities and, where appropriate, be privatized; and (iv) energy conservation should be encouraged through the cost-based pricing of energy and the restructuring of the economy, which should reduce the energy intensity of production. In line with these objectives, plans are under way to privatize ESM and to establish an independent energy-pricing regulatory body (see Energy Prices above). Additional policy goals for the energy sector include the rehabilitation of the existing energy

infrastructure, together with the construction of new capacity and new infrastructure.

The introduction of environmentally sound technologies and practices in industry and energy is encouraged by the Law on Customs and the Law on Profit, which exempt equipment protecting the environment from import duties and offer profit tax deductions for enterprises investing in the protection of the natural environment.

However, energy and energy-related issues do not appear to be high priorities for the Government. Its Public Investment Programme for 2001-2003, for example, includes only eight energy-related projects out of a total of 172 investment projects. Five employees at the Ministry of Economy have to cover all energy issues; in view of the importance of the energy sector this poses a serious problem.

The 1996 NEAP recommended that greater emphasis should be placed on self-monitoring by major industries and called for regulations on self-monitoring to make industries more responsible for their environmental pollution and so reduce the monitoring burden on the State budget. The NEAP also highlighted the compilation of a register of polluters based on data collected from a range of agencies. Due to limited resources, this register is still being finalized and there has been little analysis of the data collected.

*Legal Framework*

An overview of the main relevant legislation is given below:

• *The Law on Energy* (Official Gazette No. 47/97), as amended (Official Gazette Nos. 40/99 and 98/2000) prescribes conditions and measures for the protection of the environment in the energy sector. All forms of energy, including electricity, oil, natural gas, coal and geothermal, are covered by this Law, which also foresees the establishment of an energy efficiency strategy and an energy efficiency fund.

- *The Law on Environment and the Protection and Promotion of Nature.* Article 4 of this Law requires that, when carrying out their activities legal and natural entities should ensure: a rational use of natural resources, investment funds and production programmes for the protection and promotion of the environment, and the continuous monitoring of the environmental impact of their activities. Article 5 stipulates that the law regulates the specific conditions for the protection of the environment and public health. This Law also calls for the establishment of the Environment Fund.

- *The Law on Mineral Raw Material* (Official Gazette No. 18/99) contains a number of provisions for the protection of the environment and nature during the exploitation of mineral resources, including all forms of energy resources.

- *The Law on Waters* regulates the granting of concessions for the use of water as an energy resource.

- *The Law on Communal Works,* amongst other issues, addresses the treatment and delivery of processed water, the disposal and treatment of waste water, the treatment and disposal of industrial solid waste, and the disposal of industrial waste and harmful substances.

Key legislation relevant to foreign natural or legal persons wishing to invest in the energy and industrial sectors includes: the Constitution, notably article 31; the Law on Trade Companies (Official Gazette No. 28/96); the Law on Public Enterprises (Official Gazette No. 38/96); the Law on Concessions (Official Gazette No. 42/93); and the Law on Expropriation (Official Gazette No. 13/95).

A number of laws that will impact on the environmental performance of the industrial and energy sectors are currently in draft form or being drafted, including a law on environmental impact assessment and a law on air quality. Article 36 of the latter encourages the use of best available techniques; however, there appears to be no implementation or activity in this field. The

Environment Fund is responsible for drafting the law on the polluter pays and user pays principles.

A significant omission from current planned legislation is initiatives specifically encouraging the adoption of cleaner production techniques and environmental management systems and standards, such as the ISO 14000 or eco-management and audit schemes (EMAS).

*Institutional Framework*

Industrial and energy activities have wide-ranging environmental impacts, including air, water and soil pollution; land degradation; and the production of solid waste, toxic chemicals and other hazardous materials. For this reason a significant number of institutions are responsible for the environmental management of these two sectors, including: the Ministry of Economy; the Ministry of Environment and Physical Planning; the Ministry of Agriculture, Forestry and Water Economy; the Ministry of Health; the Ministry of Transport and Communications; the Ministry of Labour and Social Policy; and the Institute of Occupational Health.

<u>Ministry of Economy, energy and cleaner production</u>

The Ministry of Economy is the main ministry responsible for industrial and energy issues. It has a number of sectors focusing on industry, such as the Economic Policy, Technical, Technological and Structural Reforms Sector and the International Cooperation Sector. However, the Energy Supply and Resources Sector is solely responsible for energy-related issues, including: the preparation of the energy strategy, the preparation and implementation of the legislative framework and the coordination of international energy activities. Regional authorities, acting under the umbrella of the Ministry of Economy and the Ministry of Environment and Physical Planning, are also involved in industrial and energy activities.

The Ministry of Economy provides specific support for the introduction of cleaner production techniques in industry and energy. Under the Law on Foreign Trade 0.1 per cent of total export/import profit is allocated to a special fund (in 2001 this amounted to around US$ 6-7 million) administered by the Ministry of Economy for: up to 70 per cent financing for companies seeking ISO accreditation; domestic and foreign consultancy for the modernization of industrial techniques and the introduction of new products; and cleaner production and energy-saving projects. If the former Yugoslav Republic of Macedonia were to accede to the World Trade Organization this funding would be restricted. However, the Ministry of Economy indicated that in view of the importance that it attaches to the introduction of cleaner production techniques and training in environmental management in industry it would find money from other sources to continue its activities. There is currently a blurring of responsibilities in relation to cleaner production within the country and there is no collaboration at present with the National Cleaner Production Centre.

### Ministry of Environment and Physical Planning

The Ministry of Environment and Physical Planning is the key institution for creating and implementing environmental policy. It collects data on atmospheric pollution from industrial and energy-related activities; its State Environment Inspectorate monitors emissions of carbon monoxide (CO), sulphur dioxide ($SO_2$), nitrogen oxides ($NO_x$), suspended particulate matter and ozone. According to normal procedure all new industrial or energy projects should be reviewed from an environmental perspective by this Ministry, but until the law on environmental impact assessment comes into force this will remain a 'grey' area. The Ministry is also responsible for the rehabilitation of polluted areas. There is active 'voluntary' collaboration with the Ministry of Economy, largely through the Department for Sustainable Development, on industry and energy issues, particularly environmental pollution and energy efficiency.

### Other Institutions

The State Public Health Institute is responsible for monitoring emissions, including $SO_2$, black smoke, carbon monoxide and lead, and is obliged to transmit all data collected to the Ministry of Environment and Physical Planning.

The Hydrometeorological Institute is also responsible for monitoring air emissions, including $SO_2$, black smoke and total oxidants, and industrial waste water, including chemical pollution. Again there is an obligation to transmit all data collected to the Ministry of Environment and Physical Planning.

The Environment Fund was established in 1998, under the Law on Environment and the Protection and Promotion of Nature, essentially to mobilize financial resources in order to invest them in projects related to the protection and promotion of the environment and nature. The Fund has installed new boilers and gas network connections in factories, including in the "Evropa" chocolate factory (Skopje) and OHIS AD, which have achieved significant energy savings and resulted in large reductions in emissions of particulates, $SO_2$, $NO_x$, CO and benzopyrene. The Fund is also supporting an energy-savings project to install a closed steam condensation system with thermal compression in an export company.

Projects in the planning stages include the reconstruction and conversion of boilers from crude oil or coal to natural gas in several factories and in a school and a clinic, the conversion of public buses from oil to natural gas, the installation of patent steam condensation systems, the replacement of crude oil with biomass in a stock-holding company and an energy efficiency project at OHIS AD. There is an intense search for new projects.

The Chamber of Commerce has the status of an independent, non-political, non-governmental, professional business organization. The Chamber is regulated by both a special law and the Chamber's Statutes. Members are all commercial organizations with head offices in the country.

The Chamber's only environment-related activities are undertaken through its Centre for Quality Improvement, which assists companies in obtaining ISO accreditation – currently 56 companies have ISO 9000 certification. Only one company, Alkaloid AD, is ISO 14001 accredited. ISO 14001 is the international voluntary standard for environmental management systems.

There is no collaboration between the Chamber and the Ministry of Economy as the latter is currently working on a new legal basis for the Chamber's operations. It is seeking to split the Chamber into three or four separate units each focusing on an area such as commerce, trade and industry. If an industry unit is established it is expected that this unit would cooperate with the National Cleaner Production Centre.

The Academy of Sciences and Arts is the country's centre for strategic research and is the principal research body for energy projects and planning. It prepared the National Development Strategy, which was published in 1997. One of its current responsibilities is to develop a strategy for the reduction of greenhouse gas emissions – the industrial and energy sectors are major contributors to these emissions.

The Association of Energy Engineers is a non-governmental association that also undertakes activities in the energy sector, for example, providing input to the Regional Network for Efficient Use of Energy Resources (RENEUR) Win-Win Business project and web site.

### Cleaner Production Centres

The former Yugoslav Republic of Macedonia is a signatory to the UNEP International Declaration on Cleaner Production. In early 1999 the Government expressed its intention to adopt cleaner production techniques as a tool to mitigate the environmental pollution caused by industrial processes.

A joint UNIDO and Czech project was designed to develop cleaner production capacities in the country by raising the awareness of government officials, financing institutions and managers of industrial companies. The Czech Government provided US$ 150,000 for phases I and II (2001-2003) of this project. Following consultations with the Czech Cleaner Production Centre, the Ministry of Environment and Physical Planning was tasked to establish a national centre for cleaner production, which was officially opened in mid-2000. Originally based at the Chamber of Commerce, it is now located at the Environment Fund. In May 2001, the National Strategy for Cleaner Production was launched. It was completed in cooperation with the Czech Cleaner Production Centre and also UNDP and UNIDO. The Centre states that its objectives are to:

- Involve and integrate all bodies interested in cleaner production;
- Provide expert assistance in the evaluation and identification of waste as well as in introducing measures for waste reduction;
- Operate as a centre for sharing experiences, technical information and expertise in cleaner production; and
- Organize training courses for experts, managers and national consultants in order to enable the reconstruction of production capacities and achieve waste reduction.

The Centre is also planning to establish an energy savings agency, which will educate staff, cooperate with the Ministry of Environment and Physical Planning as well as Czech institutions and experts, and prepare an energy savings strategy.

A Regional Cleaner Production Centre was established at the MHK Zletovo lead and zinc smelter in Veles in November 1999. The Centre, a non-profit, non-governmental organization, has 23 members, who are all volunteers from local industries in Veles. It has no regular staff. The members have all received training in cleaner production and environmental management systems (EMS) through courses and study tours conducted by Czech experts and financed by the Environment Fund (via the Czech Government) and UNDP. The Centre announced that it had received a mere €300 from the Environment Fund in 2001. Thirteen cleaner production project proposals have been developed for industries in Veles.

## 11.5 Conclusions and Recommendations

The existing industrial and energy sectors are major sources of environmental pollution due to their use of obsolete equipment and technologies and inappropriate practices. Both sectors are in urgent need of rehabilitation, which will require significant foreign direct investment. Since 1991 there has been a significant decline in industrial activity, the sector is currently operating at 50 per cent of capacity, and this has reduced pollution levels. However, the revival of the industrial sector is an important factor in the country's economic prospects. There is a critical need for investment in new equipment, technologies and practices, together with the clean-up of polluted sites, if sustainable development is to be achieved.

Indigenous energy resources are limited to lignite, hydropower, geothermal energy and firewood. The country is dependent on one large lignite-fired power plant for the bulk of its electricity. The high energy intensity of the country's industry offers significant scope for energy savings.

A key issue to be addressed is the harmonization of the national legislation, including energy legislation, with EU standards in view of future accession to the EU. The energy policy is being adjusted to a more efficient use of energy resources, in line with international conventions and regulations on environmental protection. Energy and electricity demand are expected to rise over the next few years in correlation with GDP growth, as industrial output rises and household income grows.

*Industry*

A number of industrial sites pose significant risks to public health and the environment. UNEP has identified five separate environmental 'hot spots'. Its August 2001 feasibility study proposed a range of remedial options evaluated according to effectiveness, feasibility and cost criteria for two of the sites.

*Recommendation 11.1:*
*The Ministry of Environment and Physical Planning should set up an expert working group comprising all stakeholders, including the Ministries of the Economy, Finance and Health, and senior management from the respective industries, to prioritize action, e.g., identify low-cost remediation measures and set a timetable for urgent risk reduction at the identified environmental hot spots. (see also recommendation 9.4)*

Although UNEP has highlighted areas at a number of industrial sites requiring urgent action due to pollution from POPs and other chemicals, it is clear the extent of the problem in the country has not been fully grasped. The former Yugoslav Republic of Macedonia signed the Stockholm Convention on POPs in May 2001. In October 2001 a proposal was submitted to GEF by UNIDO for US$ 497,000 to fund a two-year "POPs enabling activities" project. Its key objectives are to strengthen national capacity, strengthen the knowledge and understanding of POPs among all stakeholders and to develop and formulate a national implementation plan – all of which will help in meeting the obligations of the Convention and in managing the elimination of POPs. The issue of POPs and chemicals currently falls under the responsibility of the Department for Sustainable Development of the Ministry of Environment and Physical Planning.

*Recommendation 11.2:*
*The Ministry of Environment and Physical Planning should strengthen its institutional capacity to manage the environmental impacts of chemicals, e.g., by the establishment of a special section for chemicals management.*

The industrial sector is characterized by energy-intensive and highly polluting activities. Significant investment in advanced technologies, equipment and practices – as used in Western countries – would enable these industries to operate economically and with due regard for the environment. In its transition to a market economy

the Government is actively seeking to privatize the industrial sector; however many Central and Eastern European countries in similar situations experienced problems in attracting foreign direct investment because of concerns over liability for past environmental damage and contamination.

*Recommendation 11.3:*
*The Ministry of Economy, in collaboration with the Ministry of Environment and Physical Planning, should develop legislation clearly identifying who is responsible for past pollution at industrial and energy-related sites, i.e. the new owner, the previous owner or the State. In the case of orphan sites, where the previous owners cannot be traced or where the previous owners are bankrupt, it should be clearly stated whether the Government would assume responsibility for the associated environmental liability.*

*Recommendation 11.4:*
*The Ministry of Economy, when carrying out studies into the continuing viability and competitiveness of industrial enterprises, should also take into consideration the need for these industries to meet European environmental standards.*

*Energy and Energy Efficiency*

All studies undertaken so far conclude that there is significant potential for energy savings in the country; one such study estimated that an energy saving target of 21 per cent (mostly in the electricity sector) was achievable. Other studies have concluded that it would be possible to reach this target largely through low-cost measures and the rational use of energy.

Energy-efficient lighting in public and other buildings; the use of thermostats; the introduction of energy meters to enable billing of heating, air-conditioning and hot water on the basis of actual consumption; the thermal insulation of new buildings; and energy labelling of equipment are a number of measures that would encourage energy saving. In the industrial sector the introduction of energy audits, particularly in energy-intensive enterprises, readily highlights areas of low-cost energy savings such as the recovery of waste heat. The regular inspection of industrial boilers will serve to identify those, for example, operating with excess air. The promotion of energy management skills and competence also has an important role to play in energy conservation.

*Recommendation 11.5:*
(a) *The Ministry of Economy should ensure that the "energy efficiency strategy up to the year 2020" is harmonized with the "strategy for the complex development of energy up to the year 2020" to ensure consistency in the development of the overall national energy policy.*
(b) *As a short-term objective of this overall national energy policy, and drawing on existing experience and infrastructure, the Ministry of Economy should promote low-cost energy efficiency measures and energy management in all sectors. The promotion of energy savings and the rationalization of energy use, particularly in the industrial sector, will result in both environmental and economic benefits.*

The establishment of an energy efficiency fund as mandated by the Law on Energy, together with demand-side management mechanisms, are priorities as they provide the basis for energy efficiency policy development and programme implementation. The creation of the fund is critical for the implementation of the long-term programme for the efficient use of energy. Among its principal roles should be the development of a national plan for the promotion of energy efficiency, the preparation of the energy sector for future accession to the EU, as well as ensuring compliance with international treaties to which the former Yugoslav Republic of Macedonia is a party.

There are clearly links between energy and environment and it is important that common policies should be developed and promoted. The existence of the Environment Fund under the Ministry of Environment and Physical Planning could be a source of significant conflict, overlap and duplication of effort as energy efficiency is a

key tool for reducing environmental impact and is a stated activity of this Fund.

*Recommendation 11.6:*
*In view of the significant potential for energy savings and expected energy supply constraints, the Ministry of Economy should, in consultation with all stakeholders, establish an energy efficiency fund as a matter of priority. The fund should be an independent organization with clear and transparent management and independent supervision. The Ministry should also ensure that appropriate financial support for the energy efficiency fund is provided or facilitated.*

The Ministry of Economy has approved a draft project proposal for the development of the privately funded AMBO oil pipeline. However, to date there has been no consultation or cooperation with the Ministry of Environment and Physical Planning on potential environmental impacts. Each country is responsible for its own section of the pipeline. The current pipeline routed through the former Yugoslav Republic of Macedonia, for economic reasons, largely follows the roads and railways and also a path relatively close to the northwestern perimeter of Lake Ohrid. Although the project is currently put on hold because of lack of investment, the risks associated with this proposal should be investigated.

*Recommendation 11.7:*
*The Ministry of Economy should ensure that a full environmental impact assessment of the pipeline proposal (AMBO) be undertaken, including the consideration of a number of alternative options for the route of the proposed pipeline project. The report of the environmental impact assessment should be presented to the Ministry of Environment and Physical Planning for review and approval.*

139

# Chapter 12

# *SPATIAL PLANNING*

## 12.1  Human settlement structure

Changes in the economic structure of the country, the opening of previously protected markets, the increasing roles of the private sector and communities, decentralization and the new role of local governments, are creating new challenges and opportunities for the former Yugoslav Republic of Macedonia's spatial planning system. Economic production has declined; following the closure of unprofitable industrial enterprises, unemployment has risen to 35 per cent; poverty has reached unprecedented levels. The country has a stagnating labour market with only 40.6 per cent of the "economically active" population in work, and a relatively small private sector contributing close to 40 per cent of GDP. Large cities have emerged as the places for economic growth and investment at the expense of growing unemployment and poverty in rural communities. These trends have exacerbated previous imbalances in the distribution of the population and long-standing inequalities in the access to essential social and infrastructure services. As a result, future spatial planning for urban and rural settlements will have to address different sets of issues.

While future spatial planning for human settlements will be guided by a number of economic, political,

social and environmental factors, the legacy of the existing spatial structure, with its human resources and land-use patterns will be a deciding factor in future development. According to its current administrative division, the country has 123 municipalities grouping 1,753 settlements. Only 1.6 per cent of these settlements are classified as urban, but they are home to 60 per cent of the population. These cities, mostly clustered in the plains along Skopje, Pelagonija, Polog and Strumica-Radovish Valleys, have continued to attract rural migrants. The country's total population according to the 1994 census amounts to 1,945,932 inhabitants. More than a quarter is concentrated in Skopje. Other municipalities – Bitola, Gostivar, Kumanovo and Tetovo – accommodate another 26.5 per cent. Population growth and urbanization have been fairly stable in the past 40 years (Figure 12.1). The average population density is 76 inhabitants/km$^2$, which is relatively low by European standards. Annual population growth slowed down to 0.64 per cent between 1991 and 1994, the average household consists of four persons (Statistical Yearbook, 2001). These dynamics reflect the intensity of industrialization during communism and the concentration of social and economic development in cities.

**Figure 12.1: Urbanization and population growth, 1953-1994**

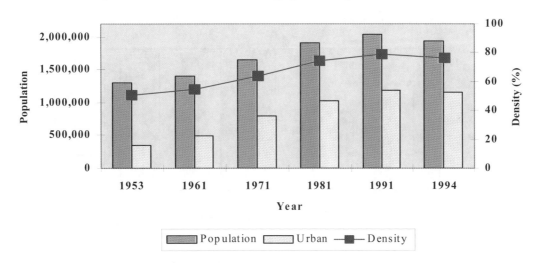

*Source*: Estimates based on the Statistical Yearbook of the Republic of Macedonia, 2001.

Rural settlements, on the other hand, have been losing their population and appear to have inferior infrastructure. More than 46 per cent of the rural settlements are situated in the west of the country, forming a dense network of villages. These communities are economically vibrant with a relatively well developed system of agricultural production. About 80 per cent of households in the rural areas farm on fewer than three hectares of land, and half of the villages have a population of fewer than 300 people (NEAP, 1997). In the mountain areas, many villages, with an average density of five people per square kilometre, struggle to sustain their physical and social infrastructure.

## 12.2  Environmental challenges

The country has a total land area of 25,713 km², of which about 50.8 per cent is agricultural land and only 2.5 per cent is urban land. The continuous urbanization has been supported by increasing public investment in urban infrastructure thus aggravating patterns of rural/urban inequality. Most urban dwellings are connected to water supply networks and proper sanitation facilities compared to 54 per cent and 35 per cent respectively for rural households. However, urbanization has proceeded faster than planned. As a result, most cities have water supply and solid waste management problems. In Skopje, environmental conditions are getting worse due to continued urbanization and, particularly, the sharp increase in traffic.

Air quality problems are limited to major urban areas. The major sources of air pollution are the industries with outdated technological equipment and polluting production processes. Skopje, Veles, Bitola and Tetovo have poor air quality, which affects the health of 30 per cent of the country's population. In Veles, in particular, air pollution from the lead and zinc smelter has caused significant health hazards. (see Chapter 11 on Industry, energy and the environment)

**Figure 12.2 a and b: Infrastructure Deficiencies: Skopje and other capital cities**
a: Waste-water treatment, 1999

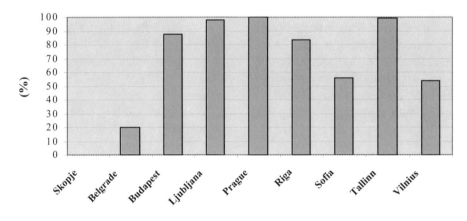

*Sources* : UNCHS-HABITAT, 2001 and Skopje draft master plan.

b: Access to sewerage network, 1999

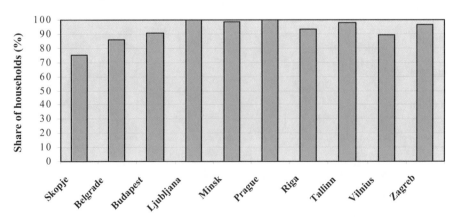

*Sources* : UNCHS-HABITAT, 2001 and Skopje draft master plan.

The most significant water pollution problems are due to discharges from the mining sector, industrial plants and waste water from large urban settlements. Most urban settlements have no waste-water treatment plants. Household waste water, together with industrial waste water, is discharged into rivers without any treatment so adding to the pollution of the Rivers Vardar, Bregalnica and Crni Drim. The impact on Lake Ohrid is significant, particularly because of the large influx of tourists. Inadequate sewerage provision and lack of waste-water treatment have a detrimental effect on the quality of life of its residents. (see Chapter 6 on Water management, including protection of lakes)

In short, environmental challenges associated with industrial pollution and cumulative infrastructure deficiencies are still significant in the large cities. The problems of high air and water pollution are due to past industrialization policies and a weak environmental management system. Given the financial difficulties of the country and reduced capital spending, the investment needed to address these challenges exceeds the financial capabilities of municipalities and the central Government. So it is important for spatial planning to set clear long-term goals and objectives that will allow incremental steps to be taken in the right direction in partnership with the private sector and international donor organizations.

## 12.3 Social challenges

While the economic prospects of the country have been evaluated positively, the social impact of the transition process presents a major challenge to market reforms. The social transformation has led to emigration, ethnic tensions, social differentiation and poverty, which are new phenomena in this previously sheltered society. Structural and macroeconomic pressures have driven unemployment up to 35 per cent. Furthermore, the development of individual urban areas has varied with some losing and others gaining economic attractiveness. Skopje and Ohrid have been privileged in that respect, attracting a larger share of investment in real estate. These social challenges require a differentiated and more sensitive approach to spatial planning and solutions that reflect the diversity of local needs. There are two items on the social planning agenda that are significant – the access to essential social services (health care, education) and the provision of housing.

In social services, the legacy of past investments will determine future access and the quality of services. Previous emphasis on urbanization has left the country with a very uneven pattern of distribution. Most of the education, health care and recreation facilities seem to be concentrated in Skopje and some of the large urban centres, leaving villages and smaller municipalities with rudimentary services. Effectively, the dispersal of the country's population and its low-density human settlement structure excludes almost half of the people from immediate access to essential social services. Slow economic growth and fiscal constraints are likely to diminish the quality of the social services system thus aggravating urban/rural inequalities. These broader developments need to be evaluated against the background of widely increasing poverty and growing employment insecurity across the country.

While the considerable inequality in the provision of essential social services, particularly in the rural areas, poses a significant challenge for future spatial planning, access to housing appears to be less of a problem. According to the latest census, the number of housing units was 580,342, indicating a housing surplus of 78,379 units. With an average dwelling size of 71 $m^3$ and housing space of 21 $m^3$ per person, the former Yugoslav Republic of Macedonia compares quite favourably with the other countries in transition. While most families appear to be adequately housed, problems with infrastructure services and substandard quality in 12 per cent of the stock continue to be a challenge. Housing progress can be attributed to intensive investment in new housing construction during the 1970s and the 1980s with significant private sector involvement. Contrary to other countries in transition, the country has a legacy of a high rate of homeownership (85 per cent in 1988). Following the rapid privatization of State and municipal property after 1991, the share of privately owned dwellings has now reached 95 per cent. Skopje has become a homeowners' city with privately owned housing rates well above the EU average. (figure 12.3)

The country has recently recognized that it has a problem of illegally constructed housing. Some of the 30-40,000 units were built as long as 20 years ago. Experts estimate that 80 per cent of the illegal construction is in Skopje and concentrated in 27 areas (Draft master plan, 2002). In most of the cases illegal construction has taken over agricultural land and lacks adequate infrastructure, with all the long-term environmental consequences that this involves. Over time, households have connected to the local infrastructure networks and established local retail and other social services. Reportedly, some of these communities are home to diverse ethnic populations with strong community support networks. Interview data indicate that the new master plans of Skopje and Ohrid, currently being prepared, have incorporated these settlements into the urban growth boundaries. While this legitimizes the existing construction, problems with the often substandard quality of the buildings and the ad hoc connection to technical infrastructure remain unresolved.

The conflict in Kosovo has posed unique challenges to the country's social and spatial planning system.

Since 1991 the former Yugoslav Republic of Macedonia has been a functional multi-ethnic country with responsive patterns of democratic government. According to the 1994 census, the population consists principally of Macedonians (66.5 per cent) and Albanians (22.9 per cent) (Figure 12.4). Ethnic diversity manifested in differences in language, culture, religion and traditions has created an eclectic multicultural fabric, which has left its unique imprint on the built environment. Spatial planning traditionally has been sensitive towards that diversity and its contribution to the cultural heritage of the country.

## Figure 12.3: Privately owned housing, 1999

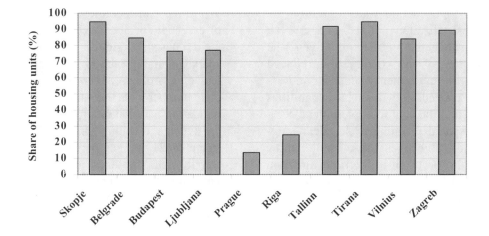

*Sources* : UNCHS-HABITAT, 2001 and Skopje draft master plan.

## Figure 12.4: Ethnic diversity

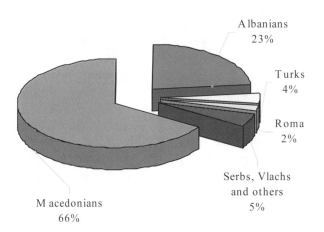

*Source:* Estimates based on the Statistical Yearbook of the Republic of Macedonia, 2001.

The influx of Kosavar Albanian refugees in June 1999 peaked at 261,000, creating significant social and environmental pressures. According to the Office of the United Nations High Commissioner for Refugees (UNHCR), approximately 57 per cent of these refugees stayed with host families and another 42 per cent lived in tented camps (UNEP, 2000). Following the international peace agreement, some of the refugees began to return home. Government priorities for the rehabilitation process include sustainable development for all ethnic groups, particularly in employment, private sector development and government. The planning framework has to reinforce these new priorities at the national and local level since the situation is likely to continue to affect the fragile economic and social balance in the border regions in the years to come.

## 12.4 Policy, legislative and institutional framework

Prior to independence, spatial planning operated under the influence of industrialization policy and centralized control over investment and resource allocation decisions. It was carried out through master plans and rural planning documentation based on controlled prices for land, capital and services. Because of the State-owned economy, the country relied on projects funded by the State and regulations were relatively easy to impose. Private ownership over land and assets was limited and the coordination of different interests more manageable and predictable. As a result, institutions in the country developed a strong physical planning framework based on normative planning, but not necessarily a strong integrated economic, social and environmental planning capacity.

Spatial planning today has to address the need to recycle and restructure space within a context of rapid economic transition. These changes have affected economic activities and correspondingly land-use patterns in rural and urban areas. Emerging private sector initiatives have created strong pressure on the supply of land and infrastructure services, particularly in desirable urban areas. New commercial services, the privatization of land and industries as well as restitution claims have moved faster than the response from the decision-making authorities. In addition, the management and coordination of the investment process in technical and social infrastructure according to the official plans has become a major problem. In the former Yugoslav Republic of Macedonia spatial planning has two

levels – national and local. While many major transport and environmental problems stretch across jurisdictional boundaries and require regional cooperation, the existing system of government does not provide an effective mechanism to institutionalize such efforts.

### The national spatial plan

Several documents define the strategic development of the country's spatial system. The national spatial plan is very important for the creation of a first coherent planning policy framework. It will replace the 1982 Spatial Plan, which is considered inadequate under the new market economy and democratic government conditions. The national spatial plan, drawn up by the Institute of Spatial Planning in 1996, is based on 22 specialized studies by independent experts with the wide participation of non-government organizations and academic institutions. Extensive consultation with line ministries has been instrumental in shaping the priorities of long-term planning policies in the area of economic, social and environmental development. The plan is before Parliament and is expected to be adopted in the course of 2002. It has a 20-year time frame. It formulates strategic priorities for the country's territorial development based on the principles of sustainable development, market competition and a regional approach to the spatial management of economic, cultural and environmental processes. Part I defines long-term goals and objectives for the spatial organization of the country taking account of its geopolitical situation and links to Europe.

Part II provides a systematic evaluation of economic and social change. It develops a comprehensive inventory of the country's natural resources – agricultural land, forests, mineral and water resources, as well as energy infrastructure. Based on projections for the country's economic, social and environmental development, the national spatial plan identifies specific sectoral policies and priorities with a special emphasis on their spatial dimensions. Two sections are particularly important for the environmentally sensitive spatial management of the territory – human settlements planning and environmental protection.

In the section on human settlements planning, the major objectives are: (i) the creation of conditions for sustainable prosperity, (ii) the coordination of economic, social and spatial development dynamics, (iii) the differentiated development prospects for different functional centres, (iv) the improvement of living conditions and the creation of equal development opportunities, (v) the intensification of transport, communication and infrastructure networks to allow the integration and mobility of capital, labour and resource sharing. Figure 12.5 draws the boundaries of 15 functional spatial units for the effective management of the territory and the hierarchy of regional and municipal centres. The system attempts to address urban/rural inequalities capitalizing on the existing human, economic and environmental potential and encourages resource sharing in a fiscally responsive manner.

Several sections deal with environmental issues, but perhaps the most important is related to *environmental protection*. The review identifies the potential for the future use of natural resources, forests, agricultural land, water and waste management systems (figure 12.6). The major objectives in that respect are (i) the implementation of effective environmental protection measures, (ii) the establishment of an environmental monitoring system and an efficient system for the institutional control and enforcement of environmental regulations, (iii) the protection of water resources, the introduction of energy-efficient measures and alternative energy sources.

The national spatial plan envisions increasing the country's total protected area from 7.16 per cent to 11.5 per cent of the national territory to enhance biodiversity and integrate the country with the Pan-European Ecological Network. It maps out a system of agricultural and forest areas as well as fresh water resources in need of special measures. Lastly, attention is paid to the rich cultural heritage with well defined spatial clusters of historic monuments (see figure 12.6).

The biggest task ahead will be to develop and implement management plans for all protected areas addressing issues related to biodiversity, the efficient management of forestry, agricultural land and water. This is clearly a task that goes well beyond the spatial planning agenda and requires clearly defined mechanisms for institutional cooperation as well as strong leadership. While the national spatial plan brings these issues within the planning framework, a new Law on Natural Heritage places the country's protected areas under the authority of the Ministry of Environment and Physical Planning. Developing effective nature protection programmes will require strong

communication and cooperation with the Ministry of Agriculture, Forestry and Water Economy as well as other line ministries and local governments.

Part III of the plan deals with implementation, including coordination with downstream urban and detailed spatial plans, the development of regional studies and institutional capacity-building. These sections, however, do not clearly assign responsibilities, time frame and strategies to ensure that the operational aspects are explicitly clarified. This important component needs considerable refinement and an action plan able to guide the implementation process.

### Related national planning policies

*National Environmental Action Plan.* Another important document that influences the development of the planning policy framework is the National Environmental Action Plan (NEAP). Its goals for national environmental policy from 1997 to 2002 have been to (i) improve air and water quality, (ii) conserve biodiversity, especially in Lakes Ohrid, Prespa and Dojran, (iii) renew and preserve forests, and (iv) strengthen the management capacity of institutions responsible for environmental monitoring and enforcement. These goals set the framework for the development of local environmental action plans (LEAPs). So far 17 municipalities have developed their own LEAPs, mostly supported through donor funding. The City of Skopje is finalizing its LEAP in a participatory manner with wider consultation of major stakeholders. While the emphasis is on environmental management, the local action plans have significant implications for urban planning and land management issues and demonstrate the growing concern of local communities about the consequences of environmental pollution owing to poor transport planning and infrastructure deficiencies.

The NEAP did emphasize the need to urgently address the environmental problems in cities. However, the role of spatial planning in this process has not been recognized thus preventing possible synergies between environmental and planning policy frameworks. Progress in the implementation of the NEAP across the major intervention areas has been uneven, so its upcoming revision might consider broadening the scope of sectoral policies to include environmental planning.

**Figure 12.5: Functional Spatial Units**

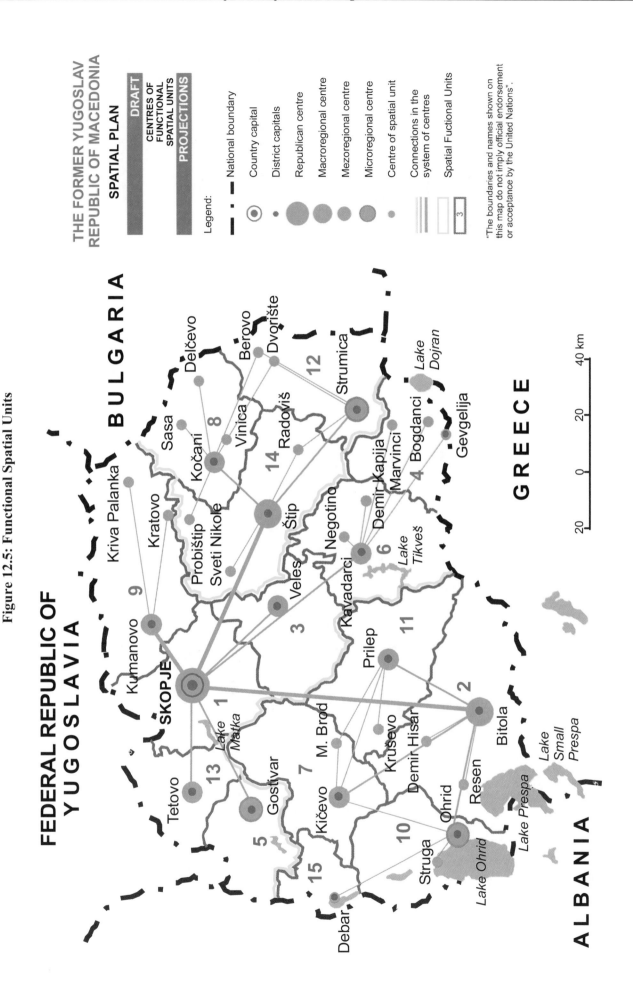

**Figure 12.6: Spatial Aspects of Environmental Protection**

"The boundaries and names shown on this map do not imply official endorsement or acceptance by the United Nations".

"Macedonia 2003": the Framework Programme for Development and Reforms, adopted in 2000, aims at accelerated economic growth and poverty reduction. It influences spatial planning objectives and priorities through fiscal, social and regional development policies. For example, support for small and medium enterprises in economically depressed regions is a priority, investment in infrastructure and environment protection projects employing the poor is another priority. Additionally, a considerable amount of funding is being allocated to investment in the health sector, education, social welfare and the provision of infrastructure in rural areas to address urban/rural inequalities. Support for economically underdeveloped areas in the country, primarily rural communities in mountainous and border areas, targets infrastructure deficiencies and job creation. These policies help in the implementation of the strategic planning objectives identified in the draft national spatial plan (section on human settlements).

*Spatial planning in the EU integration context*

The European Commission has made considerable efforts to help the country in its approximation to EU practices and legislation. These efforts are complemented by substantial cooperation in multilateral forums (UNDP, World Bank) and bilateral programmes (e.g. Agenda 21, LEAPs supported by GTZ). Undoubtedly, the scope of cooperation is broadening the country's view on different approaches to spatial planning and environmental management. As part of the PHARE funding available to strengthen the capacity of the Ministry of Environment and Physical Planning, the European Commission is assisting with environmental monitoring and data management and integrated pollution prevention. Within the overall strategy for revising the legal system for environmental management, national legislation on spatial planning, construction and land management has been given a low priority. While progress is being made on the preparation of 'NEAP-II' and investment proposals for solid waste management, the draft national spatial plan, which sets the framework for individual sectoral policies and environmental management strategies, has failed to attract any donor's attention.

*The Legislative Framework*

The 1996 Law on Physical and Urban Planning mentions several types of spatial plans:

- *The general urban plan* (master plan) for a settlement lays down the overall organization of cities, including major transport and technical infrastructure elements, zoning and land-use designation, and density targets.

- *The detailed urban plan* of a settlement unit develops the spatial organization of building lots in the unit (up to 30 ha), contains details on lands-use – housing, institutional and industrial uses – and green spaces; and delineates building setbacks, massing, and height. While it appears prescriptive in nature, the plan allows alternative design solutions depending on an investor's interest.

- *The urban documentation* of a settlement is a plan for rural settlements containing major transport and infrastructure networks. It maps out settlement boundaries, building lots and social infrastructure items appropriate to the organizational needs of rural settlements.

Spatial planning is perceived as a continuous process. The Law imposes a regular review of planning documentation so that it can be adjusted to specific needs and changes in the local community. The hierarchy of spatial plans is expected to be consistent with the national spatial plan, which has to be updated every 15 years.

General plans should be revised every 10 years. The procedure is initiated and financed by the Ministry of Transport and Communications. Local governments are consulted in the process, which requires a one-month public consultation with all interested parties. Detailed plans are commissioned by local governments and updated every five years. Reportedly, cash-constrained municipalities often delegate these responsibilities to the private sector or extend the validity of the existing plans. Financial difficulties at the central level have also affected general plan revision. Currently, 15 out of the 27 urban plans have been developed in line with the new planning framework, as have more than 360 detailed urban plans. Urban documentation exists for 799 rural settlements and is reviewed in case of growth boundary changes.

According to existing legislation, regional plans can be developed for special purposes such as natural heritage, landscape protection, major infrastructure projects, ecological preservation along river valleys, lakes and other environmentally sensitive areas.

---

**Box 12.1:     Skopje General Urban Plan Process**

The development of *Skopje General Urban Plan* is a five-year effort that brings together more than 100 experts, planners and architects. The existing general plan, adopted in 1985, expired in 2001. Recognizing the need to respond to the new challenges associated with the transition from planning to markets, the Ministry of Transport and Communications and the new leadership of Skopje made a commitment to support a collaborative effort that will result in the development of a new general urban plan with 20-year horizon. The methodological approach is guided by the principles of sustainable development, interdisciplinarity and democratic governance. The draft document incorporates the recommendations of specialized studies defining alternatives for Skopje's economic, social, spatial and environmental development.

It promotes a vision of compact development that utilizes the regeneration potential of the existing urban structure and internalizes future growth through recycling of urban land and intensification. The *General Urban Plan* sets milestones for future investment in infrastructure and environmental improvement and is the first systematic attempt to deal with spatial planning in an integrated manner. Further refinement of this 'blueprint' for Skopje's spatial development needs to define an action plan for its implementation as well as establish a democratic process that allows efficient public consultation with major stakeholders and local communities.

Source: Skopje draft master plan, October 2000

---

The new Law on Local Self-Government passed at the beginning of 2002 devolves more rights to local governments. This decentralization effort delegates planning and building control from the central to the local level and emphasizes local autonomy in the implementation of spatial plans. Municipalities will have a lot more flexibility in designing locally appropriate investment programmes and in choosing priorities for capital spending. Recent changes in the legislation address the inadequacies in the Law on Territorial Division and Boundaries; and on the city of Skopje. For example, the organization of the city of Skopje with seven municipalities apparently creates tensions and leads to overlap of competencies. The territorial division is fragmented with many small municipalities unable to perform their functions independently. The entire system is being revised by the Ministry of Local Self-Government, which oversees the decentralization process. The objective of the revision is to clarify the financing of local government tasks, which will have a significant impact on the implementation of spatial plans and investment in social and technical infrastructure.

### Infrastructure provision, landownership and real estate

The 2001 Law on Land for Construction defines options for landownership (lease or sale). The legislation also addresses municipal responsibility for infrastructure provision. Local governments are expected to develop programmes for infrastructure investment specifying capital costs for upgrades and expansion. A private contribution is leveraged through a contribution agreement between the individual owner and the municipality usually based on a fixed rate per square metre of housing

space. Municipalities can fix their own rates, which can vary significantly – e.g. from €102/m² in Skopje to €31/m² in Veles. For institutional users, the contribution is based on the actual infrastructure construction costs. Building permits are issued upon presentation of the infrastructure contract. Reportedly, some of the major difficulties in the implementation include: (i) difficulties in the phasing of infrastructure investment and collaboration with private interests, (ii) inconsistencies in the pricing and quality of services, (iii) a lack of discipline in the payment of infrastructure contributions; and (iv) inadequate resources for inspection and compliance control.

Another improvement to the legal framework of spatial planning and management is attributed to the Law on Communal Works, passed in 1997. Prior to its approval, the work of communal enterprises managing infrastructure was regulated by ad hoc municipal decisions. The variety of solutions negatively influenced the quality of infrastructure provision. The Law specifies and regulates the rights and duties of service providers and beneficiaries (individuals or legal entities) through the introduction of standards and norms. It identifies funding sources for the construction of technical infrastructure facilities and aims at creating fair competition.

The Law on Land for Construction with the Regulations for the Transformation of Urban Land of October 2001 address the privatization of urban land. Since 1958 urban land in the country has been nationalized and its sale restricted. The legislation provides a mechanism to choose an option for future landownership to bring it in line with the ownership of housing, commercial and industrial properties. A 10-year period allows for the transformation of urban land into freehold or leasehold. In the meantime, owners are required to pay land rent based on the category of settlement. The assessment methodology does not take into account the market value of land in these locations; rather the administrative land prices are based on the size of the settlement's population. For example Skopje is divided into three zones and the highest rent is €12.8/m$^2$.

Another important piece of legislation defining the framework for spatial planning is the Law on Property and Other Real Estate of September 2001. It specifies the rights and responsibilities of the two major categories of property ownership – public and private (individual and cooperative). The 1998 Law on Denationalization deals with the restitution of land and property. Administered by the Ministry of Finance, the process is considered controversial. Owners have the right to declare ownership within a five-year period. If the land is not developed and is in its original state, property title is restored, in other cases a compensation mechanism is applied.

Overall, the real estate market is immature due to the *delayed privatization of urban land* and a lack of appropriate financial mechanisms. There is no monitoring of real estate transactions and prices, information in the Cadastre and Real Estate Registration Administration is incomplete and not readily available; there appears to be no systematic effort to indicate barriers to and constraints in the implementation of the new legislation on the privatization of land and housing. These are serious obstacles to the functioning of a real estate market and investment.

### Planning and building permits

The Regulations on Spatial Planning and the Regulations on the Design of Buildings were updated in October 1999. Norms and standards for construction are currently incorporated into the Law on Standardization. Due to resource and capacity constraints, these are mainly simple cosmetic changes to the old socialist legislation.

The legal and institutional framework for an adequate permitting and enforcement system is gradually developing. In late 2000, the Law on the Environment was amended to provide the legal basis for an environmental permit system. The country intends to introduce the EU Integrated

Pollution Prevention and Control Directive. Building permits are issued by regional units of the Ministry of Transport and Communications on the basis of an application that briefly describes the proposed activity. The permit is conditional upon the presentation of detailed architectural and construction plans in compliance with the approved detailed urban plans, the registration of land title and documents for real estate, the payment of infrastructure connection fees, and other supportive documentation. The building permit is valid for six months; interested line ministries are consulted for the five major categories of construction sites and investment activities where appropriate. The Ministry of Environment and Physical Planning upon request provides opinions to the Ministry of Transport and Communications on applications for buildings and the operation of new industrial activities. Operating permits, however, require opinions from all the inspectorates concerned, including the State Environment Inspectorate. Depending on the inspectorates' opinions, conditions may be imposed on the proposed activity. In general, new establishments and economic activities are authorized without any time limit. At the moment the permitting system does not distinguish between projects of national and of local importance. The same procedure is followed, but the need for consultation with line ministries and their corresponding institutions depends on the scope of the activities.

According to the draft law on environmental impact assessment (EIA), an assessment is carried out on the basis of an application for the implementation of investment activity submitted to the Ministry of Environment and Physical Planning. The EIA contains the following elements: (i) a description of the site, the physical characteristics of the investment activity and the need for land excavation in the course of implementation and operation; (ii) a description of the main characteristics of the production process, the nature and the quantity of used materials, (iii) an estimate of expected refuse and emissions (pollution of water, air and soil, noise, vibrations, lightening, heating, radiation.) produced by the proposed activity; (iv) a description of environmental aspects that could be affected, including population, fauna, flora, soil, water, air, climate factors, material resources (architectural and archaeological heritage), landscape and interdependence among the above factors; and (v) a description of protection measures.

*The institutional framework*

<u>National level</u>

Core responsibility for spatial planning rests with the Ministry of Environment and Physical Planning. Parliament adopts the national spatial plan, ratifies international agreements and conventions and is an essential factor in the creation of a national spatial and environmental policy.

According to the 2000 Law on the Organization and Work of the State Administration, the Ministry of Environment and Physical Planning develops and implements spatial planning policies and maintains a spatial information system. It prepares draft laws, regulations and other ordinances related to planning, zoning and construction. It provides a substantial input into the preparation of legislation pertinent to spatial planning by other ministries and government institutions. The Ministry consists of several units: the Department for Regulation and Standardization, the Department for Sustainable Development, the Department for Physical Planning, the Department for European Integration and the Environmental Information Centre. The implementation of the national spatial plan is direct responsibility of the Department for Physical Planning, with a staff of five. Given the complexity of strategic objectives and priorities in the economic, social and environmental realm, this institutional capacity is insufficient to handle the task. Overall, spatial planning suffers from under-institutionalization.

Prior to 1998, the responsibilities incumbent on the Ministry of Environment and Physical Planning fell under the Ministry of Urban Planning and Construction. When the Ministry of Environment and Physical Planning was created, it took over environmental and physical planning functions, and the Ministry of Urban Planning and Construction's remaining responsibilities were transferred to the Ministry of Transport and Communications. The latter works closely with the Ministry of Agriculture, Forestry and Water Economy and other State institutions in the area of spatial planning. Several functions are particularly important: (i) the development of building standards and regulations (ii) the coordination and approval of spatial plans for urban settlements, and (iii) the regulation of the construction and building approval process. Construction permits are issued by 200 employees of the Ministry of Transport and Communications in 34 units across the country, while building inspection is concentrated in 4 regional inspectorates.

It appears that, while spatial planning functions were formally delegated to the Ministry of Environment and Physical Planning, most of the critical tasks are carried out by the staff of the Ministry of Transport and Communications. While it might be part of the institutional transformation, this institutional vacuum is detrimental to the establishment of a clear, transparent and responsive spatial planning system.

It should be noted that although there is no regional level of public administration, individual ministries and public services do operate regional units responsible for several municipalities.

<u>Local level</u>

The country's Strategy for the Reform of the Local Self-Government System adopted in 1999 decentralized critical functions to the local self-government system of 123 municipalities. Currently, municipalities are responsible for construction, land-use planning and zoning. Local self-governments and their elected councils adopt and implement spatial plans. They also manage drinking water supplies, green areas and solid waste disposal through communal enterprises. However, this decentralization of responsibilities has not been accompanied by fiscal authority to raise and manage local revenues, so municipalities continue to be financially dependent on the national Government. The development approval and building permit process, usually a responsibility of the local authorities, is still under central government control.

Some of the most significant constraints at the local level which affect spatial planning and infrastructure development are: (i) the limited and inadequate capacity of local self-government units in urban planning and management; (ii) a lack of standardization of structures responsible for infrastructure planning, financing and maintenance; (iii) the lack of effective urban planning and building control and mechanisms to deal with illegal construction, (iv) the lack of inter-municipal cooperation potential to support common planning and environmental interests and perform joint municipal activities within their competencies.

## Other specialized institutions

The Ministry works closely with the National Institute of Spatial Planning, which has eight branches across the country and some 70 employees. This public body operates independently and is authorized to develop and expand the spatial plan and the new generation of urban plans. In addition, it performs a variety of spatial planning tasks – specialized regional studies, environmental assessments, detailed urban development plans, and the management of geographic information system (GIS)-based planning data.

The Cadastre and Real Estate Registration Administration, which is a separate legal entity, affiliated with the Ministry of Environment and Physical Planning maintains a set of data on land, buildings and infrastructure, as well as information on the holders of real estate deeds throughout the former Yugoslav Republic of Macedonia. It carries out surveys, establishes cadastre units for the registration of real estate and develops geodetic plans for each municipality. Legally, the Cadastre and Real Estate Registration Administration is expected to handle the registration of the right to property, other obligations and limitations concerning the real estate of the physical and legal entities (acquisition, transfer, mortgage, limitations and termination) in the real estate cadastre. The GIS Centre has initiated a digitalization of the municipal cadastre in cooperation with the State Administration of Geodesy. More than 1,000 geodetic plans have been completed, but due to financial and organizational constraints progress has been slow.

## 12.5  Conclusions and Recommendations

The new spatial planning system has to respond to significant economic, social and environmental challenges. The country has a legacy of polarized human settlements with a high concentration of population, investment and services in the capital city and a handful of large urban centres. This inequality, particularly in the rural areas, has a marked impact on social well–being, affecting access to jobs, health care and educational opportunities. While cities are better positioned to capitalize on the economic transition and the opening of markets, rapid urbanization, infrastructure deficiencies and a legacy of high air and water pollution reduce their advantages in an environment where the competition for investment and jobs is much more intense. The Kosovo crisis also created unique social and environmental challenges for spatial planning in the border region.

### *Reforms of the planning framework*

The country's planning system aims to achieve balanced socio-economic development, improve the quality of life, ensure the competent management of natural resources and the protection of the environment. The national spatial plan is very important in the establishment of a coherent planning policy framework enabling the implementation of these planning principles. It formulates strategic priorities for the development of the national territory based on the principles of sustainable development, market competition and a regional approach to the spatial management of economic and environmental processes. While the national spatial plan demonstrates planning professionalism and a knowledge of the country's challenges and opportunities, it needs to become operational through a set of realistic, measurable objectives and actions in priority areas. Delays in its approval by Parliament are affecting the development of downstream urban spatial plans, regional studies and other planning documentation. Without consensus on strategic priorities, a whole new generation of recently approved spatial plans may be subject to revision and future speculation. Another important aspect of the plan is its ability to provide a much-needed framework for the integration of sectoral policies addressing issues related to biodiversity, and the efficient management of forestry, agricultural land and water. It can encourage regional planning and cooperation among municipalities so as to address common goals and resolve issues that transcend administrative boundaries. The implementation process is clearly a task that goes well beyond the spatial planning agenda and requires well-defined mechanisms for institutional cooperation as well as strong leadership.

*Recommendation 12.1:*
*Parliament should adopt the national spatial plan as a priority. In cooperation with the relevant ministries and local authorities, the Ministry of Environment and Physical Planning should make a greater effort to implement the national spatial plan. The development of a structured action plan with clearly assigned responsibilities, time frame and priority actions should form the basis of the implementation strategy. The action plan should include realistic and achievable objectives, taking into account fiscal and technical constraints, and define performance measures to track progress.*

*Recommendation 12.2:*
*The Government should encourage the implementation of the national spatial plan by providing incentives for regional collaboration among municipalities on issues such as transport, economic development, air and water quality. In encouraging such cooperation, the Ministry of Environment and Physical Planning should facilitate the integration of spatial planning and environmental protection to achieve positive synergies. It should also aim at inter-ministerial collaboration to ensure the complementarity of sectoral programmes within the framework of planning and development activities.*

### Reforms of the institutional framework

The country's spatial planning system demands efficient collaboration between national and the local levels of planning. The continuing shortage of staff at the Ministry of Environment and Physical Planning with competence in planning is likely to seriously delay essential work. Frequent changes and turnover have left the spatial planning area with no institutional memory and limited legal expertise. The planning system at the local level appears to be highly centralized with planning initiative and development control functions concentrated in Ministry of Transport and Communications institutions and inspectorates. While local/municipal authorities approve and implement spatial plans, their ability to make locally appropriate choices and determine investment priorities is limited by the lack of financial autonomy. The new local government reform is seeking to tap into the potential dynamism of local governments through political, fiscal and administrative decentralization. In the near future local governments will acquire all the powers related to the approval and implementation of spatial plans.

This empowerment without adequate institutional capacity needs serious attention. Some of the most significant constraints at the local level are: (i) the limited and inadequate capacity of local self-government units in urban planning and management; (ii) a lack of standardization of structures responsible for infrastructure planning, financing and maintenance; (iii) the lack of effective urban planning and building control and mechanisms to deal with illegal construction, (iv) the lack of inter-municipal cooperation potential to support common planning and environmental interests and perform joint municipal activities within their competencies.

*Recommendation 12.3:*
*Good planning needs to be supported through capacity-building efforts at the national level. For this purpose, the Ministry of Environment and Physical Planning should develop adequate institutional capacity. Both policy and legal planning frameworks require a considerable effort to enable the efficient operation of real estate markets.*

*Recommendation 12.4:*
*The Ministry of Transport and Communications in cooperation with the Ministry of Local Self-Government and the Ministry of Environment and Physical Planning should develop a strategy for the devolution of planning control and inspection functions to the municipal planning and infrastructure management units. The existing system needs to be reviewed to design appropriate institutional structures suited to the needs of the 123 local authorities.*

### Reforms of the legal framework

Over the past ten years, many new regulations have been introduced into existing planning legislation. While the country's strategy for revising its legal framework for planning appears well conceived, endeavouring to adapt legal instruments to EU practices, progress has been uneven due to financial and institutional constraints. The consequences are a high level of complexity and a low level of transparency. At the local level, inconsistencies and the lack of clear procedures for the coordination of planning and capital investment are creating significant constraints. Reportedly, some of the major difficulties in the implementation process include: (i) difficulties in the phasing of infrastructure investment and collaboration with private interests, (ii) inconsistencies in the pricing and quality of services, (iii) lack of discipline in the payment of infrastructure contributions; and (iv) inadequate resources for inspection and compliance control.

Moreover, the slow privatization of urban land restitution process and an overall lack of real estate data are significant obstacles to the efficient functioning of real estate markets on the one hand, and to market-sensitive planning responses on the other. Spatial planning still appears to be driven by physical planning norms and not necessarily by a strong emphasis on integrated economic, social and environmental planning policies. There are three central dimensions to reforms of the planning legislation: (i) a clarification of property rights in the registry with information on liens, mortgages, easements; (ii) the conversion of existing land-use controls to a transparent system of zoning regulations sensitive to demand; and (iii) the integration of sectoral policies that address local economic development, land use and environmental equity concerns.

*Recommendation 12.5:*
*The Government, through the Ministry of Environment and Physical Planning, should* *accelerate efforts to develop a legislative framework for spatial planning that integrates and reconciles fragmented planning legislation. This should include a review of the spatial plan component of the Law on Physical and Urban Planning, to emphasize integration of physical, economic and environmental planning, and promote the use of a transparent system of zoning regulations sensitive to market demand.*

*Chapter 13*

# TRANSPORT AND THE ENVIRONMENT

## 13.1  General Overview

*Introduction*

Transport plays an important role in the former Yugoslav Republic of Macedonia's economy, providing access to goods, services, and people. The road network is the most developed mode of transport. The main transport corridors (corridors 10 and 8) are an integral part of the trans-European network. Corridor 10 links Western Europe and Hungary to the Aegean Sea (Salzburg and Budapest to Belgrade–Skopje–Veles–Athens); corridor 8 links the Adriatic to the Black Sea (Durres–Tirana–Skopje–Sofia–Burgas). (see figure 13.1)

The road network comprises 12,522 km of roads, of which 53 per cent are surfaced with asphalt, concrete, or cobbled, 5 per cent are made of macadam, and 42 per cent are earth or projected roads. The road network is divided into 909 km of highways (7 per cent of the network - 60 per cent of which are part of the international road network), 3,542 km of regional roads (28 per cent of the network), and 8,071 km of "magistral" or local roads (64 per cent of the network).

The country has 925 km of rail – 697 km of normal track and 233 km of electrified track. The rail corridors roughly follow corridors 10 and 8; the section to the Bulgarian border is still under construction. The rail sector has had financial problems and debts and problems due to old track and old rolling stock, but currently rail freight is profitable. Rail passenger transport is not, perhaps partly due to irregularities in the sale of tickets.

The country has two international airports (Skopje and Ohrid), eight permanent airfields for aerial services to agriculture and forestry, and five recreational airports with grass runways. The cargo area and the navigational equipment at Skopje airport were recently (1995) upgraded, and navigation capacity is now the best in the region. A number of foreign airlines and currently one domestic airline, Macedonian Air Transportation, provide a regular service. In general, air transport is a fast growing sector within the transport industry. There are plans to expand the Skopje airport building, access roads and parking area. The air sub-sector is profitable at the moment, but Skopje may lose some of its air passengers when the airport in Pristina, Kosovo, reopens.

The gas pipeline from Bulgaria extends to Skopje. It is 100 km long and branches out to five adjacent small cities to serve industrial consumers. Although there are plans to supply other industrial sites and residences, there are no plans to supply the transport sector with this pipeline gas. One new transit pipeline to carry crude oil from Skopje to Greece is under construction (90 per cent complete at the time of writing).

Two per cent of the country's surface is water. This is a land-locked country and its road, rail and air transport sector are far more developed than its water transport sector, which serves only a small number of tourists.

*Current status and trends in the transport sector*

Freight Transport

The volume of freight transported by rail and by road in 2000 was respectively 37 per cent and 10 per cent of that transported in 1985. In contrast, airfreight tonnage was four times greater in 1999 than in 1985 (probably due to the Kosovo crisis), and 26 per cent higher in 2000 than in 1985.

Very recently, from 1995 to 2000, road freight decreased by about 31 per cent, whereas rail freight increased by about 70 per cent. The total amount of freight transported in 1999 by rail was almost the same in terms of tonnage as that on roads (2,166,000 vs. 2,327,000 tons, respectively); more freight was transported by rail than by road in 2000 (3,231,000 vs. 2,123,000 tons, respectively). Attracting even more freight to rail would involve improving the security situation, improving the flow and security measures at the border crossings, upgrading the track, the equipment and the machinery, and, especially, developing multimodal terminals to facilitate handling at various locations. (Rail freight users have requested multimodal terminals at Gevgelija, Pilep, or Bitola).

Airfreight has generally increased over time, but its volume has been highly variable throughout the 1990s (note the 1995 and 1999 surges in particular) and it is difficult to identify the true growth trend (i.e. a trend that is separate from the political and security context). (table 13.1)

### Figure 13.1.: Trans-European corridors

### Table 13.1: Freight volume, 1970-1999

thousand tons

| Transport mode | 1970 | 1975 | 1980 | 1985 | 1990 | 1992 | 1995 | 1998 | 1999 | 2000 |
|---|---|---|---|---|---|---|---|---|---|---|
| **Total freight** | **12,352** | **16,081** | **31,864** | **32,132** | **17,864** | **9,225** | **14,134** | **9,611** | **15,775** | **8,866** |
| Rail | 5,853 | 6,500 | 6,520 | 8,779 | 6,499 | 3,995 | 1,910 | 2,694 | 2,166 | 3,231 |
| Road | 6,299 | 8,881 | 23,044 | 20,572 | 8,036 | 4,015 | 3,072 | 1,895 | 2,327 | 2,123 |
| Air | 200 | 700 | 2,300 | 2,781 | 3,329 | 1,215 | 9,152 | 5,022 | 11,282 | 3,512 |

*Source:* Republic of Macedonia. State Statistical Office. Statistical Yearbook 2000 and 2001.

## Passenger Transport

Total transport by rail, road, air and lake, excluding urban traffic, was 18,288,000 passengers in 2000 compared to 63,137,000 passengers in 1985. The number of passengers travelling by rail, road and lake transport in 2000 was, respectively, 28 per cent, 28 per cent, and 33 per cent of those transported in 1985. In contrast, air passengers increased by 274 per cent in 2000 against 1985. Urban traffic in 2000 was about 23 per cent lower than in 1985. Looking more closely at the period from 1995 to 2000, rail passenger transport (albeit a small number overall) increased by 73 per cent, whereas road passenger transport remained fairly constant in 1995–1999, but decreased somewhat in 2000. (table 13.2)

## Public Transport on Roads

From 1995 to 2000, the number and the length of public transport lines decreased, whereas the number of vehicles and seats increased. The total number of passengers using these assets varied by about 610 (plus or minus 10) per cent over this period, down 9 per cent in 2000 compared to 1995.

Public transport issues are in the news. A February 2002 newspaper article reported on the Skopje City Council decision to harmonize operations of the private and public companies providing public transport. The City Council assured the public that the public transport service would be improved by May 2002, specifically by improving the maintenance of buses, improving the organization of the bus lines, providing specific parking places for buses, and improving fee and ticket collection.

## Road Safety

The total number of accidents with victims and the number of victims per 10,000 inhabitants declined between 1994 and 2000. The number of victims per 10,000 inhabitants (12, for the year 2000) is not alarming, but it is somewhat higher than in Western countries, for instance Denmark (2.3) and the United Kingdom (1.5) A February 2002 newspaper article stated that speeding and driving under the influence of alcohol were the main cause of respectively 50 per cent and 30 per cent of the accidents in 2001.

## The Vehicle Fleet

Skopje has approximately 40 per cent of all the motor vehicles registered in the country. In 2000, the average age of the fleet was 11 years. The total number of registered vehicles increased by about 5 per cent between 1995 and 2000 – from 327,269 to 342,468. Some 87 per cent of the registered vehicles are cars, 95 per cent of which are privately owned. The number of "buses", "tractors and working vehicles", and "trailers" decreased over this period (table 13.4). Vehicle ownership in 1996 was 165 per 10,000 inhabitants, which is comparatively low for the region (241 for Bulgaria and 426 for Slovenia).

## Energy for Road Transport

From 1990 to 1998, the transport sector consumed about 21 per cent of the total final consumption of energy; the residential and industrial sectors are the two sectors that consumed more (26–24 per cent and 37 per cent, respectively).

The amount of fuel purchased for road transport decreased by about 27 per cent between 1993 and 2000. The amount of fuel consumed by freight transport decreased by 38 per cent in that period, whereas the amount of fuel consumed by passenger transport decreased by only 19 per cent.

From 1990 to 1996, the consumption of diesel decreased from 83,419 tons to 47,068 tons. Other data (not presented here) indicate that diesel consumption between 1995 and 2000 increased slightly, recovering to about 1993 levels. In 1999, only 10.6 per cent of vehicles used diesel. However, buses and heavy vehicles in the country use low-quality diesel (1 per cent sulphur), which produces even more $SO_2$ when vehicles are poorly serviced.

In 1999, 88.5 per cent of all vehicles used petrol. By vehicle category, 95 per cent of the cars, 19 per cent of the buses, 30 per cent of the light trucks, and 18 per cent of the heavy trucks used petrol (table 13.5). Unleaded petrol (95 Research Octane Number (RON)) has a low, but increasing market share – 9.3 per cent in 1995 and 15.5 per cent in 1999.

There are 208 privately owned petrol stations, of which 75 per cent sell leaded and unleaded petrol. There are 190 tankers in the country. There are no petrol stations with vapour recovery installations systems for tanker or car filling.

## Table 13.2: Transport of passengers, 1970-2000

thousand passengers

| Transport mode | 1970 | 1975 | 1980 | 1985 | 1990 | 1992 | 1995 | 1998 | 1999 | 2000 |
|---|---|---|---|---|---|---|---|---|---|---|
| **Total** | **108,727** | **147,550** | **192,721** | **208,216** | **189,213** | **162,840** | **142,362** | **155,872** | **157,291** | **129,696** |
| Rail | 6,388 | 5,742 | 5,471 | **6,765** | 5,055 | 1,875 | 1,075 | 1,716 | 1,662 | 1,862 |
| Road | 21,543 | 33,730 | 48,587 | 55,975 | 40,665 | 30,540 | 18,505 | 18,310 | 18,336 | 15,407 |
| Air | 57 | 175 | 281 | 367 | 522 | 459 | 623 | 577 | 1,052 | 1,009 |
| Lake | 89 | 40 | 33 | 30 | 34 | 7 | 7 | 15 | 10 | 10 |
| *sub-total* | **28,077** | **39,687** | **54,372** | **63,137** | **46,276** | **32,881** | **20,210** | **20,618** | **21,060** | **18,288** |
| Urban traffic | 80,650 | 107,863 | 138,349 | 145,079 | 142,937 | 129,959 | 122,152 | 135,254 | 136,231 | 111,408 |

*Source:* Republic of Macedonia. State Statistical Office. Statistical Yearbook 2000 and 2001.

## Table 13.3: Transport, network and assets in urban traffic

| | 1995 | 1996 | 1997 | 1998 | 1999 | 2000 |
|---|---|---|---|---|---|---|
| Number of lines | 274 | 232 | 245 | 230 | 233 | 208 |
| Length of lines, km | 8,188 | 4,305 | 6,056 | 4,016 | 4,531 | 4,273 |
| Number of vehicles | 767 | 843 | 780 | 837 | 821 | 894 |
| Number of seats and standing room | 92,249 | 106,311 | 93,899 | N/A | 96,729 | 105,008 |
| Average number of vehicles in traffic in the course of year | 443 | 497 | 417 | 428 | 417 | 600 |
| Passengers carried (in thousands) | 122,152 | 123,064 | 109,052 | 135,254 | 136,231 | 111,408 |

*Source:* Republic of Macedonia. State Statistical Office. Statistical Yearbook 2000 and 2001.

## Table 13.4: Registered motor vehicles and trailers, 1995-2000

| | 1995 | 1996 | 1997 | 1998 | 1999 | 2000 |
|---|---|---|---|---|---|---|
| **Total registered vehicles** | **327,269** | **324,997** | **330,773** | **330,155** | **330,831** | **342,468** |
| Motorcycles | 2,305 | 2,703 | 3,439 | 3,566 | 3,506 | 3,729 |
| Cars | 285,907 | 284,022 | 289,204 | 288,678 | 289,860 | 299,588 |
| Buses | 2,541 | 2,442 | 2,430 | 2,478 | 2,479 | 2,498 |
| Commercial vehicles | 19,546 | 19,375 | 19,815 | 20,075 | 20,011 | 20,763 |
| Special vehicles and road tractors | 7,110 | 7,198 | 7,319 | 7,392 | 7,610 | 8,552 |
| Tractors and working vehicles | 3,251 | 2,800 | 2,424 | 2,192 | 1,777 | 1,417 |
| Trailers | 6,609 | 6,457 | 6,142 | 5,774 | 5,588 | 5,921 |

*Source:* Republic of Macedonia. State Statistical Office. Statistical Yearbook 2000 and 2001.

## Table 13.5: Total final consumption of energy (TFC) by end-use sector

M toe

| | 1990 | 1996 | 1997 | 1998 |
|---|---|---|---|---|
| **Total TFC** | **3.06** | **2.75** | **2.84** | **2.49** |
| Residential | 0.83 | 0.74 | 0.77 | 0.61 |
| Industry | 1.13 | 1.02 | 1.05 | 0.92 |
| Services | 0.17 | 0.14 | 0.16 | 0.20 |
| Transport | 0.64 | 0.58 | 0.59 | 0.52 |
| Agriculture | 0.11 | 0.10 | 0.10 | 0.09 |
| Non-specified | 0.18 | 0.17 | 0.17 | 0.15 |

*Source:* The former Yugoslav Republic of Macedonia. The Energy Charter Secretariat. Protocol on Energy Efficiency and Related Environmental Aspects. Regular review 2001. Draft.

## 13.2 Environmental Impacts of Transport

The transport sector contributes to many environmental problems, during both construction and operation. Especially in their construction phase, transport projects are associated with a wide array of potential impacts on the biological, physical and social environment. These include: damage to flora, fauna, endangered species and sensitive habitats; erosion, sedimentation, and water drainage, supply and quality impacts; waste management impacts (e.g. the improper management of spoil materials and spilled materials, leading to drainage, erosion and water pollution), and social impacts (e.g. resource use conflicts, land acquisition, resettlement and compensation issues, health impacts, including occupational health and safety issues, dust and noise, and damage to the cultural heritage and landscape).

During the operation phase, impacts are mainly related to safety (e.g. road accidents) and air quality. The transport sector contributes an estimated 60 per cent of the carbon monoxide (CO) and 25 per cent of the total energy-related carbon dioxide ($CO_2$), of which 80 per cent comes from road transport. The sector is a major source of volatile organic compounds (VOC). Benzene (a carcinogen) and polyaromatic hydrocarbons (PAH) are some of the most harmful transport-related pollutants. When the vehicle fleet is old, hydrocarbon emissions (in particular benzene) from petrol engines are relatively high. The transport sector generates total suspended particles (TSP), which can cause respiratory problems. The use of leaded fuel releases lead into the environment, with vehicle emissions being the largest source of lead exposure in many urban areas. The transport sector contributes to acid rain by producing some sulphur dioxide ($SO_2$), and it contributes more than half of total nitrogen oxide emissions ($NO_x$). Transport is a major generator of noise, accounting for 80 per cent of noise nuisance in some countries. Traffic noise has been associated with serious annoyance, sleep loss, communication problems, and learning difficulties in children. (High noise levels have recently been associated with hypertension and ischaemic heart disease.) At the time of writing, country-specific noise data for the transport sector were not available.

There are no quantitative data on the construction-phase impacts of transport projects, nor are comprehensive statistics on the contribution to pollution during the operational phase available. The country, for instance, has no data on the number of people affected by noise from roads, railways and airports. The air-quality monitoring network does not specifically measure air quality along the major corridors and big road arteries, nor does it measure all the important transport-related pollutants.

There are some air quality data. The lead content of the ambient air is not routinely measured, but cars in the former Yugoslav Republic of Macedonia are known to emit high levels of lead (25 g/capita/year). A study on the abatement of greenhouse gases estimated that transport contributed 8.8 per cent of the $CO_2$ in 1994. Table 13.6 gives the 1993 data (presented in the 1996

National Environmental Action Plan) on the vehicle emission contribution to the main pollutants.

The 1999 Annual Report for Air Quality in Skopje showed that the CO concentration at the monitoring station closest to the busiest traffic zone was above the maximum allowable concentration (MAC) for 11 of the 12 months. The other three stations, with less traffic, exceeded the MAC for CO for 3 to 9 months of the 12-month period. The data from the four monitoring stations in Skopje also show that the MAC for $SO_2$, $NO_2$, and TSP were regularly exceeded during the winter months, mainly it was thought because of winter heating and temperature inversion, rather than traffic.

**Table 13.6: Air quality**

|        | in tons |
|--------|--------:|
| $SO_2$ | 457     |
| VOC    | 16,732  |
| $NO_2$ | 11,348  |
| CO     | 48,148  |
| Pb     | 83      |
| TSP    | 1,830   |

*Source:* National Environmental Action Plan, 1996.

## 13.3 Policy, legislative and institutional framework

*Environmental Policies and the Transport Sector*

The Ministry of Transport and Communications does not have a strategic planning document that outlines the goals and policies of its multimodal transport network. The country as a whole does not yet have a sustainable development strategy, but the conceptual approach to such a strategy is in place.

Transport and environment policies, albeit fragmented, are emerging from outside the Ministry of Transport and Communications. The 1996 Law on the Environment and Nature Protection and Promotion and the National Environmental Action Plan (NEAP), both currently under revision, provide the framework for all environmental policies in the country. The NEAP identified poor air quality in Veles and Skopje as a critical environmental issue. It advocated two main transport-related actions: (i) to tax dirty fuels more heavily to encourage the use of cleaner fuels (see also Chapter 3 on Economic instruments and privatization); and (ii) to phase out lead from petrol.

The country ratified the Energy Charter Treaty and the Protocol on Energy Efficiency and Related Environmental Aspects in September 1998. In 1999, the Government approved a long-term Programme for Energy Efficiency. The Ministry of Economy expects to complete the Energy Efficiency Strategy in 2002. One of the general objectives of the energy efficiency policy is the 'rational use of energy in industry, transport and other consumption sectors'. It specifically highlights that '…efficient energy use is possible through the rational use of vehicles, a reduction of the age of the vehicles on the road, an increased use of public transport, a gradual transition from road to rail traffic'. It is unclear whether the Ministry of Transport and Communications was involved in the development of these objectives. It should be noted that the draft regular review under the Protocol on Energy Efficiency and Related Environmental Aspects lists instruments and measures for the residential, industrial and service sectors, but does not list any energy efficiency instruments, measures or programmes for the transport sector.

## Urban and regional planning for transport

To address pressures on the urban areas and to ensure the management of growth-related environmental impacts, the Law on Physical and Urban Planning was passed in 1996. The national spatial plan and the master plan for Skopje for the period 2001–2020 were developed under this Law.

The national spatial plan has been before Parliament awaiting approval for the past two years. The plan addresses environmental protection in a general manner, and for the transport sector, it specifically highlights the need to monitor the transport of hazardous wastes and materials and to implement measures to reduce air emissions. The plan also identifies the need to construct the Skopje bypass road to improve air quality and to better manage inter-urban and transit traffic. (Note that the construction of the Skopje bypass should begin in July 2002; the project, partially donor-funded, has gone through an EIA procedure.)

A detailed study completed in 2000 forms the basis of the Skopje master plan. The study provided many interesting findings, such as the fact that pedestrians make 33.5 per cent of the urban trips and that the average speed downtown is 3–7 km/hour. The study also estimated that the petrol wasted at one busy downtown crossroad was worth US$ 500 000 a year (excluding the air pollution costs), whereas building a multilevel crossing to alleviate the problem would cost about US$ 2 million.

The study highlighted that Skopje's primary street network is only 50 per cent complete. Hence, in some areas, large volumes of traffic must go through one point. The study and the master plan recommend that two new links should be built in downtown Skopje to relieve the extreme congestion (and concomitant traffic-related air pollution problems). As for public transport, the study identified some direct lines that are not being serviced at this time, recommended measures to better organize the public transport system, such as adding four suburban terminals, and identified the need to develop tram or light railway lines in some areas to accommodate future transport needs. A road design that accommodates non-motorized traffic is also proposed – the design includes bicycle tracks and footpaths. The master plan for Skopje is also awaiting approval.

*Project Expenditures and the Transport Sector*

The transport sector accounts for about 52 per cent of the Government's project expenditure for 2001–2003 and beyond. This represents about 50 per cent of foreign loans and 53 per cent of foreign grants. Repayment of this debt may become a long-term drain on the economy. The US$ 1,080 million transport-sector expenditure is divided between the sub-sectors as follows:
- Air: 0.5 per cent     US$ 5.57 million;
- Rail: 33 per cent     US$ 355.84 million;
- Road: 65.5 per cent US$ 707.15 million; and
- General:1 per cent   US$ 11.23 million.

The largest rail project in terms of finance is on the completion of the railway to the Bulgarian border, but only after 2003. The two largest road projects include the Skopje bypass (to be completed by 2003) and the Veles–Prelip road (after 2003). Road maintenance (main and regional roads) receives on average about 5–14 per cent of the budget, depending on the year. Local roads and city streets receive 3–8 per cent of the budget. The maintenance budget is low.

There are no projects in the list aimed at enhancing public transport, improving the conditions for non-motorized transport, or improving traffic management, nor are there projects to promote the use of cleaner vehicles, cleaner fuels, or the use of rail transport. There are no projects to promote and develop combined (integrated) transport (i.e.

transport centres, where different transport modes will meet, and where the transfer of passengers and goods is convenient).

*Legislation, regulations, and standards concerning transport*

A number of sub-sector-specific laws outline responsibilities and penalties to ensure that infrastructure work is completed to a high standard. These usually include certain aspects of environmental management. They comprise, but are not limited to, the Law on Road Safety, the Law on Roads, the Law on the Transport of Hazardous Materials, the Air Shipment Law, and the Law on Work and the Protection of the Workplace.

Furthermore, infrastructure projects are usually awarded as large contracts, which must respect a set of general contract conditions (usually set by the Fédération Internationale des Ingénieurs-Conseil (FIDIC)), special contract conditions, standard specifications and special specifications. Environmental management is addressed to some extent in those legally binding documents.

In most countries, however, the environmental management of transport sector impacts is synonymous with completing an EIA procedure. The former Yugoslav Republic of Macedonia does not have an EIA law and the current draft law is incomplete and should be harmonized with the EU Directive on EIA. Once the country has an EIA law, much work will be needed to institutionalize and implement the general and sector-specific procedures.

### Fuel Quality Standards and the Phase out of Leaded Petrol

The composition of fuel affects vehicle emissions. For instance, fuels with a high sulphur content inhibit emission-reduction technology. High benzene and aromatic levels in petrol cause high benzene concentration in exhaust emissions. The lead content of petrol is a major source of lead pollution – a health risk – and is incompatible with catalytic converters.

The country signed the Protocols on Persistent Organic Pollutants (POP) and Heavy Metals and must phase out leaded petrol. The new lead standards for petrol have a long implementation schedule:

| | |
|---|---|
| To 31 December 2004 | 0.6 g/l |
| To 31 December 2005 | 0.3 g/l |
| From 1 January 2006 | 0.15 g/l |

Some measures have been taken to encourage the use of unleaded petrol. For instance, a fee is paid to register motor vehicles – 4 per cent of the basic insurance in general or 2 per cent for vehicles equipped with catalytic converters. The tax differentiation between leaded and unleaded petrol is at EU levels and is judged sufficient (RON-98 is €43 /1,000 litres higher than unleaded RON-95). According to the law, it is prohibited to import second-hand cars more than six years old from Western Europe or Asia.

More could be done to expedite the phasing-out of lead. A study by the former Yugoslav Republic of Macedonia, the Ministry of Economy, Exergia, Energo-Sistem, Envirosmarch (2001) found that only 15–30 per cent of the cars currently in use are unsuited to unleaded petrol, and these old vehicles will probably be replaced by the time the lead phase-out comes into force. The lack of information is thought to be the reason why consumers have not switched to unleaded petrol. (The above study also identified an approach to overcoming the difficulties in phasing out lead.)

### Other standards

There are vehicle noise standards in effect (for example, 74 db for vehicles with fewer than nine seats), but these need to be revised. As of 1998, the country has CO emission limits for vehicles with diesel engines that are the same as the EU legislation. The new specifications for the sulphur content of diesel fuel will come into effect in 2005. Although these new specifications are an improvement, they are not up to EU standards. New limit values for other car emissions are expected when the new law on air pollution is passed.

### Vehicle Inspection Programmes and Emissions Testing

Regulation No. 28 of 13 May 1999 controls the technical inspection of motor vehicles, tractors and agricultural tractors. Tests are conducted yearly on all petrol- and diesel-powered vehicles by authorized vehicle-testing centres located throughout the country. The vehicle tests mainly focus on roadworthiness (e.g. brakes, lights). In terms of emissions, the Regulation requires the testing of the opacity of the exhaust gas from vehicles with diesel engines. The Regulation also requires the measurement of the CO content of exhaust gases from vehicles with petrol engines. The maximum permissible CO content of exhaust gases from petrol-powered vehicles is 4.5 per cent vol. This standard is used by the EU Member States for vehicles manufactured without catalytic converters before 1986. This standard, as used here, does not differentiate on the basis of the year the car was produced or on whether the vehicle is equipped with a catalytic converter.

### Responsible Institutions

There are four main institutions responsible for environmental management in the transport sector. These are the Ministry of Transport and Communications, the Ministry of Environment and Physical Planning, the Ministry of Economy, and the Ministry of Local Self-Government.

### The Ministry of Transport and Communications

The Ministry of Transport and Communications is responsible for transport matters. Through its various departments, agencies and authorities, it plans, designs, executes and monitors transport sector projects, and, as such, is largely responsible for its own environmental management. The Ministry of Transport and Communications assists with network planning and financial aspects and issues building and operations permits for transport projects. The following bodies support the Ministry:

- The *Urban Planning, Traffic, and Environmental Institute*, a private sector company, helps in transport planning and has provided the Government with a spatial plan for the country and a master plan for the city of Skopje;
- The *Civil Aviation Administration* plans, designs and executes air transport projects, inspects aircraft, and handles air passengers, mail and cargo;
- The *Railways Directorate* plans, designs and executes railway projects, and maintains the rail infrastructure;
- The *Fund for National and Regional Roads* plans, designs and executes road projects; and
- The *Maintenance Agency* maintains the road network.

Large rail and road projects that are externally funded at least in part usually comply with international environmental management practice. To date, the Fund for National and Regional Roads has been involved in four environmental impact assessments (EIA); the rail sector has completed two. The EIA results were integrated into the project design, as is typical of general good practice. The road and rail agencies have developed a certain sub-sector-specific environmental management capacity in the process.

About 70 transport-related staff participated in environmental management study tours in 2000 and 2001, and another study tour is planned for 2002. Furthermore, France and Germany are planning environmental seminars for the sector in 2002.

There are plans to restructure the road and the rail sub-sectors. Some aspects of the rail system may be privatized. The Fund for National and Regional Roads is currently completing its restructuring plan. As of 2003, highways will be separated from "magistral" and regional roads. The reorganization includes a plan to establish an environmental unit in the development section of the new highways authority.

### The Ministry of Environment and Physical Planning

The Ministry of Environment and Physical Planning is responsible for environmental protection by creating and implementing environmental policy. The Department for Regulation and Standardization, the Department for European Integration, the Environmental Information Centre, the Department for Sustainable Development, the Environment Office all interact with transport-and-environment issues when carrying out their various tasks. Furthermore, the Ministry reviews transport project applications and may recommend some conditions. Although the general impression is that its recommendations and conditions are seriously taken into consideration by the Ministry of Transport and Communications, the Ministry of Environment and Physical Planning does not at present have the authority to refuse a project.

Because of its strategic focus, the Department for Sustainable Development is the most suited to coordinate strategic and sector-level EIAs. This would be a new function for the Department, and the work would have to be coordinated with the Ministry of Transport and Communications, which would need to assign an environmental officer to the task.

### Ministry of Economy

The Ministry of Economy is the ministry responsible for energy. Policy changes here could have significant implications for the transport–environment question. (This is further discussed in the section on environmental policies and the transport sector (above) and in Chapter 11 on Industry, energy and the environment).

### Local government

Local government has various departments, including urban planning, construction, and traffic and environment. It is responsible for local infrastructure, including the regulation of public transport. Little attention has been given to developing environmental management capacity and, specifically, EIA and environmental management capacity for the transport sector at the local level.

### Other institutions

Other institutions have various important functions. For instance, the Ministry of Finance registers vehicles and limits the age of the vehicles allowed to enter the country. The Ministry of Internal Affairs collects information on the vehicle fleet, including aspects related to insurance, the age of the vehicle fleet, and the use of diesel fuel. Independent specialized businesses provide vehicle inspections and vehicle emission testing, issuing the necessary certificates when the vehicles are in compliance.

## 13.4 Conclusions and recommendations

The transport sector continues to be significantly affected by the political and socio-economic changes and security issues of the past decade. In brief:

- Freight transport and passenger transport by road and rail were down in the 1990s compared to the levels experienced in the mid-1980s.
- Fuel consumption declined in the 1990s compared to the mid-1980s.
- Recent data covering the 1995–2000 period show:

  - A decreasing trend in road freight;
  - A slight decrease in road passengers;
  - An old vehicle fleet (more than 11 years) and a slow increase in the number of vehicles (1 per cent per year on average);
  - Small variations (e.g. 122,152,000 in 1995 vs. 111,408,000 passengers in 2000) in the use of public transport;
  - An increasing trend in rail freight;
  - An increasing trend in rail passengers, albeit a small number of rail passengers overall;
  - A decreasing trend in gas oil and petrol consumption;
  - An increase to 1993 levels in diesel consumption.
- Airfreight volumes, although generally higher, have been too variable between years to identify short-term trends.
- The number of air passengers, although also quite sensitive to the political climate, is generally increasing.
- Because of domestic political instability, transport data for 2001 are expected to be somewhat down compared to 2000.

The transport sector already contributes to many environmental problems. The construction phase has biological, physical and social impacts. The operational phase has an impact on air quality, with $CO$, $NO_2$, $Pb$, $TSP$, $VOC$ and noise probably the most important. Assuming that the political security and economic situation will soon return to normal, a general increase in transport parameters (e.g. volume of freight, number of passengers, fuel consumption, vehicle fleet, and vehicle use) can be expected and pressures on the environment will increase proportionally.

As noted in the previous sections, the country has gone some way in managing the environmental impacts of transport through its institutions, policies, laws, regulations and standards. Other recommendations that logically flow from the discussions in this chapter are treated in other chapters, for instance, recommendations on air quality monitoring, air quality standards and emissions standards, and recommendations on the need to approve the national spatial plan and the master plan for Skopje.

Increasingly, strategic environmental assessments (SEAs) are becoming the norm for setting transport policy and goals. SEAs typically cover all transport modes and evaluate the environmental effects of the transport system as a whole, (e.g. the shift to other transport modes or to public transport, as well as air quality criteria for the protection of human health). Such a strategic document (which should also integrate the Ministry of Economy's energy efficiency strategy) could shift investment decisions towards, for instance, projects that make public transport or rail more attractive. It should also be emphasized that good and timely maintenance, i.e. investment in maintenance, is an excellent environmental management practice because it minimizes resource use and protects valuable assets for the duration of their expected life span.

*Recommendation 13.1:*
*The Ministry of Transport and Communications should establish an environmental unit to coordinate policy-level environmental issues [e.g. a strategic environmental assessment of the transport sector]. Following the completion of the restructuring being undertaken by the Fund for National and Regional Roads, an environmental unit should also be established in the new highway authority. The environmental units should be adequately staffed, trained, equipped and funded so that they can ensure environmental standards in all aspects of transport management.*

*Recommendation 13.2:*
*The Ministry of Transport and Communication should prepare a Transport Plan subject to a strategic environmental assessment. The Ministry of Environment and Physical Planning should support the carrying out of the strategic environmental assessment. The Ministry of Finance and the Ministry of Transport and Communications*

*should allocate funds within the transport sub-sectors (road, rail, air) taking into account the results of the strategic environmental assessment.*

For a comprehensive treatment of environmental matters in the transport sector, sector-specific guidelines, procedures and specifications are needed. When environmental tasks are clearly and correctly specified in guidelines, procedures and specifications (and bills of quantities), the engineers and the contractors *will* obligatorily implement environmental management or face sanctions.

*Recommendation 13.3:*
*Upon completion of the general Environmental Impact Assessment procedures, the Ministry of Environment and Physical Planning should work with the Ministry of Transport and Communications to develop sector-specific environmental impact assessment (EIA) guidelines.*

Many targets for a lead phase-out strategy and action plan, for example, an information campaign as to which cars can use unleaded petrol, were identified in a comprehensive study completed by the former Yugoslav Republic of Macedonia, the Ministry of Economy, Exergia, and Energo-Sistem, and Envirosmarch in 2001.

*Recommendation 13.4:*
*The Ministry of Environment and Physical Planning, together with the Ministry of Economy and other stakeholders, should develop a clear strategy and action plan with set targets and an implementation schedule to phase out the use of leaded petrol.*

*Chapter 14*

# HUMAN HEALTH AND THE ENVIRONMENT

## 14.1 Overall health status and environmental conditions

*Population development*

The population of the former Yugoslav Republic of Macedonia totalled 2 million inhabitants in 2001, of whom 62 per cent lived in urban areas. Since 1991, the year of the country's independence, the population has increased by 5.4 per cent. The most recent estimates confirm a decline in the population growth rate, which in 2001 was estimated at 0.43 per cent.

Life expectancy at birth has increased by approximately one year since 1991, and in 2000 reached 73.4 years, which is in line with the averages in Europe as a whole and in Central Europe (73.5 and 73.1 years, respectively), though still five years lower than the EU average (78.2 years). Women's life expectancy is four and a half years longer than men's.

Total fertility rates declined from 2.5 in 1978 to 1.9 per 1000 in 2000. Abortions also decreased to 389.2 per 1000 live births in 2000, a rate which is approximately half that of the Central and Eastern European countries and just over one third of that of the countries of the former Soviet Union. Infant mortality has decreased steadily, from 30.6 per 1,000 live births in 1992 to 11.8 in 2000, in line with the Central and East European average (11.1) and twice the EU average (5.1). Within the country, the highest infant mortality was reported in the area of Prilep, where the rate is about one third higher than the national average (16.9 per 1000 live births). In rural areas infant mortality is still significantly higher than in urban areas.

The probability of dying before the age of 5 years was estimated at 13.7 per 1000 live births in 2000, a third of the figure for 1991. Deaths due to diarrhoeal diseases among children under 5 years peaked at 100.6 per 100,000 in 1992 and fell to 16.4 per 100,000 in 2000. Much progress remains to be made, however, as this is still four times higher than the Central and East European average and almost 30 times higher than that of the European Union.

*Development of selected causes of death*

Standardized mortality rates fell slightly overall during the past decade, decreasing from a high of 1,094.3 per 100,000 population in 1992 to 1,014.5 per 100,000 in 2000 (i.e. a rate similar to that reported in 1991). These rates are in line with the Central and East European average, though some 1.5 times higher than in the European Union.

More than 80 per cent of all deaths are caused by five main groups of diseases, which are also linked to the environmental conditions in the country. Those affecting the circulatory system are the principal cause of death, accounting for nearly 60 per cent of all deaths: This trend has remained stable during the past decade and, though in line with the Central and East European average, it is twice that of the EU. Mortality due to malignant neoplasms has increased overall over the past ten years to second place, with a standardized death rate lower than those in the EU and in Central and Eastern Europe. Also cancer incidence records show an increase in the disease to double the 1991 numbers, according to the most recent available data (from 1998, when cancer incidence at all sites was 306.0 per 100,000 population).

External causes (injuries and poisoning) are the third cause of deaths. Among these, suicides account for about 20 per cent, traffic accidents for 14 per cent (one of the lowest in Europe), and homicides for 8 per cent (almost twice the number in 1991). Regarding traffic accidents, the low and overall decreasing trend observed since 1996 (when death rates went up to 8 per 100,000) are more a reflection of the stagnation of road traffic than of an improvement in the transport system's safety. In 2000, 12 people per 100,000 inhabitants died or were injured as the result of a traffic accident. A total of 2,502 accidents were reported, with 162 deaths and 2,340 people injured.

**Figure 14.1 Mortality rate trends in the former Yugoslav Republic of Macedonia compared to other Central and East European countries, 1991-2000**

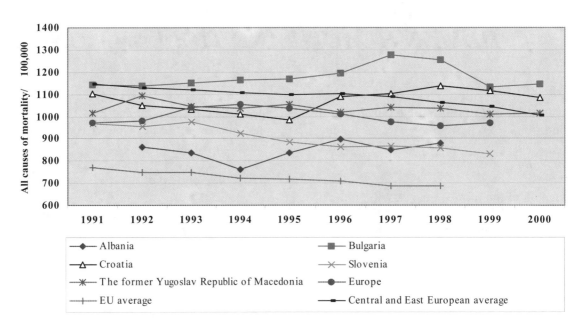

*Source:* WHO. Health for All data base. January 2002.

**Table 14.1: Standardized mortality rates for the most important causes of death, 2000**

all ages, per 100,000 population

|  | The former Yugoslav Republic of Macedonia | EU average (1998) | Central and East European average |
|---|---|---|---|
| All causes | 1014.5 (100%) | 687.0 (100%) | 1007.8 (100%) |
| Diseases of the circulatory system | 582.2 (57 %) | 266.8 (39 %) | 578.1 (57 %) |
| Malignant neoplasms | 163.6 (16 %) | 187.6 (27 %) | 205.0 (20 %) |
| External causes | 37.9 (4 %) | 40.6 (6 %) | 65.6 (7 %) |
| Diseases of the respiratory system | 36.8 (3%) | 56.8 (8.2 %) | 50.6 (5 %) |
| Diseases of the digestive system | 18.8 (2 %) | 32.1 (5 %) | 49.2 (5 %) |

*Source:* WHO. Health For All Database. January 2002.

Diseases of the respiratory system are the fourth cause of death, with bronchitis, emphysema and asthma accounting for more than 60 per cent of them. Digestive system diseases represent the fifth cause of death, with a substantial proportion (approximately 40 per cent) attributed to chronic liver diseases and cirrhosis. Important risk factors for these conditions are alcohol consumption (estimated at 3.2 litres per person in 2000) and hepatitis infections (which in the former Yugoslav Republic of Macedonia are among the highest incidence rates in Europe).

There are significant variations in mortality rates between the different parts of the country, as summarized in table 14.2. The area of Bitola,

identified as one of the "environmental hot spots" of the country, reports the highest mortality for all causes of death.

*Trends in infectious disease morbidity*

The incidence of tuberculosis in 2000 was 31.6 per 100,000 population, and had not changed significantly over the previous decade. Tetovo reports the highest incidence with 48.4/100,000. Several factors determine the incidence of this disease, among them poor housing conditions, overcrowding, deteriorating socio-economic conditions and reduced immunological responsiveness.

**Table 14.2: Standardized mortality rates for the most important causes of death, 2000**

all ages, per 100,000 population

|  | All causes | Infant mortality / 1000 live births | Malignant neoplasms | Infectious and parasitic diseases | Respiratory diseases | Circulatory diseases |
|---|---|---|---|---|---|---|
| Skopje | 771.7 | .. | 169.5 | 7.7 | 22.2 | 397.5 |
| Tetovo | 651.1 | 8.2 | 119.4 | 16.8 | 26.4 | 352.7 |
| Ohrid | 48.9 | 9.2 | 130.1 | 4.5 | 36.1 | 461.3 |
| Bitola | 1114.1 | 10.5 | 184.3 | 5.4 | 34.8 | 701.5 |
| Prilep | .. | 16.9 | .. | .. | .. | 506.4 |
| Veles | 919.4 | 15.2 | 164.8 | 10.5 | 32.5 | 398.3 |
| Kumanovo | 900.9 | 10.9 | 63.8 | 8.8 | 51.5 | 540.1 |
| Kocani | 884.6 | 14.9 | 124.0 | 13.1 | 42.8 | 562.4 |
| Stip | 873.0 | 12.4 | 144.2 | .. | .. | 498.1 |
| Strumica | 777.2 | 14.7 | 70.2 | 10.5 | 44.5 | 172.5 |

*Source:* Health For All Database of the former Yugoslav Republic of Macedonia. February 2002.

## 14.2 Environmental conditions associated with health risks

The country has a few environmental hot spots, characterized by high levels of pollution (air, water and soil), due to emissions from industrial facilities, as summarized in the table below.

*Health effects of air pollution (see also Chapter 7 on Air management)*

Problems due to air pollution affect approximately 60 per cent of the population, i.e. some 1,225,000, in particular, those living in the cities of Skopje, Veles, Bitola and Tetovo.

The health effects of particulate air pollution depend on particle size, composition and concentration, and can fluctuate with daily changes in $PM_{10}$ or $PM_{2.5}$ levels. This is the particulate fraction of the greatest concern for health, as it penetrates the respiratory system. Particulate matter may have acute health effects, such as increased mortality, increased hospital admissions because of the exacerbation of respiratory disease, fluctuations in bronchodilator use, cough and peak flow reductions. There are also long-term effects on mortality and respiratory morbidity, but there are fewer studies on them.

It is very difficult to estimate the health effects of particulate matter in the country, because only black smoke and inert dust are measured. Inert dust monitoring data for 2000 in Skopje indicate a yearly average of 208.8 $mg/m^2$ with the highest average monthly concentration in April (554.5 $mg/m^2$).

$PM_{10}$ and $PM_{2.5}$ are not monitored in the former Yugoslav Republic of Macedonia. It is therefore not possible to make quantitative estimates of their health effects with the data collected by the present air quality monitoring system. From a qualitative point of view, particulate matter pollution frequency levels reached in Skopje, Bitola, Veles and Stip are expected to be related to increased incidence of lower respiratory illness in children, of chronic obstructive pulmonary diseases, of asthma episodes, as well as increases in adult mortality. Lead is still present in fuels and in the air from the smelter operating in Veles. According to the World Health Organization (WHO), blood lead levels in children of 100 to 150 µg/l have been consistently reported as having a negative effect on measures of cognitive functioning, such as the psychometric intelligence quotient. Other sources of exposure to lead may include lead-ceramic pottery, lead-soldered cans and contaminated soil.

Analyses of monthly morbidity reports produced by the Public Health Institutes show that both pre-schoolers (under 6 years of age) and schoolchildren (aged between 7 and 14 years) living in polluted cities, such as Skopje and Veles, have a higher (up to 2 – 3 times) level of morbidity from respiratory diseases (excluding influenza and pneumonia) than children living in relatively less polluted villages. The difference is particularly high in winter, when heating and climatic factors (including temperature inversion) contribute to an increase in air pollutants (especially $SO_2$ and black smoke).

**Table 14.3:  Some environmental hot spots in the former Yugoslav Republic of Macedonia**

| HAZARDOUS SITE | HAZARDS | POSSIBLE HEALTH EFFECTS | POTENTIAL NUMBER OF PEOPLE EXPOSED | MEASURES TO REDUCE EXPOSURE |
|---|---|---|---|---|
| Jegunovce (ferro-alloy plant) | Groundwater contamination by chromium (III); air pollution; chromium slag contaminating River Vardar (and Rasce Spring) | Chromium (IV) is carcinogenic, lung diseases | 2,000 workers; 7,000 inhabitants | Removal of chromium; thoroughly monitor wells, the Rasce Spring and mapping of Cr in groundwaters; introduce secure waste handling methods; apply the Basel Convention |
| Skopje (organic chemical plant) | Organic chemical plant; HCH isomers are stored; waste water into Vardar River; SO$_2$ in flue gases | Carcinogenic (liver), liver, kidney and immune system diseases; SO$_2$ affects lung function | 444,000 inhabitants | Urgent short-term measures: covering storage area with durable materials, monitoring wells. Long-term: renewal of the waste-water treatment plant, continuous monitoring and control of health parameters, separate collection of hazardous waste |
| Bitola (electric power plant) | Emissions of fly ash containing heavy metals and uranium compounds, and SO$_2$; possible soil and water contamination by heavy metals in the ash | Health checks among workers: Potentially uranium compounds could cause lung cancer and tumours of the lymphatic and bone tissues Effects from exposure to particulate matter (respiratory and cardiovascular diseases) | 77,500 inhabitants; 1,400 workers | Technological; separation into compartments with different layers of fly ash and slag; waste-water treatment plant; Informing the residents and workers |
| Veles (lead and zinc smelter "MHK Zletovo") | Air emissions of SO$_2$, lead, cadmium. An assessment of contamination by heavy metals conducted in 2001 indicates a higher level of lead contamination in soil, agricultural products and waste water from the smelter than in soil and agricultural products sampled in a control area | Toxic and carcinogenic effects in pregnant women and children; central nervous system damage; increased risk of lung, bladder and pleura cancer mortality. Preliminary results from 239 children indicate a significantly higher lead blood level and anaemia in the study group than in the control group | 46,800 inhabitants; 1,000 workers | Filters, air monitoring should be done closer to the site; reconstruction of waste-water treatment plant; soil and groundwater monitoring. Provide the residents and workers with reliable and consistent information on the level of environmental contamination |
| Probistip (zinc and lead mine) | Zinc and lead | Ingestions of zinc in high quantities might lead to nausea and vomiting. Lead: toxic and carcinogenic effects in pregnant women and children; central nervous system damage | 12,950 inhabitants; 1,500 workers | Construct waste-water treatment plant, monitoring and investigating wells downstream, monitoring private wells |

*Source:* UNEP. Post conflict Environmental Assessment – FYR of Macedonia 2000.

---

**Box 14.1:    Case study: Air quality warning system in Skopje**

Skopje has air quality problems from stationary pollution sources (central heating power plants, cement factory, chemical complex and refinery) and transport. This is aggravated by the geographic location of the valley with poor air circulation and heat accumulation. In 1989 the city of Skopje adopted a decision regulating extraordinary measures to be taken in case of critical high air pollution levels. SO$_2$ and black smoke concentrations are measured daily, and if the level is critical over consecutive days, the three-step alarm system starts. The first level of alarm consists of warnings issued to the public (through the media), inviting the population to restrict outdoor activities. The second level includes restrictions on private traffic in the city centre, while the third level adds the temporary shutting down of plants and heating plants. Furthermore, reserves of crude oil with a reduced sulphur content (below 1 per cent instead of 2 per cent) for approximately one month have to be kept aside for use under alarm levels two and three. Since its implementation the alarm system has reached the highest level of alarm only in 1993, when a winter smog episode lasted for 20 consecutive days. The city of Veles is thinking of adopting a similar system.

*Indoor air pollution*

Indoor pollution in homes is not monitored. The use of asbestos is no longer allowed, but it is still present in buildings which have been neither cleaned up nor demolished. Any problems of exposure to asbestos are considered to be of an occupational nature.

Smoking prevalence was assessed in a survey among 1,203 medical doctors (i.e. about 25 per cent of the total) in 1999. The survey estimated that approximately 36 per cent of the population over 15 years of age were regular smokers, with a higher prevalence among males (40 per cent) than females (32 per cent).

The Law on Smoking (1994) restricted the advertising of tobacco products on TV and radio, but not in newspapers. It also prohibited the sale of tobacco products to persons under 16 years of age. Smoking is officially banned in aircraft, public transport, offices, schools, cinemas, health organizations, and the workplace, where one room for smokers should be provided. Smoking is still allowed in bars and restaurants. Responsibility for enforcing the Law lies with the inspection services of the Ministry of Health and Ministry of Labour and Social Policy. Although the Law lays down penalties for offenders, in practice, these are not enforced, and the Law is flouted. It should be noted that the former Yugoslav Republic of Macedonia is a tobacco-growing country, and that this crop is supported by the Government.

The Ministry of Health is taking steps to implement the WHO programme "Tobacco-Free Europe" and is preparing a national action plan for smoking controls in the country. There are difficulties in effective collaboration with the other ministries involved (Agriculture and Finance). The possibility of developing a new law to bring the norms closer to those in the EU and to enforce smoking bans more vigorously is under consideration.

*Drinking water, waste water and health*

Approximately 60 per cent of the drinking water is supplied from carstic springs, 20 per cent from surface waters, and 20 per cent from groundwaters, through wells. Professional communal services, the local Public Health Institutes, in cooperation with the State Public Health Institute control the quality of drinking water. In rural settlements water control is the responsibility of local communities. The control measures, frequency and standards do not yet comply with EU regulations and WHO Drinking Water Guidelines.

The Ministry of Transport manages drinking water infrastructure (primary infrastructure) and operational adjustments are managed by municipal enterprises (secondary infrastructures; pipes to houses). As user charges are low and very often not collected, enterprises are unable to maintain adequate technical standards. Municipalities are also in charge of disinfecting drinking water.

Surface waters in high mountainous areas often contain excessive concentrations of saprophytic bacteria, caused by extensive livestock breeding during the summer and by the life processes in the upper layer of the soil. The nitrate content in these waters is low.

The chemical quality of drinking water varies with the origin of drinking water sources. Almost all karstic and surface water, and significant amounts of well water, are notably short in fluoride, which helps prevent tooth decay. Some wells in Veles, Shtip and Kocani have relatively high contents of iron and manganese, and nitrates range between 1 and 5 mg/l. During the summer higher nitrate concentrations have been found in wells in Prilep and Radovish (10-15 mg/l). Both wells are situated in regions where the land is intensively used for agriculture. The nitrite content is generally below 1 mg/l. In some wells iron and manganese impair the organoleptic quality of the water (Veles, Stip, Kocani and some rural settlements). Toxic parameters, such as lead, arsenic, chromium and cadmium concentrations, meet WHO standards. A few wells in rural settlements have unusual levels of for ammonia, nitrite, nitrate and $KMn_4$.

Five per cent of all wells assessed by the Public Health Institute are microbiologically contaminated. From 1970 to 1997, there were several water-borne epidemics, caused by serious failures in the distribution networks, or the non-respect of the sanitary protection zones, combined with poor local hygiene practices which increase the likelihood of faecal-oral transmission. Hepatitis A outbreaks occurred in Debar (1978), Kratovo (1980), Probistip (1993) and Veles (1990).

Mineral and thermal mineral water springs are used as spas, for tourism, and as a source of bottled water. Water quality and safety meet national standards. Only some artesian wells presented high mineralization with the presence of iron, manganese and inorganic ammonia.

*Food Safety*

About 25,000 samples of food are tested annually for their microbiological safety, 40 per cent of which are from imported foods and 60 per cent from domestic production. In 1997, 4-6 per cent of domestically produced food samples of industrial origin and some 10 per cent of food samples from small enterprises were found to be contaminated and 8-10 per cent of contamination cases occurred in the distribution chain. The most frequent contaminants are: Staphylococcus aureus, E. coli, Proteus, and, to a lesser extent, mould and mildew.

Microbiological contamination of food is widespread. The large number of private farmers and small production enterprises, as well as the enormous number of small trade and catering firms make legal controls very difficult. Due to the ambiguity of the law, a number of those entities do not have suitable premises, equipment, staff, professional skills or standard hygiene conditions. The conditions prevailing in traditional markets are unhygienic. Fast-food shops are increasing and generally do not comply with hygiene standards.

As for pesticides, only organo-chlorinated and organo-phosphoric insecticides are monitored in food products. A limited number of rice samples taken in the area of Kocani have been tested for carbamate insecticides and herbicides. Of a total of 10,000-12,000 samples analysed each year for the presence of insecticides, concentrations above MAC were found in 0.01 per cent. The presence of the organo-chlorinated insecticides lindane and HCH was detected. The concentrations of lindane detected in plant products were very low, ranging between 0.2 and 2.6 per cent of the MAC. Concentrations were 17 per cent of the MAC in milk, 24 per cent in milk products, 7 per cent in meat and 4.8 per cent in meat products.

Between 1,500 and 2,000 samples are tested yearly for mycotoxins, of which only 100-200 are taken from domestic production. In analysed wheat, flour, coffee, tea, spices, and fruits, concentrations of aflatoxins B and G were below the detection limits, except in two-three samples which had higher contents. M-toxin in milk and milk products was not detected. Each year 4,000-6,000 samples of milk, meat, meat products, eggs, fats and honey are tested each year for antibiotic residue; all the samples tested negative. No residues of hormones were identified in the 600 samples of animal origin tested annually.

About 6,000-8,000 samples of additives are tested annually, of which only 1,000 samples are of domestic products. With imported products, 2 per cent of tested products are barred from sale due to the presence of prohibited additives, or the presence of excess quantities of certain additives. In the case of domestic producers, additive-related problems are usually found in small enterprises, due to non-professional treatment; the most frequently found violations are in refreshing beverages, meat products, cakes and ice-cream, in particular.

Around 12,000 samples per year are tested for heavy metals. All samples tested for lead had levels 100 to 1000 times lower than the MAC.

The estimated daily intake of lead through food and drinking water in the adult population in 1999 amounted to 36.9-179.9 mg, which is 29 per cent of the tolerable daily intake (TDI=400 µg /day). The estimated daily intake of cadmium through food (in drinking water the cadmium content is less than 1 mg/l) in the adult population in 1999 was 13.6 µg (TDI=57-71 /65/ µg), which is close to the data on Finland, Sweden, Turkey, Hungary, Austria, and lower than those on other EU countries.

In Veles, investigation of heavy metals contamination of locally produced vegetables indicate contamination by lead, cadmium and zinc 10-15 times higher than in control areas not influenced by emissions from the lead and aluminium smelter.

Analyses of domestically produced food shows that approximately 10-15 per cent of samples fail to meet food safety criteria, mostly because of deviation in ingredients, incorrect labelling or the presence of additives which are not in compliance with existing regulations.

Since 1980 the morbidity rates for alimentary toxic infections (ATI) have been around 80-85 cases per 100,000 population, except for 1989 and 1990 when morbidity was higher (120 per 100,000 and 123 per 100,000, respectively).

Morbidity from water – and food-borne diseases

Water- and food-borne diseases remain a major cause of concern and a top environmental health priority. The incidence of viral hepatitis remains very high, and, in 1999 it was the second highest reported in Europe, with 170.8 cases per 100,000 population, corresponding to 3,445 new cases. The incidence of hepatitis A (the form of hepatitis transmitted through contaminated water and food) was estimated at 57.7 per 100,000, while that of hepatitis B (the form transmitted through infected blood, e.g. when contaminated needles and syringes are used in health care) was reported to be 9.5 per 100,000. In 2001 the incidence of hepatitis A was the highest in Prilep (69.7/100,000), Strumica (59/100,000) and Kokani (55/100,000). It should be noted that surveillance of hepatitis is mostly based on the clinical diagnosis of jaundice patients and does not systematically reflect a serologically confirmed diagnosis. The extent to which the present data reflect an accurate diagnosis is unclear. Health personnel are not vaccinated against hepatitis B.

Since 1980 the incidence of salmonellosis has been increasing with peaks in 1990 and 1993, in line with what has been observed in other Central European countries. Since 1990 only sporadic cases of typhoid and paratyphoid have been registered -- 4.1 cases per year on average. Since 1990, there have been 258 cases of dysentery a year on average, with a peak of 388 cases in 1998. The average morbidity rate for dysentery for 1990-2000 was 12.8/100,000 per year. Enterocolitis still represents a significant epidemiological problem, with an average of 6,853 cases per year since 1990 and an average morbidity rate of 347.7/100,000.

No new cases of poliomyelitis have been recorded in the former Yugoslav Republic of Macedonia since its independence, and 96 per cent of the infants are reported to be vaccinated against this infection.

### Hospital waste

At present, hospital waste is still dumped at communal disposal sites without any prior selection at the point of production (health care centres) and without proper treatment, with an evident epidemiological risk. It is estimated that the annual generation of hospital waste in the country ranges between 8,000 and 10,000 tons, 12-15 per cent of which is potentially infectious or toxic waste, and the remainder is general (non-medical) waste. An incinerator was installed at the Drisla landfill in 2000, as a bilateral donation, but there has been contentious debate over the lack of flue gas cleaning technology in the incinerator. It was felt that the incinerator did not meet emission standards. The incinerator has the capacity to burn half of all hospital waste in the country. It started working in 2000, burning Skopje's hospital waste, but was stopped shortly afterwards due to the lack of agreement on institutional responsibility for its running costs and for the collection and transport of the waste. This dispute has now apparently been settled and the incinerator is working again.

Primary selection and disposal of hospital waste in special wrapping material and in separate premises was introduced in 2001. However, the plastic bags for the collection of this waste are not produced locally and need to be imported at a certain cost. This practice may not be sustainable.

### *Occupational Health*

There are no official data on occupational diseases in the former Yugoslav Republic of Macedonia, despite the numerous studies carried out by the Institute of Occupational Health. The official register for occupational diseases (under the Ministry of Labour) has not been updated to cover all relevant occupational diseases (in line with EU regulation). In addition there is a lack of appropriate systems to verify the diagnoses, and to report and record occupational diseases. Occupational health risks are not regularly assessed. The health protection of workers mainly refers to the diagnosis of and therapy for general, non-specific diseases, neglecting the specific occupational pathology. There is no or insufficient ambient and biological monitoring, and no register of occupational chemical hazards.

According to the Ministry of Health, the chemical hazards of greatest occupational health relevance in the chemical industry include vinyl-chloride, acrylonitrile, mercury, and phosphoramide (OHIS). In metallurgy, serious risks are posed by cadmium, lead (smelting factory in Veles), nickel, nickel-arbonyl (Fenimak), chromium and chromium compounds (Jugochrom). Possible by-products in certain technologies (hydromonoxyde, nitric gases, etc.) represent an additional toxic risk. Kidney diseases have been diagnosed by the Institute of Occupational Health in workers occupationally exposed to cadmium or mercury, blood disorders in workers in the pharmaceutical industry, and acute CO intoxications in metallurgical workers, among others.

**Table 14.4: Notified cases of food-borne diseases, 1993-1998**

| Disease | 1993 | 1994 | 1995 | 1996 | 1997 | 1998 |
|---|---|---|---|---|---|---|
| Salmonellosis | 698 | 562 | 422 | 352 | 276 | 365 |
| Incidence rate | 34.9 | 28.1 | 21.1 | 17.6 | 13.8 | 18.3 |
| Staphylococcosis | 126 | 133 | 104 | 84 | 35 | 28 |
| Incidence rate | 6.3 | 6.7 | 5.2 | 4.2 | 1.8 | 1.4 |
| Campylobacteriosis | .. | 20 | 37 | 41 | 47 | 48 |
| Incidence rate | .. | 1.0 | 1.9 | 2.1 | 2.4 | 2.4 |
| Shigellosis | 204 | 289 | 297 | 108 | 212 | 388 |
| Incidence rate | 10.2 | 14.5 | 14.9 | 5.4 | 10.6 | 19.4 |
| Brucellosis | 565 | 603 | 752 | 565 | 773 | 531 |
| Incidence rate | 28.3 | 30.2 | 37.6 | 28.3 | 38.7 | 26.6 |
| Other bact. food-borne diseases | 1265 | 1375 | 1591 | 1470 | 1839 | 1906 |
| Incidence rate | 63.3 | 68.8 | 79.6 | 73.5 | 92.0 | 95.3 |
| Hepatitis A | 959 | 897 | 622 | 333 | 536 | 1061 |
| Incidence rate | 48.0 | 44.9 | 31.1 | 16.7 | 26.8 | 53.1 |
| Echinococcosis | 3 | 3 | 4 | 8 | 7 | 25 |
| Incidence rate | 0.2 | 0.2 | 0.2 | 0.4 | 0.4 | 1.3 |
| Giardiasis | .. | 39 | 141 | 152 | 173 | 202 |
| Incidence rate | .. | 2.0 | 7.1 | 7.6 | 8.7 | 10.1 |
| Infectious enteritis of unknown origin | 3007 | 6684 | 6480 | 5003 | 7152 | 9710 |
| Incidence rate | 150.4 | 334.2 | 324.0 | 250.2 | 357.6 | 485.5 |

Source: WHO. Surveillance programme for control of foodborne infections and intoxications in Europe 7th Report. 2000.

There is no official recording of the use of occupational carcinogens. There is insufficient information on dose-effect relations in some segments of the chemical industry. There are no official statistics on occupational cancer. Data found in the recently established cancer register, or from hospital morbidity records, do not reflect the real situation.

High concentrations of free silicate dioxide ($SiO_2$) have been reported during studies in the metallurgical, metal-processing, cement, mining and construction industries. The high level of particles above the MAC, present in various technological processes in working environments, entails a specific risk of pneumoconiosis. Thus, in construction and mining, the predominance of silicosis ranges between 9.7 and 23.3 per cent, in different stages of evolution and with the characteristics of a non-typical disease. A clear sign of the harmful effects of asbestos on the respiratory system of exposed workers can be seen in the recorded specific functional changes of lungs and pleura of 50.9 per cent of 97 employees in the asbestos-cement industry, within the framework of preventive medical check-ups. After identifying this problem, the Institute of Occupational Health

and the management of the factory decided to close this technological line.

Organic particles are present in eco-technological processes, impacting on the respiratory system of exposed workers, by both specific and non-specific immunoallergic effects. Over 60 per cent of the monitored workplaces contained particles at levels above MAC (tobacco, milling, rice industries, spice processing, waste paper, wood industry), indicating high environmental health risk from the incidence and evolution of certain diseases. Thus, in targeted epidemiological studies, a 14 per cent predominance of allergic alveolitis was recorded among tobacco workers and occupational bronchial asthma with a 5.7 per cent predominance among rice workers.

Noise is a risk in the mining, metallurgical, metal, wood, textile and construction industries. The measured levels of noise are 88-110 dB in the textile industry, 96-115 dB in the metal industry, 87-118 dB in the metallurgical industry and 80-123 dB in mining. Harmful effects of noise were found in 37 per cent of exposed workers in the metallurgical industry, 49.2 per cent of workers employed in tunnel construction, and even 76 per cent of workers in textile production shops.

Local and general vibrations are present in a significant number of workplaces in the textile, metallurgical, tunnel construction, mining, forestry and transport industries, with measured vibrations above the standards recommended by ISO. In the construction materials industry, local vibrations with a frequency of 10-32 hertz were measured, with acceleration significantly higher than prescribed, as well as in rock drilling in tunnel construction, by using manual vibrating pneumatic machines, during which rather complex vibrations were registered, within the frequency range of 5-25 hertz and with vibration acceleration higher than permissible. Among tunnel workers, handling manual vibration tools, changes in vascular, nervous and bone joint systems were detected, in a form of hand-arm vibration syndrome, in 22 per cent of exposed workers or even in 44 per cent of workers using electric chain saws in the wood industry.

According to the latest available data, 672 workers in the health sector work are exposed to ionizing radiation. The monthly absorbed doses, measured during the obligatory dose-measuring control of these workers, range between $0.10 - 2.73$ μGy, which is within the permissible limits for occupationally exposed persons, but with an evident environmental health risk at work.

The risk from biological agents is a specific problem for health care workers with occupational blood exposure (hepatitis B, AIDS). A 26.6 per cent prevalence of hepatitis B was registered in health care workers, and HBsAg was found in 19.2 per cent of 120 tested health workers.

The rate of injuries at work was about 12 per 1000 employees in 1994. Injuries at work occur more frequently with men (82 per cent with men and 12 per cent with women in 1995). The highest risks are in construction, mining, agriculture and ferrous metallurgy.

Many people are no longer regularly, but only occasionally, employed even by the same industry. There are a number of laid-off workers who have been exposed in the past to several risk factors such as cadmium, $SiO_2$ and asbestos.

*Ionizing radiation*

Exposure to ionizing radiation is in principle limited to the occupational exposure of health care workers, some researchers and workers in some industries where radioisotopes are used.

An area of growing concern is the disposal of used sources of radioactivity, and contaminated waste. These are stored on the premises, since there is no system for the safe disposal of radioactive waste. Although inspections carried out by the State Public Health Institute report an overall satisfactory adherence to the mandated practice of storing radioactive sources in sealed containers temporarily stocked on-site in "secure" places, and of appointing a person responsible for radioactive waste, there is a risk that rapid changes in staff and organizational structures, together with the accumulation of waste, may cause a relaxation of practices and an uncontrolled disposal of radioactive waste.

Concerns have been expressed about the possibility that the natural radioactive contamination by uranium and thorium of the lignite burnt in the Bitola Electric Power Plant could pose health threats to the resident population exposed to the fly ash, which the plant produces in very large quantities (some 150 tons of fly ash per day), and whose emissions to air were estimated at around 2,400 tons in 1999. However, no reliable measurements are available to confirm or dispel these concerns. No good estimates exist as to the exposure of residents living near the plant to emissions of air pollutants from the plant, which is located approximately 10 km from the residential centre, with the prevailing wind direction going from the city towards the plant (and Greece). In addition, there is speculation that radon could be emitted from the mass of ash, creating potential occupational health problems for the workers employed in the management and disposal of the ash, but the country has neither the equipment nor the capacity to measure it.

Another issue mentioned during the EPR mission is the presence of 280 radioactive lightening rods installed on buildings. If these were removed without adequate control and sold as metal or disposed of unsafely, they could possibly cause accidental exposure to ionizing radiation from cobalt 60 – europium 152.

The Ministry of Health is responsible for controlling and authorizing the use of ionizing radiation sources, with technical assistance from the State Public Health Institute. The Institute's Radiation and Dosimetry Department maintains the national register of radioactive sources and controls occupational exposure. The Department participates in international projects led by the International Atomic Energy Agency (IAEA), such as one aiming at improving radiation protection.

During the EPR mission, concerns were raised about the difficulty of maintaining the register, as radioactive materials are increasingly used in areas subject to the authority of other ministries. These issues should be overcome by a new law (still being drafted), which should establish an independent directorate on radiation safety. This directorate would become the main responsible authority for controlling and regulating sources of ionizing radiation (as requested by IAEA). An emergency plan for nuclear accidents is being drafted (collaboration with IAEA).

Alongside the Radiation and Dosimetry Department, the Department of Radio Ecology of the State Public Health Institute is responsible for monitoring ionizing radiation in the environment and at the workplace. It also monitors radioactive contamination in domestic, imported and exported food, cosmetics, drugs and construction material, and issues certificates of compliance. Approximately 2000 samples per year are analysed, mostly for alpha and beta activity; others for total uranium. The Department of Radio Ecology prepares annual reports on the results of its monitoring activities, provides information to the public and services to factories, municipalities and others.

### Noise

At the moment, there are no competent authorities for noise monitoring and control. The Law on the Prevention of Harmful Noise requires the institutes responsible for noise monitoring to have the necessary monitoring equipment and employ at least one physicist and one engineer-architect or an electronics engineer. None of the Public Health Institutes satisfies those requirements at present. In spite of this lack of enforcement, some noise measurements can be carried out by the State Public Health Institute and the Public Health Institute in Skopje. The latter measures traffic noise (the main source of noise in urban areas) at 14 sampling sites in the city, taking samples from 7

a.m. to 3 p.m. using portable equipment. Approximately 60-65 per cent of the measurements taken exceed the guideline value of 65 dBA. No information is available on indoor noise levels, nor during night-time. (see table 14.5)

**Table 14.5: Noise measurements in Skopje**

| Year | No. of samples | LeqNoise (dBA) | Minimum - maximum (dBA) | No. of samples above 65 dBA |
|------|----------------|----------------|-------------------------|------------------------------|
| 1997 | 1,400 | 76 | 47 - 106 | 865 |
| 1998 | 1,400 | 76 | 48 - 99 | 905 |
| 1999 | 1,400 | 76 | 49 - 102 | 907 |
| 2000 | 1,400 | 85 | 47 -1 06 | 859 |

*Source:* Data provided by the State Public Health Institute. 2002.

Other noise measurements in Skopje are taken by the Ministry of Environment and Physical Planning at five locations.

### *Conditions related to armed conflicts*

Since early 2001 armed domestic conflict has led to the internal and external displacement of some 137,000 civilians and has had a serious impact on the population remaining in the conflict areas. Although some people were able to return home, several thousands are still waiting in the larger urban centres of Skopje, Tetovo and Kumanovo until security and the humanitarian conditions in their communities of origin improve, in particular as far as the rehabilitation and reconstruction of houses and public structures and the renewal of agricultural and other work and services are concerned.

The conflict has had a devastating impact on agriculture. In many of the conflict-affected areas farmers could not plant or harvest their fields as they had either been moved from their homes or faced the threat of unexploded ordnance and landmines. In addition, damage to health facilities, electricity and water supplies coupled with displacement and travel restrictions on medical personnel made both the remaining and the returning population in conflict areas even more vulnerable. At the same time, the needs of high-risk groups, such as internally displaced people and refugees, further strained the already fragile health infrastructure. Drug availability has diminished and immunization rates have dropped to as low as 20 per cent in some of the conflict-affected areas. In addition, communicable diseases, especially tuberculosis, pose a significant risk to those living in the overcrowded conditions common in host families and reception centres.

## 14.3 Environmental health policy and management

### Legal Framework

Article 43 of the Constitution affirms the right of every person to a healthy environment.

The Law on Health Protection (Official Gazette Nos. 38/91, 46/93 and 55/95) sets the foundations for the current health care system in the country, including the health insurance system, the rights and responsibilities of service users and service providers, the organizational structure of health care and its funding. The State is responsible for the provision of preventive care for the population through the Public Health Institutes and for ensuring that health services are available.

The Health Insurance Law of April 2000 underscores the basis of the health service funding process, establishes a compulsory health insurance scheme and confirms the independence of the Health Insurance Fund and its management board.

The Law on Health Protection also provides the legal framework for the Programme for Human Preventive Health Protection, which is adopted yearly by the Government upon the proposal of the Ministry of Health. The Programme forms the basis for vertical primary prevention programmes as well for monitoring the population's health and for monitoring food, drinking water, air and ionizing radiation. Health indicators are monitored on the basis of the relevant legislation, including:

- The Programme for Statistical Health Research for 1998-2000 (Official Gazette Nos. 64/97, 11/00 and 54/01);

- The Law on Health Records (Official Gazette Nos. 22/78 37/79, 18/88 and 15/95);

- The Law on Health Protection;

- The Law on Protection at Work (Official Gazette No. 13/98); and

- The Health Insurance Law (Official Gazette Nos. 25/00, 34/00 and 69/00).

### Policy commitments relevant to environmental health

The former Yugoslav Republic of Macedonia adopted the "Health for All" policy after joining the World Health Organization in 1993. Cooperation with WHO started in 1992 when the WHO Humanitarian Assistance Office was opened. The WHO Liaison Office was established in Skopje in 1996.

The National Environmental Health Action Plan (NEHAP) was developed by the Ministry of Health, and adopted by the Government in 1999. The NEHAP was drawn up with WHO support and the participation of a large working group which, in addition to the Ministry of Health, involved many other agencies and research institutions, including the Ministry of Environment and Physical Planning. Several of the recommendations made in the NEHAP are coherent with those made in the NEAP, which was adopted in 1996 and developed also with the participation of health sector representatives.

The NEHAP forms the policy roadmap for progress on key environmental health issues. Its priorities and proposed actions cover a broad range of aspects and issues, including the institutional set-up (with emphasis on the development of inter-sectoral cooperation, the reform of the environmental health services and capacity building), information systems, the development of criteria and procedures for health impact assessment and its integration in the decision-making process, control measures, the upgrading and updating of environmental health monitoring systems, research and technological development, the reduction and control of environmental health risk factors (water, air, food, soil and waste, ionizing and non-ionizing radiation, noise, natural and non-natural disasters, living and working environments, occupational health). However, a lack of finance for implementation, too many priorities and the need to further work out a number of actions to be taken are slowing down the implementation of the NEHAP. In addition, the decentralization and reform process is now shifting attention and resources towards Local Environmental Health Action Plans (LEHAPs). Furthermore, the more advanced NEAP implementation process makes it more difficult to attract funds from international donors.

Following the Ministerial Conference on Environment and Health in 1999, the former

Yugoslav Republic of Macedonia became the first European country to promote the Health, Environment and Safety Management in Enterprises (HESME) Programme (in 2001), with the organization of the Institute of Occupational Health and strong support from the Ministry of Health and WHO. The national HESME plan was prepared and adopted by the Health Council of the Ministry of Health in 2002. The plan identifies concrete activities to be carried out at all levels (national, local, enterprise) and supports the continued improvement of health, environment and safety management in enterprises through the collaboration and coordination of different sectors in the country.

In addition to the ongoing cooperation with a number of international organizations active in the health sector, such as WHO, the United Nations Population Fund (UNFPA), the United Nations Children's Fund (UNICEF), UNDP, many international NGOs, such as Médecins sans Frontières and the International Society of Doctors for the Environment (ISDE), operate in the former Yugoslav Republic of Macedonia. Among the various NGOs, the activities of the Institute for Sustainable Development (supported by USAID) are particularly useful because of their participatory and cross-sectoral approach to the development and implementation of LEAPs, which involves self-assessment by the communities, supported by representatives of the various sectors interested, including the health sector. There are also many important bilateral governmental projects.

## Environmental Health Impact Assessment

Until 1997, the Ministry of Health, through its Inspectorate, and with the technical support of the State and regional Public Health Institutes, was involved in the system of permits for new activities and strategic plans (a system somewhat similar to environmental impact assessment). Inspectors from the different sectors potentially affected by the activity under consideration (e.g. health, environment, transport, planning) used to make random, on-site assessments. These consisted of assessments of the existing environmental and health conditions, possible changes to be expected as a result of the new activities (e.g. in waste, water, air), and the overall project proposal (e.g. the safety aspects of the technology to be used). The results of these assessments were used to provide input on the location, execution and operational aspects of the activity applying for the permit, with the ability to follow up environmental and health

changes for one year after the start-up of the newly authorized activity (one-year probation period). The system included follow-up inspections to check continued compliance with environmental and health requirements.

Since 1997, legal entities wishing to start new activities no longer require the permissions of the health authorities, and only the Ministries of Environment and Physical Planning, of the Economy, Transport and Communications are involved.

An ancillary involvement of the State Public Health Institute and of the regional Institutes remains in providing investors with technical assistance in the application, e.g. by carrying out environmental surveys and performing analyses.

## Institutional Framework

In addition to the Ministry of Health, which is responsible for the national health care system and develops health policy and health care law, other ministries and organizations with some responsibility for health include: the Health Insurance Fund, the Ministry of Finance, the Ministry of Education, the Ministry of Transport and Communications, the Ministry of Labour and Social Policy, the Ministry of Defence, and the Ministry of Environment and Physical Planning, as well as the voluntary sector, the general public, private sector providers, and professional groups.

At present, responsibility for food control is shared by several ministries, e.g. the Ministry of Health, the Ministry of Agriculture, Forestry and Water Economy. The Ministry of Health is responsible for several inspection services, such as imported food inspection. The veterinary inspectors are responsible for meat and milk products. The Ministry of Economy is responsible for market inspections. Difficulties in collaboration and professional training in particular were highlighted during the EPR mission. Soil monitoring is non-existent. A new law on food has been drafted. The country joined the Codex Alimentarius in 2001. The new food and nutrition action plan stipulates a number of nutritional and food safety recommendations.

The State Public Health Institute was established in 1945 and is the national centre for public health and the main body responsible for environmental health. It is involved in teaching at the medical faculty, supervises and oversees the activities of ten regional Public Health Institutes, and provides technical services to the clinical centres and to the country as a whole. Its main functions are:

- The collection of data on health for all indicators;

- Monitoring the health status of the population;

- Reporting and analysing the health status and the organization of the health care system;

- Epidemiological surveillance;

- Immunization;

- Environmental monitoring (air, food, drinking water, radiation);

- Surveillance of environmental health risks;

- Drug control; and

- Advising the Ministry of Health on matters related to health policy.

The ten regional Institutes have a total of 21 branch offices that provide services in the communities. Since 1993, the Institutes have been separate from health service delivery and, amongst other functions, are charged with the delivery of vertical primary prevention programmes such as that for HIV/AIDS. The regional Institutes are located in the major municipalities: Bitola, Kochani, Kumanovo, Ohrid, Prilep, Strumica, Skopje, Tetovo, Veles and Shtip. Each regional Institute employs around 100–150 staff.

The 21 branch offices, or hygiene epidemiological surveillance stations, are located in health centres throughout the country. These also provide clinical laboratory services. The Public Health Institutes have four basic functions: microbiology, hygiene, epidemiology and social medicine. In addition to these functions, the State Public Health Institute provides virological, pharmacological, toxicological and radiation protection services to the whole country.

It should be noted that the 32 institutions mentioned above (i.e. the State Institute, the regional Institutes and the local branches) are independent of each other, including financially. Although their functions are similar, the different institutions have different capabilities and equipment. This difference is partly compensated by the State Public Health Institute, which provides the others with technical and analytical assistance on those aspects with which they cannot dealt directly (e.g. for

analysis of heavy metals). A form of coordination and planning of the activities of the 32 institutes takes place when the "Programme for Human Preventive Health Protection" is drawn up.

There is also an Institute of Occupational Health. It conducts health, methodological, educational and scientific activities following a multidisciplinary approach. It is a national coordination centre for the programme on Health, Environment and Safety Management in Enterprises (HESME) and is a base of the Medical Faculty Chair of Occupational Health. Occupational health comprises 146 occupational health specialists, other physicians, chemists, psychologists and other medical personnel. It has a network of 53 occupational health units as dispensaries, in health centres at municipal level, in industrial facilities, in governmental and inspection bodies as well as in private organizations. Their function is more curative than preventive. So the establishment of an adequately organized occupational health service providing monitoring, protection and the promotion of health at the workplace should be considered as an important goal for the health sector reforms.

In addition to the above structures, the Ministry of Health has inspection services, which receive expertise and technical and analytical support from the State Public Health Institute and other regional Public Health Institutes. At present, the main functions of the Inspectorate are the inspection of water (drinking and recreational), health care facilities (except medical waste), the surveillance of communicable diseases, food safety, cosmetic products, hygiene and epidemiological conditions in facilities and workplaces, drugs and medical devices, and the factories that manufacture them. In the past, the Inspectorate was also involved in the assessment of air pollution, waste and pollution from factories and in the system of permits for new activities. However, following the establishment of the Ministry of Environment and Physical Planning, the new Environment Inspectorate has in practice taken over those functions. As the redefinition of the responsibilities of each of the two Inspectorates has not yet been agreed, the consequent lack of clarity is occasionally a cause of conflict and competition between them.

Total expenditure on health is around 5 per cent of GDP. More than 95 per cent of official health care finance is derived either from contributions levied by the health insurance fund or from user charges. Of the remainder, half is derived from the State budget (funding vertical primary prevention programmes, including environmental health and the care of the needy) and the other half comes from other sources such as international aid.

### Environmental health information systems

An integrated environmental health information system needs to be able to establish links among environmental conditions (e.g. as assessed by monitoring data), population exposures and health effects. This means that monitoring systems should be oriented towards the coherent collection of relevant indicators (e.g. $PM_{10}$ instead of black smoke), and that it should be possible for these data to be related to health effects.

At the moment, the country does not have such an information system, and environmental monitoring and epidemiological data collected by different actors do not have the coherence necessary to relate them to each other and to identify links between exposures to environmental hazards and health effects. Some recent studies (such as those carried out in Veles by the State Public Health Institute on the health effects of exposure to lead in children) have moved toward making these links. However, the studies required ad hoc monitoring and data collection, pointing to the need to rethink environmental and epidemiological monitoring as a function of the health questions to be addressed, and of the geographical level of interest. This would also require further developing the ability of the regional and local Public Health Institutes to collect and monitor data on certain sets of relevant indicators at the appropriate scale and to reorganize the information flows to maximize vertical and horizontal compatibility, for example taking into consideration opportunities offered by environmental health geographic information systems. The participation of the country in the work initiated by the WHO to identify a core set of indicators for environmental health monitoring and reporting could provide a springboard for progress in this area, starting with a redefinition of indicators to be collected. In addition, a PHARE project is under way, aiming at developing a new health statistics law, to bring statistics in line with those used by Eurostat.

### Professional education in environmental health

The State Public Health Institute, together with the Skopje Regional Public Health Institute and the special Preventive Institute in the Military Hospital, provide training and opportunities for practical work in environmental health to students of Skopje University Faculty of Medicine. Furthermore, there is a postgraduate specialization in hygiene, which includes environmental health aspects. However, there are other specialists, such as biologists, architects, urban planners, civil and mechanical engineers, chemists and agriculturalists, who also need training opportunities, for example, through the updating of educational curricula to include environmental health. Furthermore, attention should be paid to updating the curricula for medical students and implementing continuing education programmes for qualified professionals.

The Institute of Occupational Health with the Chair of occupational medicine provides undergraduate and postgraduate teaching in occupational health. In order to harmonize curricula in occupational medicine with those in the EU, the Institute organized the first meeting of occupational medicine chairs in South-East Europe in 2002, in which seven countries participated.

## 14.4  Conclusions and recommendations

The move towards greater decentralization poses the risk of increasing the gaps in health conditions and the provision of services between different parts of the country. The fact that environmental health services receive only some 2.5 per cent of the total budget allocated to health, and the possibility for Public Health Institutes to raise money by providing analytical services to investors, municipalities and public and private investors (e.g. in applications for permits for new activities) is leading the Institutes to increasingly invest in analytical equipment to satisfy this demand, and to compete with each other in the provision of these services. However, there is the risk of an unnecessary proliferation of relatively sophisticated equipment (e.g. for analysing heavy metals in different media), and the problem of the reliability and quality of analysis, and maintenance of the analytical equipment. Although the State Public Health Institute occasionally provides training on analytical methods, this can by no means be considered as a replacement for a good programme of common methodology development, inter-laboratory comparability assessment, and data quality assurance and procedures.

Important improvements in key health indicators have been reported since the country's independence in 1991, notably with respect to infant and maternal mortality, which is also the result of the attention paid to family-planning policies. Food- and water-borne infections such as hepatitis A (for which the country reports one of the highest incidence rates in Europe) and diarrhoeal diseases, as well as respiratory and infectious diseases, are still matters for considerable concern. The large differences in health indicators reported by urban and rural areas (e.g. with respect to infant mortality) remain a source of concern, especially in view of the ongoing reform, which implies the further decentralization of the health system, and additional independence for the local institutions providing health care and environmental health services.

The armed conflict in recent years has also affected the health of the population, with the displacement of thousands of people, substantial damage to housing and public buildings, the disruption of economic activities, and the provision of basic services, including health care.

There are still significant environmental hot spots in Veles, Bitola, Skopje, Jegunovce and Prilep, where emissions from stationary and mobile sources represent an important threat to the quality of the environment and human health. However, the present monitoring system cannot establish clear links between environmental conditions and health impacts, and additional evidence should be collected about the health effects on the exposed population. Moreover, while some information is available for some of the hot spots (e.g. Skopje, Veles), less is known about conditions at other critical sites, as since the ability to investigate them differs in different parts of the country.

Among air pollutants, emissions of particulate matter and lead (from both fuel and industrial sites, especially in Veles) remain an important cause of concern, even if the absence of adequate monitoring data allows only a qualitative evaluation of the situation. The current reform of the air monitoring network should be regarded as an opportunity to redesign the system so as to allow an informed assessment of possible health effects, and clarify the different responsibilities for carrying it out, and the information flow itself.

Noise, especially from road traffic and entertainment (e.g. restaurants, night clubs, discos), represents an important and increasing source of annoyance for the population. Yet, no clear responsibilities exist for noise monitoring and enforcing noise regulations, and the information available is related only to daytime measurements of traffic noise.

There is a need to establish a coherent and integrated environmental health information system to establish links between environmental conditions, exposures and health effects.

*Recommendation 14.1:*
*The Ministry of Health, in cooperation with the Ministry of Environment and Physical Planning, and other institutes with responsibility for collecting monitoring data and health statistics, should lay the foundation for the establishment of an integrated and coherent environmental health information system. For instance:*

(a) *The State Public Health Institute and the Ministry of Environment and Physical Planning should strengthen their collaboration in the redefinition of the country's air monitoring network with a view to optimizing available resources, avoiding duplication and making the information provided more consistent. Priority should be given to ensuring that relevant indicators (such as PM10) are monitored, and to bringing air quality standards into line with the WHO Air Quality Guidelines and the relevant European Union directives (see also Recommendations 4.2 and 7.3).*

(b) *The Ministry of Health and the Ministry of Environment and Physical Planning should work together to redefine the policy framework for noise monitoring and noise standards, taking into consideration the WHO Guidelines for Noise as well as the European Union's policy on noise.*

(c) *The Ministry of Health, together with the Ministry for Education and Science and other relevant institutions, should establish and coordinate the implementation of a set of common methods for the monitoring and analysis of contaminants (biological and chemical) in different environmental media and foodstuffs. They should also continue professional training and inter-laboratory calibration and quality assurance schemes to ensure the accuracy and comparability of the results of monitoring and analytical procedures.*

(d) *The State Public Health Institute, in collaboration with the regional Institutes, should conduct specific studies on health-related issues at environmental hot spots (e.g. in Bitola and Veles) as part of the overall monitoring system.*

Water quantity and quality still pose a significant risk to human health in some areas of the former Yugoslav Republic of Macedonia. On average 5 per cent of all wells assessed by the Public Health Institute each year are microbiologically contaminated. Throughout the past three decades, there have been several water-borne epidemics caused by serious failures in the distribution networks, the non-respect of the sanitary protection zones, and poor local hygiene practices. Hepatitis A outbreaks occurred in Debar (1978), Kratovo (1980), Probistip (1993) and Veles (1990). Well water used in summer is a particular problem.

*Recommendation 14.2:*
*The Ministry of Health, in collaboration with the other ministries involved in water management and control, should enforce sanitary protection zones around springs used for drinking water supply.*

The microbiological contamination of food is frequent. Water- and food-borne diseases remain a major cause of concern and a top environmental health priority. The incidence of viral hepatitis is the second highest reported in Europe, and salmonellosis incidence has been steadily increasing since 1980 with peaks in 1990 and 1993, in line with what has been observed in other Central European countries. Since 1990 only sporadic cases of typhoid and paratyphoid have been registered – 4.1 cases per year on average. Since 1990, there have been 258 cases of dysentery a year on average, with a peak of 388 cases in 1998. The average morbidity rate of dysentery for 1990-2000 was 12.8/100,000 per year.

The creation of a new food agency under the responsibility of the Ministry of Health is recommended, with duties in compliance with the Codex Alimentarius and the Hazard Analysis and Critical Control Point (HACCP). The establishment of a common information and monitoring system at all levels, through adequately trained food inspectors, is also recommended. Training and education for those handling food at all levels is urgently needed.

*Recommendation 14.3:*
*The Government should expedite implementation of the new Food Law, including the establishment of a Food Agency under the Ministry of Health.*

Although sources of ionizing radiation are limited to material used for diagnostic, research and industrial purposes, the lack of a policy framework ensuring the effective control of radioactive sources in use, and their safe disposal and storage is increasingly becoming an area of concern, as it leaves the country more vulnerable to illegal trafficking in radioactive material.

*Recommendation 14.4:*
*The Government should designate a suitable site for the safe storage of radioactive waste.*

In addition to protecting the health of those in work, attention needs to be given to the large number of persons who have been laid off from industry but who were exposed in the past to risk factors such as cadmium, free silicate dioxide ($SiO_2$) and asbestos. Health care workers for whom the risk from biological agents is a specific problem are also a subject of concern. A 26.6 per cent prevalence of hepatitis B was registered in health care workers, and HBsAg was found in 19.2 per cent of 120 tested health workers.

Since 1997, the Ministry of Health has no longer been involved in decision-making for permits to start new activities. It may still be asked by the proponents to carry out analysis, but only on an ad hoc basis. The exclusion of the Ministry of Health entails the risk that potential health problems may be overlooked, and decisions taken without giving due consideration to health aspects. This issue is also important in view of the approximation of the country's legislation to that of the European Union, where the Amsterdam Treaty requires EU policies to be assessed in terms of their potential effects on health. Furthermore, the lack of a clear redefinition of the respective roles and responsibilities of the Health and Environment Inspectorates is a source of confusion and potential conflict and inconsistencies.

The development and adoption by the Government of the National Environmental Action Plan (NEAP, 1996) and National Environmental Health Action Plan (NEHAP, 1999) represented an opportunity for looking at environmental and health issues from a cross-sectoral perspective, and identifying priorities and areas for action on the basis of a broad consensus of the different agencies and sectors involved. However, the potential for cooperation and the joint implementation of actions of common interest remains largely untapped. In addition, the NEAP and NEHAP are often seen as competing for resources. The same issues are expected in the development and implementation of LEAPs and LEHAPs.

*Recommendation 14.5:*
*The Government should encourage and establish mechanisms for closer collaboration and the integration of common concerns between the Ministry of Environment and Physical Planning and the Ministry of Health. This should include, among other activities, the following:*

- *integration of environmental health concerns into the permitting system by involving representatives of the health sector in assessment and decision-making for new projects.*

- *redefinition of the responsibilities of the respective Inspectorates in the two Ministries.*
- *inclusion of representatives of the Ministry of Health in working groups established to approximate the country's legislation to that of the European Union.*
- *establishment of common programmes for coordinated fund-raising from external sources*
- *Implementation of the programme for Health, Environment and Safety Management in Enterprises (HESME).*

# ANNEXES

# ANNEX I
# SELECTED ECONOMIC AND
# ENVIRONMENTAL DATA

### The former Yugoslav Republic of Macedonia:
### Selected economic data

| | 1995 | 2000 |
|---|---|---|
| **TOTAL AREA (1 000 km$^2$)** | 25.7 | 25.7 |
| **POPULATION** | | |
| Total population, (milj. inh.) | 1.966 | 2.026 |
| % change (1995-2000) | .. | .. |
| Population density, (inh./km$^2$) | 76.5 | 78.8 |
| **GROSS DOMESTIC PRODUCT** | | |
| GDP, (billion US$) | 3.4 | 3.9 |
| % change (1995-2000) | | |
| per capita, (US$ 1000/cap.) | 1.7 | 1.9 |
| **INDUSTRY** | | |
| Value added in industry (% of GDP) | .. | 17.3 |
| Industrial production - % change (1995-2000) | .. | 10.5 |
| **AGRICULTURE** | | |
| Value added in agriculture (% of GDP) | | 10.0 |
| **ENERGY SUPPLY** | | |
| Total supply, (M toe) 1) | .. | 2.8 |
| % change (1995-2000) | .. | .. |
| Energy intensity, (Toe/US$ 1000) | .. | .. |
| % change (1995-2000) | .. | .. |
| Structure of energy supply, (%) of total | .. | .. |
| Solid fuels | .. | 58.5 |
| Oil | .. | 35.0 |
| Gas | .. | 1.9 |
| Nuclear | .. | 3.6 |
| Hydro | .. | 0.6 |
| **ROAD TRANSPORT** | | |
| Road traffic volumes | .. | .. |
| -billion veh.-km | .. | .. |
| - % change (1995-2000) | .. | .. |
| - per capita (1 000 veh.-km/cap.) | .. | .. |
| Road vehicle stock, | | |
| - 10 000 vehicles | 32.7 | 34.2 |
| - % change (1995-2000) | .. | 4.6 |
| - per capita (veh./1000 inh.) | 166 | 169 |

*Source:* UNECE and National Statistics
Note:
1) Available for final consumption

## The former Yugoslav Republic of Macedonia:
## Selected environmental data

| | 1995 | 2000 |
|---|---|---|
| **LAND** | | |
| Total area (1 000 km$^2$) | 25.7 | 25.7 |
| Major protected areas (% of total area) 1) | 8.3 | 8.3 |
| Nitrogenous fertilizer use (t/km$^2$ arable land) | .. | .. |
| **FOREST** | | |
| Forest area (% of land area) | 37.9 | 37.6 |
| Use of forest resources 1000m3 | 977 | 1,148 |
| Tropical wood imports (US$/cap.) | .. | .. |
| **THREATENED SPECIES** | | |
| Mammals (% of species known) | .. | .. |
| Birds (% of species known) | .. | .. |
| Fish (% of species known) | .. | .. |
| **WATER** | | |
| Water withdrawal (1000 m3) 2) | 96,240 | 102,059 |
| Fish catches (% of world catches) | .. | .. |
| Public waste water treatment | .. | .. |
| (% of population served) | .. | .. |
| **AIR** | | |
| Emissions of sulphur oxides (kg/cap.) | 53.4 | 51.9 |
| "        (kg/US$ 1000 GDP) | 31.4 | 28.2 |
| Emissions of nitrogen oxides (kg/cap.) | 7.7 | 7.5 |
| "        (kg/US$ 1000 GDP) | 4.5 | 4.1 |
| Emissions of carbon dioxide (t/cap.) | 4.2 | n/a |
| "        (ton/US$ 1000 GDP) | 2.5 | n/a |
| **WASTE GENERATED** | | |
| Industrial waste (kg/US$ 1000 GDP) | .. | .. |
| Municipal waste (1000 tons) 4) | 620 | 647 5) |
| Nuclear waste (ton/Mtoe of TPES) | .. | .. |
| **NOISE** | | |
| Population exposed to leq > 65 dB (A) | .. | .. |
| (million inh.) | | |

*Source:* UNECE and National Statistics

Note:

1) Republic Institute for protection of Natural Sites of Importance

2) Total waste water from public sewage system

4) Total waste from the buildings

5) Data from 2002

# ANNEX II

# SELECTED MULTILATERAL AND BILATERAL AGREEMENTS

| Worldwide agreements | The former Yugoslav Republic of Macedonia | |
|---|---|---|
| **as of 9 August 2002** | **Year** | **Status** |
| 1949  (GENEVA) Convention on Road Traffic | | |
| 1957  (BRUSSELS) International Convention on Limitation of Liability of Owners of Sea-going Ships | | |
| 1958  (GENEVA) Convention on Fishing and Conservation of Living Resources of the High Seas | | |
| 1960  (GENEVA) Convention concerning the Protection of Workers against Ionizing Radiations | | |
| 1963  (VIENNA) Convention on Civil Liability for Nuclear Damage<br>1997 (VIENNA) Protocol to Amend the 1963 Vienna Convention on Civil Liability for Nuclear Damage | **1990** | **Su** |
| 1963  (MOSCOW) Treaty Banning Nuclear Weapon Tests in the Atmosphere, in Outer Space and under Water | | |
| 1969  (BRUSSELS) Convention on Civil Liability for Oil Pollution Damage<br>1976 (LONDON) Protocol | | |
| 1969  (BRUSSELS) Convention relating to Intervention on the High Seas in Cases of Oil Pollution Casualties | | |
| 1971  (RAMSAR) Convention on Wetlands of International Importance especially as Waterfowl Habitat<br>1982 (PARIS) Amendment<br>1987 (REGINA) Amendments | **1987** | **y** |
| 1971  (GENEVA) Convention on Protection against Hazards from Benzene (ILO 136) | | |
| 1971  (BRUSSELS) Convention on the Establishment of an International Fund for Compensation for Oil Pollution Damage | | |
| 1971  (LONDON, MOSCOW, WASHINGTON) Treaty on the Prohibition of the Emplacement of Nuclear Weapons and Other Weapons of Mass Destruction on the Sea-bed and the Ocean Floor and in the Subsoil thereof | | |
| 1972  (PARIS) Convention on the Protection of the World Cultural and Natural Heritage | | |
| 1972  (LONDON) Convention on the Prevention of Marine Pollution by Dumping of Wastes and Other Matter<br>1978 Amendments (incineration)<br>1980 Amendments (list of substances) | | |
| 1972  (GENEVA) International Convention for Safe Containers | | |
| 1973  (WASHINGTON) Convention on International Trade in Endangered Species of Wild Fauna and Flora<br>1983 (GABORONE) Amendment | **1994** | **R** |
| 1973  (LONDON) Convention for the Prevention of Pollution from Ships (MARPOL)<br>1978 (LONDON) Protocol (segregated ballast)<br>1978 (LONDON) Annex III on Hazardous Substances carried in packaged form<br>1978 (LONDON) Annex IV on Sewage<br>1978 (LONDON) Annex V on Garbage | | |
| 1974  (GENEVA) Convention on Prevention and Control of Occupational Hazards caused by Carcinogenic Substances and Agents (ILO 139) | | |
| 1977  (GENEVA) Convention on Protection of Workers against Occupational Hazards from Air Pollution, Noise and Vibration (ILO  148) | | |

y = in force;    Si = signed;   R = ratified;   A = Accession;   Su = Succession;   D = denounced.

Selected bilateral and multilateral agreements (continued)

| Worldwide agreements | The former Yugoslav Republic of Macedonia | |
|---|---|---|
| as of 9 August 2002 | Year | Status |
| 1979 (BONN) Convention on the Conservation of Migratory Species of Wild Animals | 1996 | y |
| 1991 (LONDON) Agreement Conservation of Bats in Europe | 1997 | y |
| 1992 (NEW YORK) Agreement on the Conservation of Small Cetaceans of the Baltic and North Seas (ASCOBANS) | 1999 | A |
| 1995 (THE HAGUE) African / Eurasian Migratory Waterbird Agreement (AEWA) | | |
| 1996 (MONACO) Agreement on the Conservation of Cetaceans of the Black Sea, Mediterranean Sea and Contiguous Atlantic Area (ACCOBAMS) | | |
| 1982 (MONTEGO BAY) Convention on the Law of the Sea | 1990 | R |
| 1994 (NEW YORK) Agreement Related to the Implementation of Part XI of the Convention | | |
| 1994 (NEW YORK) Agreement for the Implementation of the Provisions of the United Nations Convention on the Law of the Sea of 10 December 1982 relating to the Conservation and Management of Straddling Fish Stocks and Highly Migratory Fish | 1993 | Su |
| 1985 (VIENNA) Convention for the Protection of the Ozone Layer | 1990 | Su |
| 1987 (MONTREAL) Protocol on Substances that Deplete the Ozone Layer | 1990 | Su |
| 1990 (LONDON) Amendment to Protocol | 1994 | R |
| 1992 (COPENHAGEN) Amendment to Protocol | 1994 | R |
| 1997 (MONTREAL) Amendment to Protocol | 1995 | A |
| Multilateral Fund for the Implementation of the Montreal Protocol | 1993 | A |
| 1986 (VIENNA) Convention on Early Notification of a Nuclear Accident | 1992 | Su |
| 1986 (VIENNA) Convention on Assistance in the Case of a Nuclear Accident or Radiological Emergency | | |
| 1989 (BASEL) Convention on the Control of Transboundary Movements of Hazardous Wastes and their Disposal | | |
| 1995 Ban Amendment | 1996 | Si |
| 1999 (BASEL) Protocol on Liability and Compensation | | |
| 1990 (LONDON) Convention on Oil Pollution Preparedness, Response and Cooperation | | |
| 1992 (RIO) Convention on Biological Diversity | 1996 | S |
| 2000 (CARTAGENA) Protocol on Biosafety | | |
| 1992 (NEW YORK) Framework Convention on Climate Change | 1995 | A |
| 1997 (KYOTO) Protocol | | |
| 1994 (VIENNA) Convention on Nuclear Safety | | |
| 1994 (PARIS) Convention to Combat Desertification | 1994 | A |
| 1994 (SOFIA) Convention on Cooperation for the Protection and Sustainable Use of the Danube River | 1996 | A |
| 1997 (VIENNA) Joint Convention on the Safety of Spent Fuel Management and on the Safety of Radioactive Waste Management | | |
| 1997 (VIENNA) Convention on Supplementary Compensation for Nuclear Damage | | |
| 1998 (ROTTERDAM) Convention on the Prior Informed Consent Procedure for Certain Hazardous Chemicals and Pesticides in International Trade | 1997 | Si |
| 2001 (STOCKHOLM) Convention on Persistent Organic Pollutants | 2001 | Si |

y = in force;  Si = signed;  R = ratified;  A = Accession;  Su = Succession;  D = denounced.

**Selected bilareral and multilateral agreements (continued)**

| Regional and subregional agreements | | The former Yugoslav Republic of Macedonia | |
|---|---|---|---|
| as of 9 August 2002 | | Year | Status |
| 1950 | (PARIS) International Convention for the Protection of Birds | | |
| 1957 | (GENEVA) European Agreement - International Carriage of Dangerous Goods by Road (ADR) | 1993 | Su |
| 1958 | (GENEVA) Agreement - Adoption of Uniform Conditions of Approval and Reciprocal Recognition of Approval for Motor Vehicle Equipment and Parts. | | |
| 1958 | Convention Concerning Fishing in the Water of the Danube | | |
| 1968 | (PARIS) European Convention - Protection of Animals during International Transport 1979 (STRASBOURG) Additional Protocol | | |
| 1969 | (LONDON) European Convention - Protection of the Archeological Heritage | | |
| 1969 | (LONDON) European Convention - Protection of the Architectural Heritage | | |
| 1973 | (GDANSK) Convention on fishing and conservation of the living resources in the Baltic Sea and the Belts 1982 (WARSAW) Amendments | | |
| 1974 | (Helsinki) Convention on the Protection of the Marine Environment of the Baltic Sea | | |
| 1979 | (BERN) Convention on the Conservation of European Wildlife and Natural Habitats | 1995 | y |
| 1979 | (GENEVA) Convention on Long-range Transboundary Air Pollution 1984 (GENEVA) Protocol - Financing of Co-operative Programme (EMEP) 1985 (HELSINKI) Protocol - Reduction of Sulphur Emissions by 30% 1988 (SOFIA) Protocol - Control of Emissions of Nitrogen Oxides 1991 (GENEVA) Protocol - Volatile Organic Compounds 1994 (OSLO) Protocol - Further Reduction of Sulphur Emissions 1998 (AARHUS) Protocol on Heavy Metals 1998 (AARHUS) Protocol on Persistent Organic Pollutants 1999 (GOTHENBURG) Protocol to Abate Acidification, Eutrophication and Ground-level Ozone | 1997 | Su |
| 1991 | (ESPOO) Convention on Environmental Impact Assessment in a Transboundary Context | 1995 | R |
| 1992 | (HELSINKI) Convention on the Protection and Use of Transboundary Waters and International Lakes 1999 (LONDON) Protocol on Water and Health | | |
| 1992 | (HELSINKI) Convention on the Transboundary Effects of Industrial Accidents | | |
| 1992 | (HELSINKI) Convention on the Protection of the Marine Environment of the Baltic Sea | | |
| 1992 | (PARIS) Convention for the Protection of the Marine Environment of the North-East Atlantic | | |
| 1993 | (OSLO and LUGANO) Convention - Civil Liability for Damage from Activities Dangerous for the Environment Memorandum of Understanding Concerning Conservation Measures for the Siberian | 1993 | A |
| 1994 | (LISBON) Energy Charter Treaty 1994 (LISBON) Protocol on Energy Efficiency and Related Aspects | | |
| 1998 | (AARHUS) Convention on Access to Information, Public Participation in Decision-making and Access to Justice in Environmental Matters | 1999 | R |
| | | | |

y = in force;   Si = signed;   R = ratified;   A = Accession;   Su = Succession;   D = denounced.

# *SOURCES*

## Personal authors

1.  Avramovski. Copy of presentation. Conference on Economic Instruments, 18 & 19 February 2002. REC Szentendre.
2.  Bazerko, T. Projects Expenditures by Financial Resources. 1999.
3.  Efremov, G. et al. Academy of Sciences and Arts. Agricultural Development Strategy in the Republic of Macedonia to 2005. Skopje, July 2001.
4.  Ivanovcki, P. Furagno Proizvodstvo. Skopje 2000.
5.  Kahnert, A. Institutional and legislative features of environmental policy and management in The Former Yugoslav Republic of Macedonia. First draft.
6.  Kaufman, M. Balkan presidents assemble in Davos. Forum News Daily. 31 Jan 2001.
7.  Kocov, M. Ozone Unit. Ministry of Environment. Republic of Macedonia. Protect the ozone layer, Macedonian Experience. 1999.
8.  Lazarevski, P. and Todorovski, I. Conceptual approach to the creation and realization of the national strategy for the sustainable development of the republic of Macedonia. Skopje, 2000.
9.  Mitrikeski, J. and Mitkova, T. Faculty of Agriculture. Assesssment of the quality of the contaminated soils in Republic of Macedonia. 2001.
10. Panov, N. Tourist Encyclopaedia of the Republic of Macedonia. Skopje, 1998.
11. Panov, N. Tourist Encyclopaedia of the Republic of Macedonia. Skopje, 2001.

## Material from the former Yugoslav Republic of Macedonia

12. Fund for national and Regional Roads, FYR of Macedonia. EBRD. Macedonian Regional Roads Project Skopje Bypass, Updated Feasibility Study. Environmental Impact Assessment Study. Executive Summary. January 2002.
13. Fund of Tourism of Ohrid Municipal. Ohrid Macedonia. 1996.
14. Government of Macedonia. Approximation of the legislation of the Republic of Macedonia with that of the EU. 2001.
15. Government of Macedonia. Poverty Reduction Strategy Paper (draft). 2000.
16. Government of Republic of Macedonia. Ministry of Environment and Physical Planning. Skopje, 6.9.2000.
17. Government of the Republic of Macedonia. Macedonia 2003 - Framework Program for Economic Development and Reforms. Skopje, 2000.
18. Government Strategy for Approximation of Legislation, General Secretariat, Sector for European Integration. January 2002.
19. List of Priority Projects under the conclusion of the Government of the Republic of Macedonia for the Fund for Environment. February 2002.
20. Macedonian Academy of Sciences and Arts. National Development Strategy for Macedonia. Skopje, 1997.
21. Macedonian Information Centre. Macedonian Press Digest. Skopje, 29. January 2001.
22. Macedonian Information Centre. Macedonian Press Digest. Skopje, 30. January 2001.
23. Macedonian laws. CD Rom.
24. Ministry of Environment and Physical Planning. Air quality in Skopje: Annual report. June 1999.
25. Ministry of Environment and Physical Planning. Save the Dojran Lake. CD Rom.
26. Ministry of Urban Planning. NEAP - Report for air quality. May 1996.
27. Municipality of Veles. "For Veles". CD Rom.
28. Office Group Birarija. Too High to Jump Too Low to Get Under. Skopje 1998. Video cassette.
29. Republic Institute for Health protection. Report to EPR team on emission monitoring system for the air pollution measured and health impact assessment by the institutes for health protection in the Republic of Macedonia. Skopje. February 2002.
30. Republic of Macedonia and European Commission. Energy Policy in the EU Countries Concerning Environmental Protection and Energy Efficiency: Possibilities for Implementation in the Former Yugoslav Republic of Macedonia. Volume 1. Final report. March 2001.
31. Republic of Macedonia and European Commission. Energy Policy in the EU Countries Concerning Environmental Protection and Energy Efficiency: Possibilities for Implementation in the Former Yugoslav Republic of Macedonia. Volume 2. "Collaboration Possibilities between The FYR of Macedonia and Other International Organisations". March 2001.
32. Republic of Macedonia and European Commission. Energy Policy in the EU Countries Concerning Environmental Protection and Energy Efficiency: Possibilities for Implementation in the Former Yugoslav Republic of Macedonia. Volume 3. Key area 1:Environmental Issues on Electricity Production from Lignite. March 2001.
33. Republic of Macedonia and European Commission. Energy Policy in the EU Countries Concerning Environmental Protection and Energy Efficiency: Possibilities for Implementation in the FYR of Macedonia. Volume 4. Key area 2: Oil Products Quality. March 2001.
34. Republic of Macedonia and European Commission. Energy Policy in the EU Countries Concerning Environmental Protection and Energy Efficiency: Possibilities for Implementation in the Former Yugoslav Republic of Macedonia. Volume 5. Key area 3: Energy Efficiency and Promotion of Renewable Energy Sources. March 2001.

35. Republic of Macedonia. Act on Environment and Nature Protection and Promotion (St.G.30.06.2000).
36. Republic of Macedonia. Draft Law on Environmental Charges.
37. Republic of Macedonia. Draft Law on Financing Local Self Government.
38. Republic of Macedonia. Draft Law on Fund for Environment.
39. Republic of Macedonia. General Urbanisation Plan 2001-2020 Skopje. Changes and Amendments.
40. Republic of Macedonia. Law on Communal Taxes.
41. Republic of Macedonia. Law on Concession (St.G. 07.07.1993, amended St.G. 40/1999).
42. Republic of Macedonia. Law on Environment and Nature Protection and Promotion.
43. Republic of Macedonia. Law on Excise Tax.
44. Republic of Macedonia. Law on Local Self Government.
45. Republic of Macedonia. Law on Organization and Activity of the Organs of the State Administration (St.G. 21.07.2000).
46. Republic of Macedonia. Law on Privatisation on Public Enterprises.
47. Republic of Macedonia. Law on Public Revenue Administration.
48. Republic of Macedonia. Law on State Officers (St.G. 22.07.2000).
49. Republic of Macedonia. Law on Transforming socially owned Enterprises.
50. Republic of Macedonia. Ministry of Environment and Physical Planning. Proposal for adoption of the law on environmental impact assessment. Skopje, October 2000.
51. Republic of Macedonia. Ministry of Environment and Physical Planning. The Protection of the Ohrid and Prespa Landscape. CD-Rom. ISBN 9989-9508-4-9.
52. Republic of Macedonia. Ministry of Environment and Physical Planning. The Law on air quality (draft).
53. Republic of Macedonia. Ministry of Environment. Fund for Environment. Water and Environment Sector. List of Identified Projects. February 2002.
54. Republic of Macedonia. Ministry of Environment. Skopje, 1999.
55. Republic of Macedonia. Ministry of Local Self Government. Strategy for Reform of the Local Self Government System in the Republic of Macedonia. November 1999.
56. Republic of Macedonia. Ministry of Urban Planning and Construction. Project of Wastewater Treatment Plant for Skopje, Prilep and Bitola.
57. Republic of Macedonia. Ministry of Urban Planning, Construction and Environment of the Republic of Macedonia. Collection of legislation sets in the field of communal (public) works. Skopje, October 1998.
58. Republic of Macedonia. Ministry of Urban Planning, Construction and Environment of the Republic of Macedonia. Area plan. Skopje. June 1999.
59. Republic of Macedonia. National Environmental Action Plan. Synthesis Report. Skopje, December 1996.
60. Republic of Macedonia. National Environmental Action Plan. Synthesis Report. Skopje, January 1997.
61. Republic of Macedonia. Profit Tax Law.
62. Republic of Macedonia. Public Enterprise for Physical and Urban Plans. General Urbanisation Plan for the City of Skopje. October 2001.
63. Republic of Macedonia. Public Investment Programme 2001-2003. April 2001.
64. Republic of Macedonia. State Budget Law.
65. Republic of Macedonia. State Statistical Office. Statistical Yearbook of the Republic of Macedonia 2001. Skopje, 2001.
66. Republic of Macedonia. State Statistical Office. Statistical Yearbook of the Republic of Macedonia 2001. CD Rom.
67. Republic of Macedonia. State Statistical Office. Statistical Year Book of the Republic of Macedonia. 2000.
68. The former Yugoslav Republic of Macedonia. Ministry of Economy. Pricing Methodology for different types of energy. August 1998.
69. The former Yugoslav Republic of Macedonia. The Energy Charter Secretariat. Energy Efficiency Protocol and Related Environmental Aspects. Regular review 2001. Draft.
70. The Heritage Trails Project. Macedonian Lakeland. Land of Light. Heritage Trails in the region of Ohrid and Prespa Lakes.

## Regional and international institutions

71. Balkan Energy Efficiency Program (Beep). Project Proposal. 2000.
72. EBRD. Environmental Procedures. Ref 2252. September 1996.
73. EBRD. Investment Profile FYROM. 2001.
74. EBRD. Serving the Environment. Ref 4645. September 2000.
75. European Union. Phare programme - institutional strengthening and capacity building / Ministry of Environment, FYROM. Monthly Report 4. January 1999.
76. European Union. PHARE Project. Institutional Strengthening and Capacity Building. Component: An Approximation of the Environmental Legislation. January 2000.
77. European Union. PHARE Project. Waste Water, Water Quality and Solid Waste Management FYR of Macedonia. Final Report. January 2000.
78. European Union. PHARE. 2001. Investment Options in the Transport Sector. Project Realisation Seminar, from 31 October to 3 November 2001. (Seminar presentations).
79. European Union. PHARE. Contract no. 98-0 Environment FYROM. Financing contract no Ma 9702-01-01. Final Report. 11 January 2000.
80. European Union. PHARE. Institutional strengthening and capacity building. Component C: environmental inspection/inspectorates. Final report. November 1999.
81. European Union. PHARE. Institutional strengthening and capacity building. Component D: environmental information systems centre. Final report. October 1999.

82.   European Union. Phare. Project no. MA - 9702.01.01 Institutional Strengthening and Capacity Building. Component D: Fund for Environment and Nature Protection. October 1999.
83.   Japan International Cooperation Agency (JICA), Ministry of Environment of the Former Yugoslav Republic of Macedonia. The Study on Air Pollution Monitoring System in the Former Yugoslav Republic of Macedonia. Final Report. Main Report. Tokyo, June 1999.
84.   Ministry of Finance. Medium Term Economic and Financial Policy Framework Paper, 1998-2002.
85.   REC Country Report. 2000.
86.   UNDP. Donor Assistance Database. CDAD. Skopje. CD Rom .
87.   UNDP. FYR of Macedonia, Early Warning Report. October 2000.
88.   UNDP. FYR of Macedonia, Early Warning Report. Report no. 2. November 2000.
89.   UNDP. Living conditions. 10 September 2000.
90.   UNDP. National Human Development Report. Macedonia 1999.
91.   UNEP. Balkans Unit. Environmental Projects and Programmes Conducted in FYR of Macedonia by Inter-governmental Organizations and Bi-Lateral Donors from 1997-2001. Geneva, August 2001.
92.   UNEP. Balkans Unit. Feasibility Study for Urgent Risk Reduction Measures at Hot spots in FYR of Macedonia. Geneva, August 2001.
93.   UNEP. Information Resources for FYR of Macedonia Contained in the Balkans Unit Database (28 08 2001).
94.   UNEP. Post-Conflict Environmental Assessment - FYR of Macedonia. Switzerland 2000.
95.   UNEP. Post-Conflict Environmental Assessment and the State of the Environment - FYR of Macedonia. 2000. CD Rom.
96.   UNEP. Strategic Environmental Policy Assessment – FYR of Macedonia. A review of environmental priorities for international cooperation. Switzerland, 15 November 2001.
97.   UNEP. UNEP Balkans Technical Report. Analytical Results of UNEP Field Samples from Industrial Hotspots and Refugee Sites in the Former Yugoslav Republic of Macedonia. November 2000.
98.   UNEP. UNEP Balkans Technical Report. Environmental Impacts of the Refuge Influx in the Former Yugoslav Republic of Macedonia. November 2000.
99.   UNEP. UNEP Balkans Technical Report. Institutional Capacities for Environmental Protection in the Former Yugoslav Republic of Macedonia. November 2000.
100.  UNEP: Balkans Unit. Current Projects.
101.  USAID. Environmental Action Programme Support Project. 2001.

## Internet addresses:

102.  Act on Environment and Nature Protection and Promotion:
      http://www.mia.com.mk/moe/angliski/dolemeni/legislation/legislation.htm
103.  Early Warning Report: http://www.undp.org.mk/nivogore/EWR-Eng-Nov.pdf
104.  Fund for Environment and Nature Protection and Promotion: http://www.mia.com.mk/moe/angliski/slika_links/fondzashtita.htm
105.  National Human Development Report 1999: http://www.undp.org.mk/nivogore/Nhdr.pdf
106.  Ozone Unit (Projects, Contacts): http://www.ozoneunit.gov.mk/eng/index.html
107.  The former Yugoslav Republic of Macedonia. (Grid Arendal) - State of the environment report:
      http://www.grida.no/enrin/htmls/macedon/soe2000/eng_mac/index.htm
108.  The former Yugoslav Republic of Macedonia. (Grid Arendal): http://www.grida.no/enrin/htmls/macedon/
109.  The former Yugoslav Republic of Macedonia. State of the Environment Report: http://www.moe.gov.mk/soer2/
110.  UNDP (FYROM): http://www.undp.org.mk/
111.  UNEP Balkans Task Force: http://balkans.unep.ch/fyrom/
112.  UNEP. Map of the former Yugoslav Republic of Macedonia: http://www.undp.org.mk/nivogore/webmapF.htm

## Ministries and government institutions

113.  The former Yugoslav Republic of Macedonia. Government: http://www.gov.mk/English/Tela.htm
114.  The former Yugoslav Republic of Macedonia. Ministry of Agriculture, Forestry and Water Economy: http://www.mzsv.gov.mk
115.  The former Yugoslav Republic of Macedonia. Ministry of Environment and Physical Planning -Environmental Information Center: http://www.moe.gov.mk/eic
116.  The former Yugoslav Republic of Macedonia. Ministry of Environment and Physical Planning:
      http://www.moe.gov.mk/ang/start.htm
117.  The former Yugoslav Republic of Macedonia. Ministry of Finance: http://www.finance.gov.mk
118.  The former Yugoslav Republic of Macedonia. Ministry of Health: http://www.zdravstvo.gov.mk/
119.  National links from the Ministry web site: http://www.moe.gov.mk/ang/linkovi-nacionalni.htm
120.  NGOs links from the Ministry web site: http://www.moe.gov.mk/ang/linkovi-nevladini.htm

## Other internet sites

121.  Europeanforum. Basic facts or FYRO Macedonia. 31.10.2001: http:// www.europeanforum.net/cup/macedonia/index.htm.
122.  USAID: http://www.usaid.gov/
123.  The World Conservation Union: http://www.iucn.org/
124.  PHARE, ISPA and SAPARD: search for details of EU external aid projects: http://europa.eu.int/comm/europeaid/cgi/frame12.pl

125. European Bank for Reconstruction and Development (EBRD): Projects and Investments: http://www.ebrd.com/english/index.htm
126. Environmental Procedures; http://www.ebrd.com/english/enviro/public/procedur.pdf
127. European Investment Bank (EIB): Financing activities of EIB: http://www.eib.org/loans.htm
128. Environment and Natural Resources Information Network: http://www.grida.no/enrin/index.htm
129. Organization for Security and Co-operation in Europe. (OSCE): http://www.osce.org/docs/english/misc/anrep01e_activ.htm

## Conventions and programmes

130. Bern Convention: http://www.nature.coe.int/english/cadres/berne.htm
131. Bonn Convention (Convention on Migratory Species): http://www.wcmc.org.uk/cms/
132. Commission on Sustainable Development: http://www.un.org/esa/sustdev/csd.htm
133. Convention on Biological Diversity: http://www.biodiv.org/
134. GRID Arendal: http://www.grida.no/index.htm
135. RAMSAR Convention: http://www.ramsar.org/
136. REC: http://www.rec.org/Default.shtml
137. UN/ECE Helsinki Convention (Convention on the Protection and Use of Transboundary Watercourses and International Lakes): http://www.unece.org/env/water/welcome.html
138. UNEP / DTIE (Paris): Division of Technology, Industry, and Economics: http://www.uneptie.org

## DATE DUE

| | | | |
|---|---|---|---|
| | | | |
| | | | |
| | | | |
| | | | |
| | | | |
| | | | |
| | | | |
| | | | |
| | | | |
| | | | |
| | | | |
| | | | |
| | | | |
| | | | |
| | | | |
| | | | |
| | | | |

Demco, Inc. 38-293